Kirkcudbright's
Prince of Denmark
and her voyages in the South Seas

David R. Collin

Whittles Publishing

Published by
Whittles Publishing,
Dunbeath,
Caithness, KW6 6EG,
Scotland, UK

www.whittlespublishing.com

ISBN 978-184995-088-6

Also by the author:

Kirkcudbright, an Alphabetical Guide to its History (2003). ISBN 09533907 6 4
Kirkcudbright Shipping 1300–2005 (2007). ISBN 13:978-0-9551638-5-2
Kirkcudbright Sailing Club, the Early Years, 1956–1974 (2007).

This book is dedicated to my grandson,
Duncan Alexander Collin

Printed and bound in the UK by Charlesworth Press, Wakefield

Contents

Acknowledgements

My researches began in Kirkcudbright, where Dr. David Devereux, curator of the Stewartry Museum, gave me constant help and encouragement. Helen Devereux sprang to my rescue by translating an important article from the French original. The late Ernie Robinson of Portling, an expert in the history of shipping of the North Irish Sea, searched his extensive archives for any leads I had missed, and Joseph Sassoon and Glen Murray of Kirkcudbright cast experienced seamen's eyes over my drafts.

Frances Wilkins of the Wyre Forest Press, author of many books on smuggling and a scrupulous researcher, was generous with her help in suggesting sources of information. Morag Fyfe of the National Archives of Scotland in Edinburgh identified important Customs and Excise Records for me to investigate, and Graham Hodson of the Merseyside Maritime Museum in Liverpool tracked down some basic facts about the *Prince of Denmark*. Sources in Britain were sparse however, and my enquiries soon had to be directed further from home.

David Payne of the Australian National Maritime Museum and Geoff Andrewartha of the Maritime Museum of Tasmania each led me to information which opened up new areas to explore. Members of staff at the Archives Office of Tasmania went out of their way to be of assistance, as did Marita Bardenhagen of Launceston Historical Society and Marion Sargent of Launceston Library. In Queensland, my distant relation, Bonnie Currie, took time out of her own research work to find and follow up a few more important leads, and in Western Australia, John Luyer generously made available information he had compiled concerning the botanist William Baxter.

In Canada, Gilbert Provost searched through early copies of Lloyd's Registers of Shipping for references to the *Prince of Denmark*, and in New Caledonia, Pierre Larue of *Fortune de Mer* responded instantly to my enquiry by providing a wealth of new information. Members of staff at the various museums, art galleries and libraries listed in my sources were without exception helpful, obliging and patient, giving me great encouragement for what at times seemed a daunting task. That task was only completed with the patient understanding, help and support of my wife and family.

I am deeply grateful to all of the people and organisations mentioned above, and to many others for their advice and assistance. Perhaps most importantly however, I thank the various captains, mates and officers of the *Prince of Denmark* for their diligent log keeping. Their words, never intended for general reading, give the most accurate picture possible of the hardships, successes and failures they experienced in their struggle to earn their livings.

Lastly I was delighted to find in Whittles Publishing a Scottish publisher who was able and willing to help me put this story in print. From my first contact with them, Dr Keith Whittles (publisher), Shelley Teasdale (production editor) and Sue Steven (sales manager) were thoroughly professional, friendly, approachable and practical. Their common sense approach to everything, combined with the wonders of technology easily overcame any potential difficulties arising from the fact that they and I are located at opposite ends of Scotland.

David R. Collin

Preface

In 1995, members of an expedition team based in New Caledonia discovered remnants of a wreck on a remote reef in the South Pacific Ocean, which they identified as being that of the schooner *Prince of Denmark*. They also located the site of a shore whaling station and found artefacts such as try-pots and fragments of a ship's steering gear, which they believe to have belonged to the same vessel. Off the whaling station, their divers found and recovered large pieces of whalebone.

The *Prince of Denmark*'s meanderings across the world's oceans lasted for 74 years. King George III occupied the throne of Great Britain and Ireland when she was built: she then sailed through the reigns of King George IV, King William IV, and continued sailing for 25 years into the reign of Queen Victoria. In the year of her launch, George Washington became the first President of the United States of America, and the French Revolution had peaked with the storming of the Bastille. In Scotland, Robert Burns – the country's greatest poet – was appointed as an excise man at Dumfries, and the territory for which he was responsible included the port of Kirkcudbright. Perhaps Robert Burns even attended the launch of the new revenue cutter *Prince of Denmark* a few hundred yards from the Custom House at Kirkcudbright.

In addition to her service as a revenue cutter, she had been involved in colonial venture, exploration, sealing, whaling, international and coastal trade. Among the people who had come into contact with her, were Maoris, Australian Aborigines, missionaries, prominent politicians of the day, explorers, naturalists, ex-convicts and fraudsters.

By the last year of the *Prince of Denmark*'s life, the world had changed. Henry Ford was born, Claude Debussy and George Bernard Shaw were children, and Count Leo Tolstoy had begun to write *War and Peace*. The age of the commercial sailing ship was drawing slowly to a close.

The purpose of this book is to tell the story of the schooner *Prince of Denmark*, which was built in Kirkcudbright in southwest Scotland in 1789. My particular interest in her began when I realised that of all the ships that are known to have been built in

Kirkcudbright between 1626 and 1859, she could be the only one of which an illustration might exist. This possibility arose because of reports that she was still afloat in the southern hemisphere in the early part of the 20th century. In attempting to establish whether or not this was the case, I found and explored information about her extensive voyages – which is occasionally very detailed, mostly frustratingly sparse, sometimes contradictory and on occasions quite astonishing.

The career of the schooner *Prince of Denmark* was long, varied and full of incident. The people that came into contact with her in many different roles and locations included the famous, the infamous and a whole range of characters that lie somewhere between these two extremes. To my surprise, I found that the *Prince of Denmark* had played a small but significant part in the early colonial history of both Australia and New Zealand.

The illustration that eventually materialised of this vessel is perhaps comprised more of words than of pictures. The words of the men who commanded her and who navigated her safely through some of the most formidable areas of the world's oceans for so many years are testament to her qualities as a ship, and to their qualities as mariners. Just occasionally, their stark accounts of the events of each day give an insight to their feelings of pride, satisfaction, depression, fear and relief.

I hope that people in Kirkcudbright will be proud of what their ancestors achieved in constructing the *Prince of Denmark*, and will be interested in reading about her strange adventures. I also hope that people in many other countries will have good reason to be proud of their forebears who sailed in her, and that they will enjoy reading about her origins in Scotland and some of her subsequent voyages.

David R. Collin

1 An Old Caledonian Beginning

Kirkcudbright is neither the kind of place nor the size of place that is generally associated with shipbuilding. It is a tranquil and picturesque little town in southwest Scotland, situated at the head of the estuary of the River Dee, five miles inland from the northern coast of the Irish Sea. Its population has slowly increased from about 2,000 to about 3,500 people over the last 200 years; a large percentage of that population now consists of retired people, attracted by the charm, friendliness and security of the town. Artists of some distinction have been drawn to Kirkcudbright for over 160 years, and the town has recently been successfully marketed as a venue for those interested in enjoying and learning more about its cultural heritage.

In parallel with the development of an increasingly active tourist industry, a highly successful fishing industry has been established, based originally on the local availability of lobsters and queen scallops. This industry has now been expanded to involve between ten and 20 scallop dredgers, averaging about 60ft in length, operating all round the coast of the British Isles and sending their catches back to Kirkcudbright to local processing plants. In addition, marine engineering, chandlery and boat building businesses support both the fishing industry and the growing numbers of pleasure craft that are either based in Kirkcudbright or visit its harbour and marina.

The town's situation in the heart of the beautiful Galloway landscape means that it has always had a background in agriculture, and although markets, abattoirs and creameries no longer exist in the town, production of foodstuffs such as cheese, butter and pâté have provided substantial numbers of jobs. The past success of these various activities has resulted in Kirkcudbright having an air of prosperity, of which inhabitants of many less fortunate small towns are envious. Kirkcudbright's shops are almost all independent family-owned businesses, offering home-baking, fresh local meat and fish, and a huge variety of arts and crafts. There is also a growing number of cafés, restaurants and guesthouses offering a high standard of catering and accommodation.

Kirkcudbright High Street and Tolbooth

Kirkcudbright Harbour with the Moat Brae in the background

However, it is easy to forget that Kirkcudbright was an important town for hundreds of years before artists, or even a fishing industry, were known to have existed there. Founded in about 1200, it became a royal burgh in 1455 and was the county town of Kirkcudbrightshire – or more properly the Stewartry of Kirkcudbright – until 1975, when a policy of regionalisation merged the counties of Dumfriesshire, Kirkcudbrightshire and Wigtownshire to form Dumfries and Galloway. The town's importance in its early years stemmed from its merits as a port, and it has been the centre of a fluctuating coastal and foreign trade for over 700 years. Nautical activities in that period of time have included warfare, piracy, smuggling, colonisation, transportation, passenger services, fishing, leisure pursuits and shipbuilding.

Ships have almost certainly been built and maintained in Kirkcudbright since the early 13th century, when Alan, Lord of Galloway, based his substantial fleet in the town's harbour. That fleet was protected by his motte-and-bailey castle at what is now known as the Moat Brae: a grassy mound overlooking the present harbour. The first known reference to construction of a specific vessel is that of the *Grace of Kirkcudbright*, built for Sir Robert Gordon of Lochinvar. This vessel was built by Richard Neil and ten other English shipwrights at Kirkcudbright. They were admitted as burgesses of the town on 11 March 1626, in recognition of their good service to Sir Robert. The *Grace of Kirkcudbright* sailed from the town in an attempt to establish an early Scottish colony in North America. In 1622, the *Planter* of London, owned by the same family that owned the *Mayflower*, sailed from Kirkcudbright for the same purpose.

Many ships were built in Kirkcudbright from the mid-18th century until the mid-19th century, but by no means all of their names were recorded. The first recorded name after 1626 is that of the schooner *Prince of Denmark*, built in 1789. Nothing is known of who owned the shipyard at that time and little is known of its extent. The north side of the Moat Brae was certainly the site of a shipyard in 1792, and a drawing by A. Reid, engraved by W. and J. Walker and published in London on 1 October 1792, shows a substantial vessel under construction there.

Town maps of 1843 show shipyards both on the Moat Brae and further to the east, on the far side of a tidal dock. These later shipyards were operated at various times in the 19th century by James and Homer Campbell, Stitt and Campbell, Jenkinson and Peel, Jenkinson and McEwen, and James McEwen. At least one vessel – the *Isabella* – was built by James Skelly at the Snuff Mill Creek, upstream from the present bridge over the River Dee, and several more were built at the Fish House by the Wishart family, a few miles downstream on the west bank of the river. It seems highly likely that the Moat Brae was the site of the *Prince of Denmark*'s construction and the illustration on page 4 provides a valuable insight into the manner in which she was built, the shape of a Kirkcudbright vessel of the time, the character of the town, and the dress of some of the inhabitants.

Although no records exist of the ownership of the town's 18th century shipbuilding yards, some details are known of individuals who were ship carpenters or shipbuilders at that time. The visitation lists prepared by the parish minister, the Rev. Dr. Robert Muter, in 1786 and 1788 provide invaluable information regarding the population of the town, and describe the occupations of many of its almost 2,000 inhabitants. From those lists and from memorial inscriptions and parish records, the following names have been found of men who could have been actively involved in the construction of the *Prince of Denmark*:

Andrew Grant, ship carpenter, active in 1786.
John Neilson, ship carpenter, died on 2 July 1824.
David Caig, ship carpenter, died 12 January 1843.
James Skelly, ship carpenter and shipbuilder, born 1760, died 1828.
Robert Black, ship carpenter, died 26 July 1792.
James Brown, ship carpenter, died 29 September 1819.
John Milroy, ship carpenter, died 1837.
George Alexander, ship carpenter and shipbuilder, active 1825–1826.

Of the foregoing, James Skelly is known to have been an important figure in the seafaring community of his time. Of his many achievements, the one most relevant to this history is that he built his own vessel – the 58-ton sloop *Isabella* at the Snuff Mill Creek in 1795. She was involved in carrying coals and general cargo between

The Moat Brae Kirkcudbright in 1792 (Courtesy of the Stewartry Museum, Kirkcudbright)

Kirkcudbright and Whitehaven in Cumberland until at least 1823. Thought to be the smartest local vessel of her day, she was 54ft 5in in length and had a beam of 16ft 2in. The depth of her hold was 8ft 8in. The experience and skill that enabled him to build her may well have been gained on construction of the *Prince of Denmark*, launched only six years earlier, when James Skelly would have been 29 years of age.

Mr. A. Reid's 1792 drawing (above) shows six of the main grown timber frames of a vessel being assembled on the sloping north face of the Moat Brae. The slope at that time was clearly a lot less than it is today, and is evidence of the way in which that important piece of land has been adapted as its use changed over the centuries. At various times over the last 700 years, it has been the site of the Lord of Galloway's motte-and-bailey castle, a Franciscan Friary, the grounds of Maclellan's Castle, two parish churches, a warehouse, a school, a timber yard, and a shipyard. Construction of the vessel pictured is at a relatively early stage and only a small midship section has been erected, with the frames held in position by raking props. There is no sign of the keel, stem or sternpost, so the overall size of the hull is quite difficult to assess. It is clear, however, that she was to be a vessel of considerable size.

The timber frames visible in the 1792 drawing by Mr. A. Reid would have been sawn from the limbs of trees selected for the appropriateness of their shape. They would almost certainly have been of locally grown oak, sawn by hand using two-handed saws over a sawpit. The experienced sawyer guided the saw from above and apprentices got the unpleasant task of pushing and pulling the blade from the bottom of the pit while showered with saw dust. The sawn frames would then have been trimmed by hand with adzes, used by skilled ship carpenters. After all of the frames, the keel, the stem and the sternpost had been assembled, work would begin on fastening the planking with wooden treenails (trunnels), starting close to the keel and working slowly upwards.

In some ships, the planking would have been of local larch, but in other cases it could have been of imported pine, or even mahogany. The strength of ships and the efficiency of construction would have been greatly enhanced by availability of sound timber in lengths that were as great as possible. In the late 18th century, Kirkcudbright had a lively trade with the Baltic countries, Canada, and America, from where local merchants were supplied with high quality timber. The *John* of Kirkcudbright arrived in the town in 1769, under the command of local man, John Paul (later to become John Paul Jones, the American naval hero), with a cargo from Jamaica which included 75 mahogany planks. The *Hannah* berthed in 1791, and landed a choice cargo of pitch pine and cypress from Savannah, Georgia. The pitch pine was in lengths varying from 23ft to 55ft and would have been ideal for shipbuilding. Perhaps the pitch pine, famed for its durability, provided the planking for the *Favourite* and would help to explain her long life. No landings have been recorded which can be directly linked to the *Prince of Denmark*.

The *Favourite*, a sloop of 65 tons, was launched at Kirkcudbright in 1793. Her length was 55ft 4in, her beam was 17ft 3in, and the depth of her hold was 9ft 1in. She had a running bowsprit, one deck, one mast, a square stern, and was carvel-built with no galleries and no figurehead. Bearing in mind that Mr. A. Reid's drawing was undertaken in October 1792 and shows the very early stages of construction of a fairly large vessel, it is possible that she is the *Favourite*. The *Favourite* was locally owned and like the *Isabella* was used in the coastal trade, typical cargoes being coals from Whitehaven and potatoes to Liverpool. She was still afloat at Alloa in Clackmannanshire in 1846, providing evidence that Kirkcudbright's ships of that time were soundly built of durable materials.

The name *Prince of Denmark* is unusual as most local vessels were named after family members of the owners or masters, or local place names. The eight ships known to have been built in Kirkcudbright between 1791 and 1799 were typically named: *Brothers*; *Elizabeth*; *Favourite*; *Henny*; *Isabella*; *James*; *Raeberry Castle*; and *Robert and Jannet*. Their average net registered tonnage was 54 tons.

In 1789, the holder of the title 'Prince of Denmark' was Frederik Oldenburg, a son of King Frederik V of Denmark by his second marriage. The Prince of Denmark, aged 18, became regent to the Danish Crown when his half brother, King Christian VII of Denmark was found to be insane in 1772.

There seemed a possibility that the choice of name implied that the new vessel was intended for the Baltic trade. A substantial building, the Basil Warehouse, was erected on the Moat Brae in Kirkcudbright in 1734 for the purpose of developing that trade, and was not demolished until 1895. No evidence has yet been found of who commissioned the *Prince of Denmark*, or of any trading intention.

A note in *Shipping Arrivals and Departures – Tasmania, 1834–1842*, by Ian H. Nicholson, gave the first indication of her early history by referring to her as an ex-revenue cutter. It should be noted that in the term 'revenue cutter', unusually, the use of the specific term 'cutter' does not refer to the vessel's rig, but merely to her style and purpose. A revenue cutter was certainly on the stocks at Kirkcudbright in 1792, and may not have been the only such vessel built in the town. The commissioning of a revenue cutter from such a small yard implies that the reputation of the builders at Kirkcudbright must have been very high. Revenue cutters had to be fast and highly manoeuvrable craft, able to outperform the many vessels involved in smuggling. It was not until 1840 that the Admiralty introduced a standard design, so prior to that date, the onus lay entirely with the builder to use his design skill to produce an exceptionally fast vessel. Paradoxically, the skill necessary to fulfil such a requirement was often gained by providing vessels for smugglers. In 1839, James Campbell of Kirkcudbright built the 117-ton schooner *Lynx*. She was commissioned by English owners and intended for the fruit trade. This trade necessitated ships that were extremely fast, in order that their cargoes might be delivered in good condition. This tends to confirm that Kirkcudbright-built ships had a reputation for speed.

Among the revenue cutters and sloops which were known to be in service in the west of Scotland during the late 18th century were: the *Prince of Wales*; *Prince William Henry*; *Prince Edward*; *Prince Ernest Augustus*; *Prince Augustus Frederick*; *Royal George*; *Royal Charlotte*; and *Princess Elizabeth*. Additionally, at the same time, on the east coast of Scotland, a customs sloop – the *Princess Royal* – was in service; so the name *Prince of Denmark* would seem to fit neatly into a well-established pattern.

After the end of the Napoleonic Wars, the British Navy had more vessels than it needed in peacetime, so some of these were redeployed as revenue cutters, replacing the older vessels. Between 1816 and 1817, no less than 20 revenue cutters were disposed of by the Admiralty. It is known that the *Prince of Denmark* was subject to an extensive refit in 1819, so it is probable that she was one of the vessels sold at that time.

Revenue cutters were also in service in other parts of the British Empire and some of them may have been built in Great Britain. In the 1830s, in Australia, there was a revenue cutter called *Prince George*, providing evidence that the naming pattern already referred to extended far beyond Scottish waters.

Captain Frederick Marryat, who was involved early in his career in the control of smuggling, gives the following description of a revenue cutter of the late 18th century in his novel *The Three Cutters* (1836):

> She is a cutter, and you may know that she belongs to the Preventive Service by the number of gigs and galleys which she has hoisted up all round her. She looks like a vessel that was about to sail with a cargo of boats: two on deck, one astern, one on each side of her. You observe that she is painted black, and all her boats are white. She is not such an elegant vessel as the yacht, and she is much more lumbered up [...] Let us go on board. You observe the guns are iron, and painted black, and her bulwarks are painted red; it is not a very becoming colour,

but then it lasts a long while, and the dockyard is not very generous on the score of paint—or lieutenants of the navy troubled with much spare cash. She has plenty of men, and fine men they are; all dressed in red flannel shirts and blue trousers; some of them have not taken off their canvas or tarpaulin petticoats, which are very useful to them, as they are in the boats night and day, and in all weathers. But we will at once go down into the cabin, where we shall find the lieutenant who commands her, a master's mate, and a midshipman. They have each their tumbler before them, and are drinking gin-toddy, hot, with sugar—capital gin, too, 'bove proof; it is from that small anker standing under the table. It was one that they forgot to return to the Custom House when they made their last seizure.

One day, in 1789, when the wind was fair, the *Prince of Denmark* sailed down the channel of the River Dee from Kirkcudbright and passed Little Ross Island at the mouth of the bay, before disappearing over the horizon. Her departure was doubtless watched with a mixture of pride and sadness by many of the men who built her. Nevertheless, the minds and energies of shipbuilders are quickly focused on their next project, and by the time the *Prince of Denmark* had been fitted out and rigged, either the 54-ton *Brothers* or the 55-ton *James* would have been on the stocks.

The *Prince of Denmark* seems to have been quickly forgotten in Kirkcudbright. If, as seems likely, she was built as a revenue cutter, she would perhaps not have been the subject of great public affection. Smuggling was engaged in by a wide diversity of people and was seen generally as beneficial to both the finances and the lifestyle of the community at large. Neither revenue cutters nor those who manned them were looked at in quite the same way.

No records have been found of her service as a revenue cutter and no references to her appear in the limited amount of surviving official correspondence from local Customs and Excise officers. This is not particularly surprising, as records of the activities of revenue cutters were of a highly sensitive nature. There may have been many people in positions of authority who would have been happy for them to have been either destroyed or conveniently mislaid. A fire in 1814 at the Customs House in London also brought about the accidental destruction of a large quantity of archive material.

A revenue cutter that vanished without trace immediately after her launch perhaps seems an unusual subject about which to write a history. It is hoped however, that the strange story that evolves when she re-appears many years later will compensate for the mystery of her missing years.

2 Following in the Wake

The only trace of the *Prince of Denmark*'s existence left in her homeport was probably the imprint of her keel and the planking of the lower part of her hull on the soft mud at the bottom of her fitting-out berth. Within a few days, the fresh water of the River Dee would have combined with the effects of the ebbing tide to erase that last reflection of her shape and form.

Local museums and libraries have been scoured for local port records, contemporary press reports of her launching, personal diaries, logs and journals which might have

Kirkcudbright from the north, c.1840 (Courtesy of the Stewartry Museum, Kirkcudbright)

divulged some information, but nothing has been found. Larger and national museums in Scotland and England have been written to and visited, with results ranging from no reply to no known records. Hours spent in Edinburgh at the Scottish National Library and in the Scottish Records Office produced a wealth of background information, but no clues to either the destination or the purpose of the *Prince of Denmark*'s maiden voyage.

For a while, defeat seemed comprehensive and my attention turned to the pleasure of sailing my own boat in Kirkcudbright Bay. However, I could not quite get out of my mind the vision of a brand new schooner sailing down the estuary I know so well and vanishing over the horizon to destinations unknown, over 200 years ago.

Checking through my archives, I came upon two articles entitled *Solway Sailing Vessels* by James Copland and published in *Sea Breezes* in 1930, in which it was stated that according to his research, the *Prince of Denmark* was still afloat in Sydney, New South Wales, in 1913. Suddenly fired with new enthusiasm, I wrote immediately to the Australian National Maritime Museum in an attempt to establish whether or not there was any truth in this contention. The lack of a reply to my letter was disappointing but was not the end of the matter. *Classic Boat* magazine was the unexpected stepping-stone to eventual success. Its January issue in 2006 featured the result of a competition for the design of a small open boat, powered by sails and oars, and announced that the judge, Nigel Irens, had chosen *Perentie* – a design by David Payne – as the winner. As Nigel Irens was the designer of *Speedwell* (my own much-loved and admired Romilly 22), I paid particular attention to both his chosen design and its designer's name. The next month, in a letter to *Classic Boat* regarding his winning design, David Payne mentioned that he was a part-time employee of the Australian National Maritime Museum and was in the early stages of setting up a database, to be called the *Australian Register of Historic Vessels*. My letter to him received an instant and most encouraging reply. David quickly established that the *Prince of Denmark* had been wrecked in 1863 in the Chesterfield Islands and he sent me a copy of the all-important cancellation of her registration document. He also checked that there were no known photographs of her in existence and, most usefully, suggested that the Maritime Museum of Tasmania might be a source of further information.

A letter to the Maritime Museum of Tasmania produced a positive response from their head researcher, Geoff Andrewartha, who swiftly posted a package of the information to which he had immediate access. Geoff's package contained photocopies of extracts from a book by Ian Nicholson, entitled: *Log of Logs, A Catalogue of Logs, Journals, Shipboard Diaries, Letters, and all forms of Voyage Narratives, 1788 to 1988, for Australia and New Zealand, and Surrounding Oceans*. Other extracts came from several volumes of *Shipping Arrivals and Departures – Tasmania*, by Ian Nicholson and Graeme Broxom. The number of references to the *Prince of Denmark* in these publications made it very clear to me that I had a great deal of reading to do and a lot to learn about her voyages in the South Seas.

Geoff also wrote to ask if I knew anything about the world-famous Scottish yacht designer, William Fife of Fairlie. For nearly 20 years I had been a regular crewman on the 54ft cutter *Solway Maid*: the very last yacht to be designed and built by Fife. It was a pleasure to be able to provide him with some background information, particularly as the name of the homeport carved into her elegant counter stern is that of Kirkcudbright.

The next two winters were spent tracking down and acquiring obscure books, obtaining copies of the *Prince of Denmark*'s logs, transcribing them, and using the Internet to fill gaps and to source relevant maps and charts. Some difficulties were encountered due to the fact that many ports, headlands, rocks, straits and other geographical features had been re-named over the centuries. I rediscovered my sea-going great grandfather's *Comprehensive Atlas and Geography of the World*, published by Blackie and Son in 1882, which provided some of the answers I needed. One or two destinations still proved troublesome however, and I struggled to successfully make sense of it all, one prime example being the detailed log of a passage up the River Tamar to Launceston in Tasmania, in which I was unable to locate many of the place names quoted. I wondered how someone on the other side of the world might go about finding similar information on the detailed names of rocks, bays and minor headlands in Kirkcudbright Bay, and realised that as chairman of Kirkcudbright History Society, I perhaps knew of a possible source of information.

Though uncertain even of their existence, I wrote to 'Launceston Historical Society', outlining my problem and asking for assistance. In an immediate reply, Marita Bardenhagen told me that she was confident that she knew someone who could help, and forwarded my inquiry to Launceston Library. Shortly afterwards, I received a package of maps, articles and diagrams from Marion Sargent of Launceston Museum, which answered all my questions. In a subsequent note, Marion asked how things were in Kirkcudbright, as she had passed through it a few years previously on her way to visit the home of some of her forebears in Girvan.

Much of the story of the *Prince of Denmark*'s long and adventurous life was now becoming clearer, but many gaps and anomalies still required further investigation before it could be properly told. The circumstances of her loss in the Chesterfield Islands were still vague and I sensed that there was a story that had yet to fully unfold. I recollected hearing that an organisation called *Fortune de Mer* was based in New Caledonia and had carried out a survey of wrecks on the Chesterfield Islands. A letter to them in Noumea, to a rather vague address, failed to produce a response. Several months later, I found a website providing general tourist information about New Caledonia, which guaranteed a reply by email to any enquiry, within 24 hours. On a whim, I wrote to them with brief details of my quest for information regarding the wreck of the *Prince of Denmark*. Within the stipulated 24 hours, I had the promised reply: a standard message thanking me for my enquiry and assuring me that I would enjoy my forthcoming holiday in New Caledonia. I felt a bit foolish, and reluctantly concluded that I was not going to get any further with that potential source. A few weeks later, however, I was astonished to receive a message from Pierre Larue of *Fortune de Mer*, in Noumea. He told me that the tourism office had forwarded my enquiry to him, as he had been the dive photographer on a survey of wrecks on the Chesterfield Reef, one of which was identified as being that of the schooner *Prince of Denmark*. Pierre's English is much better than my French, so we were able to communicate freely over many months. He was immensely generous in giving me access to all the information that he and *Fortune de Mer* found and in sending me his excellent photographs of the wreck site.

Despite the lack of any information about her early years as a revenue cutter, I was confident that the story of the *Prince of Denmark* was now worth telling. My next tasks were to fill in the many minor gaps in her history and to find out more about her various masters, owners and crewmen. At this stage, I turned my attention to the wonderful collections of local newspapers held by the National Libraries of both Australia and New Zealand. A continuing programme of digitalisation is making these collections available to everyone via the Internet, and this enables searches to be made for coverage of events, people, places and ships *etc*. in many different local newspapers throughout the respective countries.

Having spent years trying to find enough information to enable me to attempt to write an article about the *Prince of Denmark*, I suddenly found that the proposed article was growing into a book, and that the available material now needed careful editing to restrict the proposed book to manageable and affordable dimensions.

3 A Colonial Venture

In the first quarter of the 19th century, the British public perceived great opportunities for fortune-seeking and a new way of life in Australia and New Zealand. Colonisation schemes for these exciting destinations stimulated the imagination of the many Britons who sought to better their lot, and were not afraid to risk everything on a long voyage to a destination about which their expectations generally exceeded their knowledge.

In 1825, three schemes for establishing colonies in New Zealand were in existence to tempt potential emigrants. The first was organised by the New Zealand Company, the second by Baron Charles Philippe Hippolytus de Thierry, and the third by Captain William Stewart. Captain Stewart was, at one time, in the employment of Baron de Thierry, and was probably involved in the baron's colonial plans before breaking away and setting up his own project to establish a settlement on Stewart Island, off the southern tip of New Zealand's South Island. Captain Stewart may also have been in contact with the New Zealand Company, prominent figures in which included the Earl of Durham, George Lyall, Stewart Marjoribanks, George Palmer, and Colonel Torrens. George Lambton sent agents for the company to New Zealand in 1825, who allegedly bought land in Cloudy Bay, Stewart Island, and also in the North Island. However, the company failed to gain the support of the British Government, and although it did send ships and emigrants to the North Island, it eventually collapsed.

Baron de Thierry was a colourful character, born at Grave in Holland on 23 April 1793, the godson of the brother of King Louis XVI of France. He served in a British cavalry regiment – the 23rd Dragoons – and he studied theology at Oxford, then law at Cambridge. Through contacts made in Cambridge in 1820, he claimed to have purchased 40,000 acres of land in New Zealand in 1822, and began to formulate plans for the establishment of a settlement there. His colonial ambitions suffered their first setback in 1823, when his attempt to secure a concession for a trading settlement on Stewart Island was refused by the British Government on the ground that New Zealand was not a Crown Possession. Baron de Thierry was apprehensive that others would succeed

Baron de Thierry as a young man (left) and later in life (right) Courtesy of Auckland City Libraries, New Zealand

where he had failed, and on 21 April 1824, he wrote to the colonial secretary, the Earl of Bathurst, in the following terms[*]:

> 30 Budge Row,
>
> My Lord,
>
> After the nature of answers to the letters which I had the honour at various times to address to your Lordship, I would not again intrude upon your time respecting the Islands of New Zealand, if it were not that I claim an act of justice from his Majesty's Government, to obtain which, I cannot better address myself than to your Lordship whose impartiality and justice are so well known.
>
> The Act of Justice which I plead for is, that should any privileges be granted to any individual in New Zealand, that H.M. Government will bear in mind that I was the first to seek this assistance, and the first to set on foot the colonisation of New Zealand; I should not therefore be the last to be listened to with a favourable ear.
>
> A Captain Stewart, of the whale trade, is to wait upon your Lordship, to request that Government will grant him the island which bears his name, on the southern extremity of New Zealand. I will not enter into any length on the hostile tendency of the step towards myself, and will confine myself to two facts, the one that he deserted from H.M. Royal Navy, and only dared return to England on the general

---

[*] (*Quoted from:* Murihika, A History of the South Islands of New Zealand and the Islands Adjacent, *Robert McNab, [1909]. Commons Attribution-share alike 3.0 N.Z. licence. Retrieved from the New Zealand Electronic Text Centre,* http://www.nzetc.org/tm/scholarly/tei-McNMuri.html)

pardon some years back; on the other, that he has deserted me, who had employed him not knowing his former offence.

I write not to you, my Lord, as an informer, but simply that your Lordship may be enabled to draw a line between an aspirant who deserted the service of the King, and a claimant who has served him faithfully, and will ever be at his disposal.

I have the honour to be, *etc.*,

P.S. After deserting H.M. service, Mr. Stewart was prize-master on board a privateer.

Baron de Thierry's attempt to foil Captain Stewart was unsuccessful, and following the collapse of his colonial plans he was imprisoned for bankruptcy during 1824. After spending time in France, unsuccessfully pursuing the furtherance of his New Zealand venture, he returned to London to escape his creditors. In 1827, he journeyed to America and the Caribbean, where his exploits included proposing and gaining a concession for the formation of a canal through the Panama Isthmus, some 80 or 90 years before the present canal opened in 1914. Unable to find backers for his scheme, he then sailed west from Panama in 1835. After a brief sojourn in the Marquesas, where he modestly declared himself king of the island of Nukuhiva, he arrived in New Zealand from Sydney in November 1837 with over 60 aspiring colonists, to take possession of the 40,000 acres of land he believed he had purchased with the help of his Cambridge contacts, and he then assumed the title of 'Sovereign Chief of New Zealand', to universal derision.

While at Cambridge in 1820, the baron had met a missionary, the Rev. Thomas Kendall, and two Maori chiefs – one of whom was the influential Hongi Hika. Thomas Kendall and the two chiefs had spent five months in England, in the course of which, Hongi Hika had been introduced to King George IV before returning to New Zealand in 1821. The baron had been inspired by the glowing accounts he received from Thomas Kendall and the two chiefs of the opportunities that New Zealand offered for trade, and he resolved to establish his own empire there. He appointed Thomas Kendall, who was fluent in Maori languages, to act as his agent, entrusting him with property to the value of £800 to invest in the purchase of land suitable for the establishment of a colony. Thomas Kendall did indeed purchase 40,000 acres of land on the baron's behalf, but the price he agreed with the Maori owners was a mere 36 axe heads. There is some doubt about what happened to the baron's £800, some sources suggesting that Thomas Kendall never received it and others suggesting that it had been passed on by him to Hongi Hika, who had used it to secure arms for his warriors. Hongi Hika was something of an empire-builder himself, with a fearsome reputation among his fellow Maoris. He is alleged to have been grateful to the white men who had given him access to modern weapons, and in return spared them from harm in his future skirmishes.

The Maori owners of the land at Hokianga that the baron believed he had purchased claimed to have received payment of only 24 'Sydney' axes in place of the 36 axe heads that had been agreed. Several white residents and missionaries persuaded the landowners that this invalidated the title deeds. These same people then bought the land concerned piece-by-piece, and influenced nearly all of the baron's prospective settlers to desert him and to work instead with them.

Baron de Thierry, angry and frustrated but never a man to give up easily, persuaded one of the new owners to sell him a few hundred acres of land for £100, and he and his long-suffering wife, Baroness Emily, whom he had married in England in 1819, then attempted to clear virgin ground themselves and to cultivate their diminished empire while living in a tiny house built of bark. Without the help of the intended colonists, the baron's efforts were fruitless, and again facing financial ruin, he was forced to make an ignominious withdrawal to Auckland, where he scraped a living teaching music and French. Being a man of apparently boundless optimism, he sailed for California in 1850 on the barque *Noble* (following his two sons to the goldfields), but became marooned on Pitcairn Island for a month, when due to a sudden change in weather, the *Noble* departed minus five of her passengers. While on Pitcairn, the baron gave lessons in linear perspective and the use of the pencil and gave tuition in singing to members of the church choir, with the assistance of a tuning fork which he happened to have in his pocket. Evidence of at least one of the baron's many talents lies in the fact that one of his drawings is in the collection of the Auckland City Art Gallery. Eventually escaping from Pitcairn on the *Velocity*, bound for Honolulu, he took charge of the French Consulate there in 1852.

After returning to Auckland in 1853, he claimed to have devised a new process for the treatment of flax and sought substantial investment to enable him to build factories and commence production. His initial plans failed and his investors lost their money. He died in Auckland on 8 July 1864. The following paragraph from the *North Otago Times*, written a few years after his death, draws attention nicely to the enigma of his personality:

> Baron de Thierry, the First King of New Zealand: Such men as de Thierry are of the peculiarities of humanity. They are not to be accounted for. Looking at his swindling meanness on the one hand, and his mighty aspirations on the other, we can imagine that such as he would have been produced had Count Cagliostro married Joan of Arc, or if Jeremy Swindler had wedded Joanna Southcote.

Count Cagliostro (1743–1795) was an occultist, freemason, healer, forger and swindler; and Joanna Southcote (1750–1814) was an eccentric English religious prophetess with over 100,000 followers. No trace of Jeremy Swindler has been found, but his name has perhaps been confused with that of Jeremy Diddler, an artful swindler in James Kenney's 1803 farce *Raising the Wind*.

History to date has not been kind to Baron de Thierry. He is all too often likened to a character in a comic opera: naïve, pompous and with delusions of grandeur. He was, however, despite his many shortcomings, a man of astounding vision and determination who travelled to the very edge of the known world of his day in his efforts to make his dreams come true. This eccentric but multi-talented aristocrat has perhaps not yet found his true place in history.

Several more of the characters who feature either directly or indirectly in the history of the *Prince of Denmark* are people of somewhat dubious integrity. Interestingly, those who arrived in the southern hemisphere against their will and in chains generally developed into successful and wealthy pillars of society, whereas those who arrived armed with supposed wealth, influence and the claimed ability to generate new opportunity, all too frequently turned out to be fraudsters, confidence tricksters or impostors.

William Stewart was reputedly born in Scotland in about 1776 and served in the Royal Navy from 1793 until 1797, during which time he saw active service in the West Indies. It is probable that he then deserted from the Royal Navy, and in June 1801 he sailed from Calcutta to Port Jackson as chief officer in the brig *Harrington*, owned by Chace, Chinnery and Co. of Madras, which carried letters of marque. Letters of marque entitled the master of the *Harrington* to act as a privateer, and this would have meant that as her chief officer, William Stewart would almost certainly have been prize-master of any vessel captured. From 1801 until 1805, he was actively involved in seal hunting in the Bass Straits, in association at various times with both John Palmer and Robert Campbell. John Palmer was a former naval officer who had risen to the position of commissariat general and had extensive business interests, including shipbuilding and sealing. Robert Campbell, John Palmer's brother-in-law, was a wealthy and respected Sydney merchant. By 1805 however, such large numbers of American vessels had been lured to the lucrative sealing grounds there, that the seal population had been severely reduced.

William Stewart was forced to find new grounds and eventually arrived (in November 1805) at Antipodes Island, in command of the brig *Venus*, owned by John Palmer's partner, Robert Campbell. A large party of American sealers who were already at work opposed his landing there and Captain Stewart, against the advice of his colleagues, hoisted the Union Flag, declaring Antipodes Island to be the property of His Majesty The King. Predictably, a fracas developed, in which Captain Stewart was defeated, but a compromise was eventually reached and the process of unloading stores began. Despite this, whilst Captain Stewart and 15 of his crew were ashore, a gale sprang up, forcing the *Venus* to put to sea under the command of the mate. Subsequent damage to the rudder forced the mate to return to Port Jackson for repairs, leaving the captain and most of the crew stranded. Captain Stewart returned as a passenger on the *Star*, after ten months on the island, but it was to be a further ten months before his crew was rescued.

During 1806, Captain Stewart was based in Sydney and for a brief period was master of Robert Campbell's brig *Sophia*. He was also in partnership for a time with John Palmer, in a venture involving the 18-ton sloop *Fly*. Then, during 1807, he became owner and master of the *Fly*, having terminated his association with John Palmer. His principal activity between 1806 and 1819 was either defending himself or attacking others, in a bewildering mass of litigation. In November 1806, he lost his case against John Palmer, who he blamed for failing to provide provisions for the men stranded on Antipodes Island, then lost two appeals against the original decision, in February and April of 1807. By mid-1809, he was embroiled in a case against Garnham Blaxcell, one of Sydney's richest merchants, for pursuance of debt. The case was unsuccessful, but Captain Stewart proceeded both to lodge an appeal and to petition the lieutenant governor without success. He was then appointed as master of the 58-ton *Antipode*, belonging to Simeon Lord, and he sailed on a sealing expedition to Antipodes Island in September. He returned in February 1810 from a voyage about which nothing is known except that the weather was very bad and the *Antipode* returned in extremely poor condition. Captain Stewart promptly took legal action against Simeon Lord over lack of wages and poor provisions, a case that dragged on until July 1813. Captain Stewart then sailed in November 1811 as master of the 80-ton schooner *Cumberland*, bound for Macquarie Island on yet another sealing voyage, calling at Campbell Island in December. On his return to Port Jackson in July 1812, he was immediately taken to court by William O'Neal and two other seamen who had served with him on the *Cumberland* seeking wages they claimed were due to them. The case was heard in the supreme court in January 1813, and as in the case involving Simeon Lord, the decision went against Captain Stewart, who was also held liable for costs.

In late 1813, Captain Stewart returned to the command of the *Fly*, various efforts to sell her having been unsuccessful. On 25 September, he and the *Fly* arrived at Port Dalrymple in Van Diemen's Land from Kangaroo Island. At the time, the area was under martial law, in an effort to control the activities of bushrangers. The person responsible for enforcing that law was Acting Lieutenant Alexander Campbell. Captain Stewart, who was not in the best of health at the time, made the serious mistake of quarrelling with Lieutenant Campbell over a trivial matter and suffered gravely for that error of judgement. Narrowly escaping a flogging, he was later accused of a minor theft and was escorted to a court appearance in Hobart Town. The court found in Captain Stewart's favour and he returned to Launceston in early August of 1814, only to find that the *Fly* had sunk in the Tamar River during his absence and lay half-submerged, together with her cargo and all Captain Stewart's personal effects. On 7 August, one of Lieutenant Campbell's personal servants, acting on Campbell's instructions, seized a greyhound dog from Captain Stewart as he walked along the street in Launceston. This latest incident was more than Captain Stewart could bear, and precipitated him into fighting a four-year-long campaign against Lieutenant Campbell, seeking everything from the return of his dog to compensation for the loss of the *Fly*, its salvage, and his loss of earnings. In the course of his battle against officialdom, Captain Stewart added his name to a petition seeking the removal of Governor Macquarie, and in consequence found himself accused of being a party to libel, sedition and unprincipled depravity. Captain Stewart's response was to seek the court-martial of Lieutenant Campbell and to request Governor Macquarie to forward a letter explaining all the circumstances to the Duke of Wellington. While waiting for a reply, Captain Stewart then pursued his case against Lieutenant Campbell in the supreme court and was rewarded, in August 1817, by a decision in his favour and payment of nominal damages. Needless to say, that did not satisfy him, and he continued to press his case for compensation. In early 1819, Governor Macquarie, prompted surprisingly by a request from the Duke of Wellington that Captain Stewart's complaints be investigated, asked that the captain attend a meeting at Government House. According to Captain Stewart, an attempt was then made to appease him and the way was left open for unspecified assistance in the salvage of the *Fly* to be given. That was virtually the end of the matter, but although Captain Stewart sent one final epistle, again detailing all his grievances, it was never replied to, and the *Fly* remained submerged. Captain Stewart, once a respected seafarer who had triumphed over all kinds of danger and adversity, had become, for a time at least, a dangerously embittered man obsessed with grievances both real and imagined.

In 1819, after living in Sydney for four years with no known source of income, Captain Stewart fell on hard times and seemed to have little prospect of recovery. News then arrived that the distinguished Scottish Admiral Lord Cochrane had been invited to take command of the Chilean Navy, in a bid to achieve that country's liberation from Spanish rule. Admiral Lord Cochrane, like Captain Stewart, joined the Royal Navy in 1793, and being widely respected by those who had previously sailed under his command, was able to recruit experienced ex-naval men and merchant seamen in search of adventure to the Chilean cause. In December 1819, Captain Stewart sailed east from Port Jackson on the *Isabella Robertson* on his way to active service with Admiral Lord Cochrane.

No details are known of Captain Stewart's service with Admiral Lord Cochrane, but it would presumably have ended when the Chilean campaign was over and the admiral left Chile in late November 1822. At approximately the same time, the convict transport ship *Providence*, under the command of Captain James Herd, arrived at Valparaiso with a cargo of spars from Hokianga, homeward bound for London. There is at least a possibility that Captain Stewart met James Herd in Valparaiso and secured a passage home with him to London. A general pardon for all naval deserters was in effect, so it would have been the first opportunity that existed for many years for Captain Stewart to return to Britain without fear for his life. While the *Providence* had been at Hokianga, the missionary Thomas Kendall acted as an interpreter for James Herd, and negotiated with the Maoris on behalf of Baron de Thierry in the purchase of his 40,000 acres of land. The deeds had been signed on the deck of the *Providence*, and Captain Herd was on his way to deliver them to Baron de Thierry's home in London. Detailed knowledge of all these events would have been of considerable use to Captain Stewart.

Captain Stewart was short of neither tenacity, nor relevant experience, and armed with his reputation as the person after whom Stewart Island had been named, he eventually succeeded in finding independent backers for his colonial project. He set sail from London on 8 October 1824, as master of the schooner *Prince of Denmark*, newly acquired by Messrs. Thomas and David Asquith of Kent. Nothing is known of the Asquiths, but it seems likely that they were inexperienced entrepreneurs operating in a small way, who had been impressed by Captain Stewart's expert first-hand account of the opportunities that existed in New Zealand and had decided to put all their trust in his judgement.

Lloyd's Register of Shipping for the period from 1822 until 1824 records the *Prince of Denmark* (reg. 194/1822, London) as a single-decked schooner of 127 tons, built in Scotland in 1789, re-decked and having undergone major repairs in 1819. She had also been sheathed in copper and had further thorough repairs carried out in 1822.

Between 12 August 1822 and 1 June 1824, the *Prince of Denmark* is reported to have made two previous voyages to the South Seas. Captain P. Williams, who was in command for the voyage which began in 1822, was probably Captain Peter Williams, born in Milford Haven on 17 October 1794. The *Prince of Denmark* left London on 12 August 1822, clearing Gravesend on 19 August. She left the Cape of Good Hope on 16 November and is believed to have visited the South Shetland Islands, in Antarctica, on a sealing expedition between 1822 and 1823.

The *Prince of Denmark* was far from young when she made these voyages to the South Seas. More than 30 years after Kirkcudbright's craftsmen had fashioned her on the Moat Brae, one might have expected her as a retired revenue cutter to be modestly engaged in coastal trade. The fact that she had undergone major repairs, including the renewal of her deck in 1819 and had been sheathed in copper in 1822, implies that she had been hard-used, but was also being properly maintained. Thomas and David Asquith would have depended heavily on Captain Stewart's knowledge and experience of all aspects of his profession and would almost certainly have been guided by him as to the choice of a suitable vessel for their proposed colonial venture. Captain Stewart and Captain Peter Williams were both British, both sailed originally from London, and both had been prominent sealers or whalers in the waters around the South Island of New Zealand. It seems most likely that they and the vessels they had each commanded were known to each other. Details of the *Prince of Denmark*'s later career will illustrate that she was a conspicuously fast and able vessel. She was known to have performed well in the waters around New Zealand and she was apparently instantly available in London.

Over the years, questions have arisen regarding the identity and the character of Captain Stewart. There are frequent references to him in the study of New Zealand's early years, many of which are greatly to his credit. Other references describe incidents which range from the disgraceful to the absurd, one involving a charge of murder and another crediting him with taking the Jacobite Princess, Charlotte Stuart, a daughter of Bonnie Prince Charlie, to Campbell Island. It seems likely that historians have been confused in the past by similarities in the careers and exploits of Captain William Stewart, William W. Stewart, and Captain John Stewart, and have inadvertently moulded them into a composite character incorporating both fact and fiction.

William W. Stewart, who has no known connection to our Captain Stewart, arrived in New Zealand waters in 1809 as mate or first officer of the *Pegasus* under Captain Chase. He carried out extensive surveys in the vicinity of Stewart Island, confirming reports and rough sketches made in 1804 by the American sealer Owen Folger Smith, which showed that it was indeed an island, correcting Captain Cook's mistaken assumption that it was a peninsula. A detailed chart of Port Pegasus was also prepared during a period of two months, in which repairs and refitting work were carried out to the *Pegasus*. William W. Stewart was an experienced surveyor who had previously charted the coastline of Vanua Levu in the Fiji Islands from Sandalwood Bay to Wailua Bay, while serving on the 160-ton brig *Elizabeth*, which was then engaged in the sandalwood trade.

William W. Stewart then returned to Britain in August of 1810 with the *Pegasus*, by way of Cape Horn and Rio de Janeiro. His chart of Port Pegasus was published in 1816.

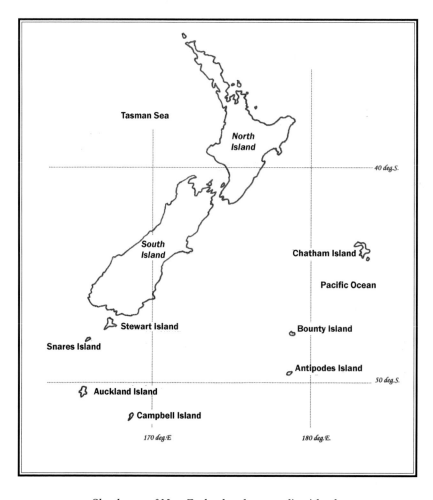

Sketch map of New Zealand and surrounding islands

His survey work and the quality of the resulting charts were regarded at the time as competent and the various place names that he chose to identify the features of his charts perhaps imply that he was a person of some education.

It now seems evident that William W. Stewart of the *Pegasus* and not Captain Stewart of the *Prince of Denmark* was the person who charted Stewart Island, and after whom it was named. Captain Stewart may not have directly claimed to be the person concerned, but he apparently did nothing to dissuade those who had jumped to the wrong conclusion. The association of his name with Stewart Island was to be of considerable advantage to him in his efforts throughout his career to establish trading posts, colonies and a variety of other enterprises. Perhaps what started off as a fortuitous misunderstanding escalated into a legend that it became impossible for him to refute without the total destruction of his reputation.

Captain Stewart's colonial venture had been arranged with Messrs. T. and D. Asquith, and he seems to have left it entirely to them to communicate with the British Government. The *Prince of Denmark* and her crew arrived safely in Sydney on 2 March 1825, carrying one passenger, a Mr. Mathew. Just over a month later, her owners, Messrs. Asquith, wrote to Lord Bathurst in the following terms[*]:

Lewisham

11 April 1825

To the Right Honourable the Earl of Bathurst

Permit us to call your Lordship's attention to the following statement.

In the month of October last year we entered into a speculation the object of which was cultivating flax and procuring timber at that part of New Zealand called Stewart's Island, to accomplish which we have engaged a person named Stewart, a man apparently well qualified for the undertaking, and from whom the island takes its name.

To forward the enterprise we have since purchased another vessel named the *Lord Rodney*. She is now in the London Dock nearly ready for sea, the expense attending both ships amount to about £5,000.

We further beg to inform your Lordship that one Company is already in existence and another forming for the same purpose, namely collecting flax and timber at New Zealand their intentions agreeably to their professions will be to form settlements on the more northern parts of the country, but to guard against any interference on their part at Stewart Island we have taken the liberty of thus addressing your Lordship under the persuasion that having advanced capital to

---

[*] *(Quoted from:* Murihika, A History of the South Islands of New Zealand and the Islands Adjacent, *Robert McNab, [1909]. Commons Attribution-share alike 3.0 N.Z. licence. Retrieved from the New Zealand Electronic Text Centre, http://www.nzetc.org/tm/scholarly/tei-McNMuri-t1-body-d1-d25.html)*

the above amount you will not refuse granting us protection for that portion of New Zealand we have already made choice of.

We have the honour to be, *etc.*,

T. and D. Asquith.

Immediately on arrival in Sydney, Captain Stewart inserted a notice in the local press[*]:

> For New Zealand, to sail in fourteen days the fine fast sailing schooner *Prince of Denmark*, William Stewart Master. Any gentleman wishing to visit these interesting islands will find this an excellent conveyance, as the above vessel will return to this port in four months. For freight or passage apply to the Commander on board or to Robert Campbell, Campbell's Wharf, March 15th 1825.

On 24 March 1825, the following advertisement appeared in the *Sydney Gazette and New South Wales Advertiser*:

> Just received by the *Prince of Denmark*, 1,500 gallons of fine genuine O.P. old Jamaica rum, now in bond, which will be sold by the cask, on reasonable terms, by J. Roberts, at the Fox and Hounds, Castlereagh Street…

This advertisement gives perhaps the only clue to the route taken by the *Prince of Denmark* on her voyage from London. It also indicates that her owners, naïve in many other respects, certainly knew which cargo was most likely to turn over a fast profit on arrival.

It was nearly two months before the *Prince of Denmark* was able to sail from Sydney. The reason for the delay was that Mr. Robert Campbell, who had been invited to act as agent in a letter from the Asquiths, had refused to advance money for the fitting out of the vessel and had withdrawn from his agency. The paths of Robert Campbell and Captain Stewart had crossed before and Robert Campbell had perhaps some reason to show caution. Captain Stewart was forced to find a new agent prepared to advance funds for the venture, and after some initial difficulty, eventually succeeded in gaining the support of Thomas Raine. In an agreement made on 16 May 1825, Thomas Raine advanced £541.16s.6d. for fitting out the *Prince of Denmark*, and the vessel was mortgaged to him as security. Captain Stewart then wasted no time in putting to sea, sailing for the Bay of Islands on 19 May. His safe arrival there on 15 June 1825 was duly recorded by missionaries:

> The settlement now enjoyed a short interval of repose, during which the natives assisted the brethren to lay down such a breadth of wheat as was likely to afford

---

[*] *(Quoted from:* Murihika, A History of the South Islands of New Zealand and the Islands Adjacent, *Robert McNab, [1909]. Commons Attribution-share alike 3.0 N.Z. licence. Retrieved from the New Zealand Electronic Text Centre, http://www.nzetc.org/tm/scholarly/tei-McNMuri-t1-body-d1-d25.html)*

a supply of flour for a whole year. Things thus presenting an encouraging aspect, and the ship *Prince of Denmark* arriving at the same time with fresh stores from New South Wales, it was judged prudent and safe to bring the females and children back from Kiddu-kiddu, and to remain, for the present at Wangaroa.*

The *Prince of Denmark*, now carrying a Mr. John Lee (or Leigh) as a passenger, then sailed southwards down the east coast of New Zealand, stopping at Hicks Bay – where Captain Stewart purchased 500 acres of land – and again at Akaroa, where a further 900 acres of land were acquired in exchange for unspecified merchandise. Captain Stewart then sailed for the Antipodes Islands, where he landed a sealing gang led by the mate, Alexander Foster, and the carpenter, George Allen. Finding seals less prolific there than anticipated, Captain Stewart then headed further south in search of new sealing grounds into sea areas notorious for the severity of their weather. The aim may have been to find the occasionally reported but as yet undiscovered Heard Island, or the islands then referred to as 'the Nimrod Group', which later proved to be wholly fictitious. Sadly, this ill-considered venture was to cost the life of the second mate, William Rook, who was so severely frostbitten that he lost the use of his limbs, and eventually died.

The ship's company was now reduced considerably in both numbers and in physical strength, firstly by the absence of the sealing gang left on Antipodes Island, and secondly by the loss of the second mate. Spars, sails and rigging were probably in need of extensive maintenance following the severe weather that had been encountered and Captain Stewart and his hard-pressed crew headed for the Bay of Islands, where they intended that provisions could be taken on board and repairs carried out.

While anchored at the Bay of Islands, the *Prince of Denmark* was raided by a party of Maoris, led by their chief Hongi Hika, who stripped the vessel of everything moveable but left the crew unharmed. This was the same Hongi Hika who Baron de Thierry had met at Cambridge a few years earlier. Ironically for Baron de Thierry, his money (or axe heads) and the gratitude of its Maori recipients had perhaps saved the life of his rival.

The *Prince of Denmark* sailed for Sydney on 1 December 1825, arriving on 18 December with a cargo of only 450 sealskins and the lone passenger, Mr. John Lee (or Leigh). The voyage clearly had not been profitable and there could be no prospect of repaying the money advanced by Thomas Raine. On his arrival, Captain Stewart found that a second vessel despatched by the Asquiths, the *Lord Rodney*, had arrived at Port Jackson. Her master carried a letter of instruction to Captain Stewart that he should leave for Stewart Island with both vessels, to establish the planned colony. Thomas Raine was again called upon for financial assistance and despite his lack of a return on the first voyage, he increased his stake in the *Prince of Denmark* by £1,300.

Captain Stewart seems to have shown surprisingly little concern for the welfare of his sealing gang abandoned on Antipodes Island. There were, however, many other

---

* (*Quoted from:* Remarkable Incidents in the Life of the Rev. Samuel Leigh, Missionary to the Settlers and Savages of Australia and New Zealand, *by the Rev. Alexander Strachan, [1855]*).

Stripping sea elephant blubber and rolling it in barrels to try-works Courtesy of NOAA National Marine Fisheries Service USA

Seal hunting at the Auckland Islands (Courtesy of the State Library of Victoria, Australia)

sealers at work in that vicinity and he may have been confident that his crew either had, or would be able to acquire, sufficient provisions for their extended stay ashore. He was not to know that only the day before his arrival at Sydney, the mate and the carpenter had both been drowned in an accident involving their longboat.

A few years prior to 1888, Mr. Bethune, the second engineer of the *Stella*, reported a grave on Antipodes Island, marked by a wooden board bearing the following faded inscription*:

> To the memory of W. Foster, chief officer of the schooner *Prince of Denmark* who was unfortunately drowned in the boat harbour, December 17th 1825.

Captain Stewart commenced a second voyage to the Bay of Islands on 19 January 1826. On arrival there, he waited in vain for the arrival of the *Lord Rodney* for a period of three weeks, then took on board William Cook, an English shipbuilder who had been persuaded to accompany him to the proposed new colony on Stewart Island, with his wife, family and several friends. These included Robert Day and Benjamin Turner (sawyers), Hugh McCurdy (shipwright), and the original passenger John Lee (or Leigh). The *Prince of Denmark* then set sail for Port Pegasus on Stewart Island, to the immediate south of South Island. It later transpired that the *Lord Rodney* had been sent on a sealing expedition by Thomas Raine, presumably in an attempt to defray some of the losses made by the *Prince of Denmark*.

The *Prince of Denmark* arrived at Port Pegasus in April of 1826, and Captain Stewart and his new associates quickly established a timber business and a shipbuilding yard there. Shortly after their arrival, the *Rosanna* and the *Lambton*, which had been despatched by the New Zealand Company to carry their first party of emigrants from Britain, visited Port Pegasus. The settlers aboard the *Rosanna* sailed originally from Leith in Scotland, and joined the *Rosanna* at London. It was claimed that they were on passage to the North Island and had called at Stewart Island only to prepare their guns and other weapons, in case of an attack by Maoris. There is however, some reason to suspect that Captain Herd of the *Rosanna* made a prior arrangement with Captain Stewart to meet at Stewart Island, and perhaps to reappraise the location of the New Zealand Company's proposed settlement, with or without the knowledge of the directors of that company.

During his six-week stay at Port Pegasus, Captain Herd of the *Rosanna* identified some minor inaccuracies in the charts made by William W. Stewart in 1809, and was surprised to learn that they had originally been made, according to Captain Stewart of the *Prince of Denmark*, using only a quadrant and a boat's compass. To produce charts as accurate as they were would have been no mean feat, considering the limitations of such basic equipment, and the credibility of Captain Stewart must have been stretched

---

* *(Quoted from:* Murihika, A History of the South Islands of New Zealand and the Islands Adjacent, *Robert McNab, [1909]. Commons Attribution-share alike 3.0 N.Z. licence. Retrieved from the New Zealand Electronic Text Centre, http://www.nzetc.org/tm/scholarly/tei-McNMuri-t1-body-d1-d25.html)*

close to breaking point as he attempted to describe the techniques used in making charts, which he had never even seen before. This of course serves to illustrate what a persuasive and able man he was in all matters other than ethics.

Thomas Shepherd, a Scottish nurseryman and gardener with the Herd expedition, met Captain Stewart on Stewart Island and recorded in his journal for Tuesday, 18 April 1826, that he had spent three days in the company of the captain of the *Prince of Denmark*, who had with him a New Zealand lady dressed as a European, and who the captain said had been acting as a stewardess for a year.

Captain Lovett of the Van Diemen's Land seal-hunter *Sally* visited Stewart Island while the *Prince of Denmark*, the *Rosanna* and the *Lambton* were there, and it was he who first brought the news of the establishment of a settlement there on his return to Hobart Town[*]:

> Captain Stewart of the ship *Prince of Denmark* had also arrived from England and had commenced his settlement on his own or Stewart's Island, which since the discoveries of Captain Cook was supposed to form the southern extremity of Te Wai Pounamu or the Southern Island; but which Captain Stewart first discovered to be an extensive island separated from the main by a strait of twenty miles.

In April 1826, James Herd and the *Rosanna* sailed from Port Pegasus, having decided that it was not the place for their proposed settlement. Although the harbour was deemed excellent, the soil, the fresh water and the climate were all thought to be less than ideal. After considering a few other locations, they headed for Hokianga, where they succeeded in purchasing land more suited to their needs. The *Prince of Denmark* sailed on her return voyage from New Zealand on 21 August 1826, travelling firstly to the Antipodes Islands to pick up the survivors of the unfortunate sealing gang, then to the Chatham Islands, eventually arriving at Sydney on 8 September 1826. Her cargo consisted of a mere 460 sealskins and one and a half tons of flax. She carried a crew of 25 men.

Captain Stewart now owed over £1,000 to Thomas Raine, who was on the verge of instigating legal proceedings to recover his money. However, Captain Stewart, in what must have been a virtuoso performance in the art of persuasion, induced Thomas Raine to charter the *Prince of Denmark*, and to attempt to establish a trading base at Hokianga. Captain Stewart's debt to Thomas Raine now increased to £1,720, as he embarked on his third voyage to New Zealand and the southern islands, leaving Sydney on 3 November 1826. A fast passage was made to Hokianga, where the *Prince of Denmark* was brought safely to anchor, 20 miles up the Hokianga River. In November 1826, land was purchased at Te Horeke, and work quickly began on the construction of a fort, a

---

[*] (*Quoted from:* Murihika, A History of the South Islands of New Zealand and the Islands Adjacent, *Robert McNab, [1909]. Commons Attribution-share alike 3.0 N.Z. licence. Retrieved from the New Zealand Electronic Text Centre,* http://www.nzetc.org/tm/scholarly/tei-McNMuri-t1-body-d1-d25.html)

jetty, a dockyard and a superintendent's house. The keel was also laid for a 40-ton schooner, and a cargo of spars was sent to Sydney. Captain Stewart was to remain at Hokianga for the next three years, presumably reluctant to return to Sydney where his debts, his unscrupulous behaviour regarding the Asquiths, and the abandonment of the settlers at Port Pegasus would inevitably catch up with him. The *Prince of Denmark* returned to Sydney on 1 May 1827, without him.

Luck had not been with either Captain Stewart or with Thomas and David Asquith, and the inevitable result of this third unsuccessful voyage was the following notice in the Sydney press[*]:

> Vice Admiralty Court, New South Wales, September 4th 1827: On Monday next, the 10th instant, at the King's Wharf, at 1 o'clock, will be exposed for Public Sale, for the Benefit of the Claimants, the Schooner *Prince of Denmark*, with her Tackle, Apparel, and Furniture, as she now lies in Sydney Cove, Burthen 127 tons. An inventory of her Stores may be seen on board, at Messrs. Raine and Ramsay's or the Sheriff's Office. By order of the said Court.

Rather surprisingly under the circumstances, Thomas Raine bought the *Prince of Denmark* for the sum of £1,650.

After three years of working at Te Horeke, where he was involved in both the building and the fitting out of ships for Thomas Raine, Captain Stewart did eventually return to Sydney on 12 January 1830, as a passenger on the *New Zealander*, one of the ships that he had helped to complete. Later the same year, he was appointed as master of the *New Zealander* and began a regular trade in flax between Port Jackson and New Zealand. By the end of that year, Thomas Raine was facing severe financial difficulties and Captain Stewart again found himself unemployed.

Armed with his uncanny skills of persuasion and his extensive experience, both real and fictitious, Captain Stewart soon found a new sponsor in Joseph Montefiore, an entrepreneur who had only recently arrived in Sydney. Mr. Montefiore chartered the schooner *Darling* and appointed Captain Stewart to her command, with the intention of setting up trading posts throughout the North Island of New Zealand. The *Darling* sailed on 12 February 1831, carrying four pioneer traders in flax: Mr. John Harris; Mr. Thomas Ralph; Mr. Barnet Burns; and a Mr. Black. On her return to Port Jackson in August 1831 with only 2.5 tons of flax, Joseph Montefiore disposed of his New Zealand interests and Captain Stewart had once more to seek new employment.

On 3 September 1831, Captain Stewart was appointed master of the 18-ton schooner *Emma*, which was owned by Captain David Clarke – a former employee of Thomas Raine – and Clarke's partner, John Stewart – the former Captain of the *Elizabeth*. John Stewart had recently been released from bail following his arrest on a charge of murder, arising from a disgraceful incident in which his interference in Maori affairs resulted

---

[*] *(Quoted from:* Murihika, A History of the South Islands of New Zealand and the Islands Adjacent, *Robert McNab, [1909]. Commons Attribution-share alike 3.0 N.Z. licence. Retrieved from the New Zealand Electronic Text Centre,* http://www.nzetc.org/tm/scholarly/tei-McNMuri-t1-body-d1-d25.html)

in him and his crew being complicit in the deaths of 50 Maori people. The 50 people concerned had been held captive in the *Elizabeth* and were later handed over to their enemies, by whom they were allegedly killed and eaten.

The coincidence of Captain Stewart and John Stewart both having links to the *Emma* has in the past given rise to much confusion between the activities of the two men. Like John Stewart, Captain Stewart also became too closely involved in Maori affairs for his own good, and narrowly escaped culpability for an attempted massacre of the people of Tuhua Island, off Tauranga. But by early 1833, he either wisely or fortuitously left the command of the *Emma*, and made his way once more to Hokianga.

At Hokianga in July 1833, Captain Stewart joined the 135-ton brig *Bee* in the rather strange and probably spurious role of navigating master. The *Bee* was under the command of Captain William Cuthbert, a man whose activities had already come to the attention of the authorities at Hokianga. James Busby, the recently arrived British resident had identified him as a bigamist, and also held him responsible for the death of a crewman. His plans to arrest him had to be abandoned due to lack of evidence. The *Bee* sailed for Sydney, but mysteriously arrived in Adventure Bay to the south of Hobart Town in Van Diemen's Land. Captain Cuthbert then went ashore and visited Hobart Town on a seemingly clandestine mission, in the course of which he was imprisoned on an unknown charge. Acting on Captain Cuthbert's instructions, Captain Stewart sailed in the *Bee* for Maria Island, arriving in early September, and was there joined by Captain Cuthbert, who had escaped from custody and brought with him the constable of the jail and three other prisoners. The *Bee* then departed with its motley crew of fugitives and miscreants, arriving at Honolulu in the Sandwich Islands in January 1834. There is a theory that Captains Cuthbert and Stewart intended from the outset to seize the *Bee* and to sail for the west coast of South America, where they anticipated that Captain Stewart's experience with Admiral Lord Cochrane would stand them in good stead for a new career in piracy. Whether or not this is true, Captain Stewart, motivated either by a new found sense of morality or by an increasing fear of the consequences of any other course of action, wrote to the British Consul at Honolulu on 8 January 1834, volunteering details of the *Bee*'s activities, betraying his shipmates, but of course omitting to give any incriminating evidence against himself. The *Bee* was promptly seized by the Crown, but was eventually allowed to return to Sydney, where she arrived safely on 3 May 1834, under the command of Captain Stewart. Her previous captain and his crew escaped to America.

At Sydney, instead of the hero's welcome that he might have aspired to, Captain Stewart was promptly arrested for debt and imprisoned. On his eventual release, he was re-arrested for a separate debt of £80 owed to Abraham Polack, a Sydney merchant who was a part-owner of the *Bee*. Captain Stewart was finally released towards the end of 1834. After a brief return to the sealing trade, he is next recorded at the Bay of Islands in April 1836, on his way to Mercury Bay. There, he joined Gordon Browne, the former superintendent of Thomas Raine's shipyard at Te Horeke, who was trying to re-establish an abandoned timber station.

HMS Herald *in Sylvan Cove, Stewart's Island, New Zealand, 1840 Courtesy of the Alexander Turnbull Library, Wellington, New Zealand*

In 1840, a messenger arrived at Mercury Bay for Captain Stewart to pass on an invitation from Captain Joseph Nias of the frigate HMS *Herald*, and Major Thomas Bunbury, to accompany them as pilot to the southern parts of New Zealand, and to use his influence to persuade the Maori chiefs in the Mercury Bay area to consider adding their signatures to the Treaty of Waitangi. After his lengthy period of isolation at Mercury Bay, Captain Stewart must have been delighted that he was still remembered, albeit for the wrong reasons, and regarded as a suitable person to fulfil the role of pilot to a ship of the Royal Navy. The prospect of lucrative employment so late in his career would have been an unexpected windfall and the offer was accepted with alacrity.

HMS *Herald* sailed on 14 May 1840, heading southwards down the coast of New Zealand. She arrived at Stewart Island on 5 June and when the Union Flag was hoisted at Shipbuilder's Cove, Stewart Island became a tiny part of Queen Victoria's realm. Captain Stewart's knowledge of the area and his familiarity with a variety of Maori dialects seem to have been of great assistance to Captain Nias and Major Bunbury in their negotiations with Maori chiefs throughout their voyage in New Zealand waters, and the name of William Stewart appears several times as a witness of signatures to the historic treaty of Waitangi.

The ship's interpreter, Mr. E. M. Williams, described Captain Stewart as[*]:

> A straightforward, truehearted sailor, who lived a temperate life in surroundings in which sobriety was rare.

---

[*] *(Quoted from* Historic Poverty Bay and the East Coast, North Island, New Zealand, *by Joseph Angus Mackay [1949]. Creative Commons Attribution – share alike 3.0 N.Z. licence.* http://www.nzetc.org/tm/scholarly/tei-MacHist-t1-body-d43-d1.html*)*

HMS *Herald* returned her pilot to his home at Mercury Bay on 28 June 1840, where he resumed his lonely life after this last brief but important involvement in the colonial history of New Zealand. In late 1849 or early 1850, Captain Stewart, having fallen once more on hard times, went to Poverty Bay, where his former associate John Harris provided him with accommodation in the form of a cottage in the grounds of his property. Captain Stewart, now an old man with a long beard, reportedly spent his last few months strolling around the garden while constantly muttering to himself. An old Maori friend attributed this to the fact that evil spirits were troubling him. Despite his long and brilliant career as a mariner, it is possible that happy contemplation of his colourful past and his many achievements was being gnawed away at by a guilty conscience. He died on 10 September 1851, aged 75 years, after two months of severe illness.

4 Merchants, Mystery, Missionaries and Maoris

Another phase of the *Prince of Denmark*'s life began in 1827, when her new owner, Thomas Raine registered the vessel in Sydney. Her registration (number 6) records that she was brig or *polacre* / schooner rig, of 127 and 14/94 tons under the old rule, and 69 and 2241/3500 tons under the new rule. References to tonnage can be misleading, so require some explanation. The displacement of a ship represents her true weight, but is of course difficult to calculate accurately. Expressions of tonnage are usually derived from a formula designed to provide an indicative measure of her cargo-carrying capacity. In the mid-18th century, a typical formula would involve multiplying the ship's length on deck by her breadth at the mid-point of her length, and again by the depth from the underside of the deck to the outside of her external skin at the pump well. The total figure would then have been divided by 130 in order to produce the registered tonnage. The formula for such calculations was subject to occasional change, hence the reference to different tonnages reflecting old and new rules.

The *Prince of Denmark*'s official number was 32050. Her measurements were 66ft 10in in length, 21ft 11.25in in beam and 8ft 10in in depth of hold. Her general description was that she had one deck, two masts, a square stern, a standing bowsprit, and was carvel-built at Kirkcudbright in Scotland in 1789. Her previous port of registry was London in 1822, where her number on the register was 194.

The description of her rig that is recorded in 1827 with her registration is interesting in that it seems at first to imply that changes had perhaps been made to her rig since her launch in Kirkcudbright. Being a schooner when launched, she would have been gaff-rigged on each of her two masts, probably with topsails set on her foremast. Her rig in Sydney seems to have left the surveyor in some doubt as to whether she was a brig or a schooner. A brig would have been square-rigged on each of her two masts, and a *polacre* schooner would not have had housing topmasts – each of her masts being in the form of a single spar. *Polacre* rigs originated in the Mediterranean and were often associated with the type of vessels used by Barbary pirates: fast and highly manoeuvrable. In their true form, they would have carried a lateen mainsail on the foremast. It is

Captain Thomas Raine (Courtesy of the Australasian Pioneers' Club, Sydney, Australia)

much more likely that the *Prince of Denmark*'s rig was close to that of a schooner, but with some of the features of a brig. The terms 'brigantine', 'hermaphrodite brig', and 'schooner / brigantine' are all used with varying accuracy to describe vessels, the rig of which does not quite accord with convention (further information is given on pages 62 and 63 which clarifies the nature of the *Prince of Denmark*'s rig).

The *Prince of Denmark* made at least one voyage carrying flax from New Zealand to Sydney in early 1827. The *Hobart Town Gazette* of 6 October 1827 reported her arrival with a crew of 13 men at Hobart Town, under the command of Captain Wright, having left Sydney on 26 September. Her cargo consisted of 74 bags of rice, 27 bags of pepper, 21 crates of earthenware, 150 bags of sugar, 8,000ft of cedar, 22 boxes of oranges and assorted other goods. She also carried two passengers: Mr. and Mrs. Christopher Wright. Christopher Wright promptly placed the following notice in the *Colonial Times and Tasmanian Advertiser* on 5 October 1827:

> For Sydney direct – to sail in ten days, the fine fast sailing schooner *Prince of Denmark*, burthen 127 tons, Captain Wright – For passage only, apply to the Commander on board, or to Christopher Wright, Agent.
>
> Captain Wright of the schooner *Prince of Denmark* hereby cautions the public against giving credit to the crew of the said vessel, as he will not be answerable for any debts contracted by them.

The same newspaper carried the following advertisement on 12 October 1827:

Just landed from the *Prince of Denmark*, the following valuable merchandise:

4 puncheons of rum, 95 chests of Hyson-skin tea, 6 cases of calico, 27 bags of pepper, 174 bags of rice, 21 crates of earthenware, 8 bags of sago, 2 cases of port wine, 34 bales of wool bagging, 150 bags of Isle of France sugar, 1 case of Rankin's cheese, 2 cases of brushes, 2 cases of lair brooms, 1 bale of superfine cloth, 2 casks of split peas, 22 boxes of oranges, 1 case of bombasines, 16 coils of New Zealand flax rope, 20 bags of corks, 2 bales of canvas sacks, 4 cases of London furniture prints, 1 case of silk handkerchiefs, 2 cases of plated ware, 2 cases of stationery, 8,000ft of cedar, 6 cases of Manilla segars [*sic*], 1 ton of Sydney salt fish, 44 casks of glass ware, 1 case of paper hangings, 1 trunk of wearing apparel, 3 cases of muslins, 1 case of Indian silks, 3 bales of slops, 3 cases of Irish linen and dimity, 1 case of black galloons.

With an assortment of merchandise too numerous to mention; for which colonial produce of every description will be taken in payment, at the highest prices.

Christopher Wright.
Wharf, October 11th, 1827.

The *Prince of Denmark* was reported in the *Hobart Town Courier* of 20 October 1827 as having left again on 17 October, bound for Sydney via George Town, her cargo consisting of 47 casks of whale oil, 1,000 bushels of wheat, 950 bushels of malt, 319 kangaroo skins, one case of parchment, and nine cases of mustard. She arrived safely at Sydney on 27 October. On 7 December 1827, she arrived again at Hobart Town under the command of Thomas Wright, having left Sydney on 30 November. The *Hobart Town Courier* issue of 8 December 1827 records that her cargo of merchandise included 9,846ft of cedar, a box of oranges, four bags of almonds, 66 coils of New Zealand flax rope, and other goods for Mr. C. Wright. She was registered in Hobart in December 1827 by J. Raine (possibly Jane Raine), and her owner's name was given as Thomas Raine. The maiden name of Thomas Raine's wife, Jane, was Wright, so there is a possibility that Captain Thomas Wright and the merchant, Christopher Wright, were relatives. The *Prince of Denmark* departed from Hobart on 6 January 1828, bound for Sydney via Launceston, carrying a cargo of sundries which the *Hobart Town Courier* of 12 January 1828 described as including 2,505 kangaroo skins, 12 crates of earthenware, pitch, tar, and seven bales of wool. Mr. and Mrs. Wright were again listed as passengers and arrived safely at Sydney on 13 January 1828. Her next port of call was Sydney, from where she departed in late February, one of four vessels that sailed eastwards across the Pacific Ocean to Valparaiso for wheat and tobacco, via the Isles of the Navigators (Samoa) and Tahiti.

To deal with such an ambitious and lengthy voyage in one brief sentence may seem remiss, but as no details have been found of the duration of the voyage or the route taken, a great deal must be left to the imagination.

Thomas Raine, the *Prince of Denmark*'s new owner was born in England in 1793, the son of a barrister. After attending Westminster School, he joined the merchant navy and sailed for Australia in 1814 as a junior officer in the convict transport ship

Surry. At the age of only 21, he found himself in command of the *Surry*, when the captain and all the other officers died after an outbreak of typhoid. He successfully completed the voyage, returning home via China, after exploring part of the Great Barrier Reef, where he gave his name to Raine Passage and Raine Island. He then made five more voyages to Australia as captain of the *Surry*, and set up (in 1818) the first whaling station on the Australian mainland at Two Fold Bay. In 1821, he carried out the dramatic rescue of three survivors of the whaler *Essex*, which had sunk after being rammed by a whale. The incident is generally regarded as Herman Melville's inspiration for his novel *Moby Dick* and is infamous for the fact that the survivors resorted to cannibalism. The rescue took place at Henderson Island, between Pitcairn Island and Ducie Island, while the *Surry* was on passage from Valparaiso to Sydney with a cargo of wheat. Captain Raine had been requested to call at Ducie Island, where he was told the survivors had last been seen. On arriving there, he saw no signs of life, and after going ashore, found no evidence of habitation. Displaying considerable skill and admirable concern for his fellow seamen, he deduced that the island had been wrongly identified and sailed instead for Henderson Island, some 80 miles away, where three men, close to death, were rescued.

Thomas Raine had earned the respect of Governor Macquarie for his humane treatment of the convicts in his care, for whom he even organised tuition in reading and writing whilst on board ship. Governor Macquarie was himself a passenger with Thomas Raine on a voyage back to Britain in 1822. Thomas Raine continued to command the *Surry* until 1827, but a few years earlier formed a partnership with the *Surry*'s Scottish surgeon David Ramsay to establish a Sydney-based firm of merchants, ship-owners and agents. Their business interests included trade in timber, pork, coconut oil, sugar, spices, rum, flax and timber spars for ships and they traded to Tahiti, Mauritius, New Zealand, the Eastern Orient and Great Britain.

On 16 January 1828, the *Sydney Gazette and New South Wales Advertiser* carried the following report:

> Captain Foreman of the *Prince of Denmark* states that Messrs. Tyreman and Bennett of the London Missionary Society were at the Isle of France (Mauritius) when he left. Messrs. Tyreman and Bennett had been last from Calcutta and were proceeding to the Cape of Good Hope whence they return to England.

This story appears to provide evidence of another lengthy trading voyage by the *Prince of Denmark* serving Thomas Raine's interests in far away places. On further investigation, however, it appears that the journalist responsible had confused the names of two different vessels. Captain Foreman did indeed make a great many voyages to and from Mauritius, but his ship was named the *Denmark Hill*.

On 8 July 1828, the *Prince of Denmark* arrived at Sydney from Valparaiso with a return cargo, which did not include the wheat that had been hoped for, and on the very next day the *Sydney Gazette and New South Wales Advertiser* published the following notice:

The Schooner *Prince of Denmark*

For sale by public auction, at the Commercial rooms, on the 16th instant, (if not previously disposed of by private contract) this remarkable fine vessel. For further particulars, apply to Mr. Thomas Raine, Bligh Street.

General recession in the late 1820s had brought financial difficulties for Raine and Ramsay and the partnership was dissolved in October 1828. In early 1829, Thomas Raine was practically bankrupt, but came to an arrangement with his creditors, sold some of his assets, invested wisely in property and established his successful shipbuilding and trading base at Hokianga in New Zealand. He later diversified further into wheat and dairy farming and established a successful flour-milling business. He died in Sydney in 1860.

An impression of the calibre of the man, and the benefits of his background and education, can be gleaned from the following letter he wrote to the Right Honourable Sir George Murray, H.M.P. Secretary of State for the Colonies[*]:

Sydney

Jany. 3rd 1829.

Sir,

Under the full impression that the Islands of New Zealand were a dependency of this colony, I, about two years ago, formed an establishment on the north-west part of the Northern Island, at a place called E. O. Kianga (Hokianga), which has now risen in consequence to a place of some consideration. With such views and impressions I have built two vessels, one called the *Enterprise*, and the other the *New Zealander*. The former, on her arrival, I obtained a register for; that vessel has since been unfortunately wrecked on the coast of New Zealand.

The New Zealander, a brigantine of 140 tons, arrived in this port early last month, and when I applied for a certificate of registry for her, I learnt from the authorities here that no such registry could be granted. I am consequently now obliged to sail that vessel on my own responsibility between this colony and New Zealand exclusively. For the more perfect information of the Home Government, I have the honor to enclose copies of my correspondence and communications on the subject, and beg most respectfully to solicit that this case may be taken into consideration, and a register ordered to be given for the vessel.

And I beg further to state that I am still prosecuting shipbuilding at my establishment, and have now men engaged for the purpose of building a vessel of 300 tons register, which I hope will be launched by the time I shall have the honor of being favoured with a reply to this letter. The persons employed are British subjects; the materials, with the exception of the timber, are all from and belonging to the Mother country.

---

[*] *(Quoted from:* Historical Records of New Zealand, Vol.1, *editor Robert McNab, [1908], Commons Attribution – share alike 3.0 N.Z. licence. Retrieved from The New Zealand Electronic Text Centre,* http://www.nzetc.org/tm/ scholarly/tei-McN01Hist-t1-b10-d59.html)

Perhaps it would not be considered impertinent nor irrelevant in my here mentioning the other main pursuits I am following at New Zealand – namely, the procuring of flax and spars. Of the former I have sent a considerable quantity to England, and of the latter I have sent one whole cargo, *viz*., per ship *Harmony* and from the experience thereby gained I shall this year import into England a cargo of spars that will, I trust, be found to answer, and be of importance to His Majesty's Navy.

I cannot let this opportunity pass without respectfully drawing your attention to my exertions at New Zealand, with the hopes that His Majesty's Government will be pleased to consider them meritorious and deserving of encouragement.

I have, *etc*.,

Thomas Raine

In September 1828, the *Prince of Denmark* was engaged in seal hunting under the command of Captain Duncan Forbes. On 7 January 1829, once again under the command of Thomas Wright, she arrived at Launceston in Van Diemen's Land from a sealing voyage to New Zealand. She took on supplies there before sailing on a further sealing voyage to King George's Sound in Western Australia. King George's Sound is actually an inlet rather than a sound and is one of the best and largest natural harbours in Australia. A military outpost was established there in 1826 by Major Edmond Lockyer and was named Frederickstown. It was renamed as Albany in 1832. The *Prince of Denmark*'s voyage must have involved a round trip of a minimum of 3,000 miles, probably skirting the entire southern coast of Australia in search of seals. At that time, this southern coast was a wild and little-known area, populated sparsely by indigenous aboriginal people, interspersed with the primitive settlements of whalers, seal hunters and escaped convicts. Finding safe anchorages in little known waters and sourcing provisions and water in communities so isolated and unruly must have been difficult and dangerous.

At Frederickstown, one of the first actions of Major Lockyer in 1826 was to set free a considerable number of aboriginal women who were enslaved to seal hunters and whalers. This gives a small but telling insight to the nature of life in these early settlements, and is borne out to some extent by the following account of a sealer's way of life in the Bass Straits, written in 1815 or 1816, which appeared in the *Hobart Courier* on 10 April 1854:

> The custom of the 'sealers' in the Straits was that every man should have from two to five of these native women for their own use and benefit and to select any of them they thought proper to cohabit with as their wives, and a large number of children had been born as a result of these unions – a fine, active, hardy race. The males were good boatmen, kangaroo hunters and sealers; the women extraordinary clever assistants to them. They were generally very good-looking, and of a light copper colour.

Major Lockyer was very highly regarded by aboriginal people for his action in attempting to reduce the extent of lawlessness and depravity, which was all too common among some seal hunters, and whalers of the day. Whaling and seal hunting ships frequently provided employment for escaped convicts who had succeeded in surviving, for a time at least, in the bush. For these men, return to urban areas was impossible. Captains in need of crew would offer them employment, but in accepting such employment, the runaways effectively imprisoned themselves all over again. Although they were fed and perhaps even earned some cash, they were still unable to take any part in shore-based society. This made them dangerous crewmen and captains had to be alert at all times to the possibility of mutiny or the theft of their vessels in a desperate bid to escape from Australia.

On 8 May 1829, the *Prince of Denmark*, under the command of Captain Duncan Forbes, arrived at King George's Sound. A few days later, Captain Forbes wrote the following letter to Lieutenant George Sleeman, the commandant of the military outpost at King George's Sound, informing him of an important discovery[*]:

Prince of Denmark,

King George's Sound,

13th May 1829.

To Lieutenant Sleeman,

Sir,

I beg to state to you for the information of His Majesty's Government that part of my sealing gangs, stationed at Kangaroo Island, have reported to me that during their excursions into the interior of New Holland, they discovered a very large lake of fresh water; they describe it as being very deep and of great extent, as they could not discern the termination of it from the highest land; the banks abound with kangaroo and the lake with fish; they also say that the natives are very friendly and have a number of canoes upon it, and the land appears to be rich and fit for cultivation.

I regret my term did not permit me to examine it, but I propose doing so upon my return to the eastward; the latitude of the place the men started from is 35 deg. 30 min., the longitude 138 deg. 40 min., and from their account 1½ days journey from the coast to the northeastward. I do not implicitly rely altogether upon their report; but I am satisfied, from the plain tale they told and their wish to conduct me to it, that a very large lake or sheet of water lies in the position just pointed out, and if I may be allowed to hazard an opinion, making its way to the Gulph [sic] of St. Vincent as the people say it bends in that direction; should any circumstances prevent my present intention of surveying it, any of the Government vessels going to King George's Sound might do it and set a question

---

[*] *(Quoted from: State Records NSW: Colonial Secretary; NRS 905, Main series of Letters received, [4/2092].* Letter dated 13 May 1829 to Lt George Sleeman from Duncan Forbes, Master of the *Prince of Denmark.*

Major Edmond Lockyer (Courtesy of the Mitchell Library, State Library of New South Wales, Australia)

of so much interest to New South Wales (if it does exist which I have not the smallest doubt of).

I am *etc.*, Duncan Forbes, Master of the *Prince of Denmark*.

Lieutenant Sleeman was impressed by Captain Forbes's account, later describing him to the colonial secretary as an intelligent man. The *Prince of Denmark* was in harbour for several weeks while her foremast was replaced and other repairs were carried out. Captain Forbes was finding difficulty in obtaining suitable timber from which to saw planks to repair the ship's boats, but Lieutenant Sleeman came to his assistance by allowing him to take a useless spar left behind by the brig *Lucy Anne*, to cut up for that purpose.

The government cutter *Dart* arrived in Sydney on 4 May 1830, commanded by John Nicholson. Her log records that on 9 April 1830, a large lake had been discovered by sealers, one day's journey from Encounter Bay. The *Dart* also carried a letter for the colonial secretary from Captain Duncan Forbes, based on the information provided by his sealers. However, by the time the letter arrived, another explorer, Charles Sturt, had followed the Murray River from its source to the sea and had named the lake he found there *Lake Alexandrina*, after Alexandrina, who was later to become Queen Victoria. Captain Forbes' letter had brought late news of a discovery, for which others had already been given credit.

The *Prince of Denmark* finally sailed on completion of repairs on 14 July 1829 and arrived at George Town in the north of Van Diemen's Land on 23 August 1829. The *Hobart Town Courier* of 29 August 1829 reported her arrival as follows:

> The Schooner *Prince of Denmark* came into George Town also on Sunday, She has been engaged on a sealing expedition to King George's Sound, where she was dismasted, and we regret to add lost three men, during a severe season of bad weather. She has arrived with only 1,031 skins.

She left George Town, still under the command of Captain Duncan Forbes, in late August 1829, bound for Sydney and arriving at Port Jackson on 7 September. The *Sydney Gazette and New South Wales Advertiser* of 8 September 1829 records that two passengers – Mr. William Underwood and Mr. William Baxter – were also carried from King George's Sound to Sydney. Lieutenant Sleeman, commandant at King George's Sound, wrote to Colonial Secretary Macleay on 9 July 1829, giving a glowing account of William Baxter's enthusiasm and diligence in his botanical researches there. He also explained that, as Mr. Baxter had been offered a free passage to Sydney for his plant collection by his friend Captain Forbes, it would not be necessary for him to wait for a passage on a government ship. Mr. Forbes had given impressive assurances that the collection would be well cared for while it was aboard the *Prince of Denmark*, and that it would be safely kept under Mr. Baxter's control.

William Baxter was a Scottish gardener who collected plants in Australia on behalf of various nurseries and private individuals. His expedition to Western Australia in 1828–1829 was arranged by Charles Fraser, a Scottish gardener and soldier who had become the superintendent of the Royal Botanical Gardens in Sydney. Mr. Baxter had arrived at King George's Sound on board the *Lucy Anne* on 22 December 1828. Having impressed Lieutenant Sleeman, he had been accommodated in the best hut in the settlement on full military rations and had been given the assistance of one of the most useful of the prisoners. Despite the very favourable report by Lieutenant Sleeman on William Baxter's conduct, Charles Fraser (his sponsor) gave a very different opinion of his character following their bitter disagreement regarding the division of the botanical collection after its arrival at Sydney. He wrote to the colonial secretary on 19 January 1830, severely criticising Mr. Baxter and accusing him of keeping the best specimens for himself, sabotaging others, and behaving abusively and violently. Despite the foregoing petty quarrel, William Baxter was eventually honoured by having the genus *Baxteri* named after him.

In November of 1829, the *Prince of Denmark* put to sea again on a speculative voyage from Sydney. Later in 1829, Captain Philip Skelton took over her command, and the *Sydney Gazette and New South Wales Advertiser* of 19 June 1830 records that he delivered a cargo of flax and floorboards from New Zealand to Sydney in June 1830, along with several passengers: the Rev. Samuel Marsden; Miss Marsden; Mr. Ferris; and Mrs. Evans, widow of the late Dr. Evans, 57th Regiment. The Rev. Marsden arrived in New Zealand on 8 March 1830, and sailed from there on the *Prince of Denmark* on 27 May 1830. Philip Skelton first came to New Zealand in 1805 as captain of the whaler *Ferret*, owned by D. Bennet of London. Bennet was engaged in the maritime fur trade and had previously operated at least one other ship, the *Betsy*, off the northwest coast of America. After spending two months at the Bay of Islands, the *Ferret* returned to London with

Philip Skelton personally escorting a Maori called Mohanga, who was possibly the first native New Zealander to visit Britain. Captain Stewart was also at the Bay of Islands during 1805, in command of the *Venus*. In 1830, Philip Skelton took over command of Thomas Raine's brigantine *New Zealander*, and later the same year handed over that command to Captain Stewart.

The *Prince of Denmark* sailed for New Zealand under the command of Captain George Jack in July 1830, and the *Australian* of 30 July records that she was carrying five cases of muskets, five casks of gunpowder, two bales of cartouche boxes, six iron pots, one box of tobacco pipes, one case of ironmongery, two pigs of lead, one hogshead of brandy, and stores. On 3 September 1830, the *Prince of Denmark* landed 15 tons of flax at Sydney. Captain Jack reported that whilst there was plenty of flax available, the natives were unwilling to trade. In October 1830, Captain George Jack became the owner of the *Prince of Denmark* and registered her at Sydney (Registration No. 21). He then sailed for New Zealand with a cargo described in the *Sydney Gazette and New South Wales Advertiser* of 19 October 1830 as consisting of 11 cases of muskets, 17 barrels of powder, nine bags of salt, three bags of rice, three bags of sugar, two cases of soap, one bale of slops, one cask of vinegar, six bags of nails, one hogshead of brandy, two puncheons of rum, four kegs of tobacco, and stores. On 26 November 1830, the *Prince of Denmark* arrived at the Bay of Islands in the North Island of New Zealand in a fine breeze from the southwest, sailing again on 30 November.

On Wednesday, 16 March 1831, the Rev. Henry Williams, leader of the mission at Paihia in the Bay of Islands, recorded in his journal that Captain Jack of the *Prince of Denmark* had sailed that day, carrying 14 severed heads of relatives of principal Maori chiefs of Ngapui who had been killed at Tauranga. Although the journal makes no comment on this macabre situation, the Rev. Henry Williams is generally regarded as having been a good friend of the Maori people and is unlikely to have been happy about what had taken place.

The Rev. Henry Williams' journal provides a fascinating record of what life was like in a remote mission station in the early years of the 19th Century, and also gives welcome and authoritative details of ship movements in and around the Bay of Islands. Williams was an unlikely recruit to the missionary service, having started his career as a midshipman in the Royal Navy in 1806 and seeing active service at Copenhagen. He also formed part of the crew of the American ship *President*, which had been taken as a prize, and he played a part in the suppression of a mutiny by her imprisoned crew. In 1815, after peace had been achieved, he retired from the navy and was inspired by relatives of his wife to become a missionary. On ordainment, he sailed for Port Jackson (Sydney) in 1822 on the *Lord Sidmouth*, which carried a full complement of female convicts. It is recorded that during the voyage of the *Lord Sidmouth*, he brought about the prevention of the female convicts from singing bawdy songs, despite the captain's lack of enthusiasm for his cause. The accumulation of his experiences in the Royal Navy and on board the *Lord Sidmouth* ensured that the Rev. Henry Williams had seen both violence and the seamier side of life. This was to stand him in good stead when he

The Rev. Archdeacon Henry Williams (Courtesy of the Alexander Turnbull Library, Wellington, New Zealand)

travelled with the Rev. Samuel Marsden to the Bay of Islands in 1823 and took charge of the mission at Paihia.

Just prior to the opening of the whaling season on 28 March 1831, the *Samuel*, commanded by Captain Anglem, landed 500 seal skins and 10 tons of flax at Sydney. She was followed next day by the *Prince of Denmark*, which the *Sydney Gazette and New South Wales Advertiser* of 5 April 1831 reported to be carrying 45 tons of flax and 3,000ft of planks. The crews of the two vessels brought the news that the *Industry* had been wrecked on 28 February at Easy Bay, Stewart Island. Captain W. Wiseman, ten seamen and six native women had been lost.

In addition to her routine cargo, the *Prince of Denmark* carried her captain's grisly collection of 14 human heads, which he perhaps naively intended to sell to curio collectors. Unfortunately for him, a Maori chief who visited the vessel was shown the contents of the captain's locker and was horrified to recognise there the faces of several of his friends (a fine painting, entitled *A Dreadful Recognition* by the Irish artist Arthur David McCormick R.I. vividly portrays the scene on the deck of the *Prince of Denmark* for an illustration in the book *New Zealand* by Reginald Horsley, but copyright restrictions preclude its reproduction here). The shock of such an experience is hard to imagine. The chief was at the time a guest of the Rev. Samuel Marsden and wasted no time in seeking his guidance and assistance. The Rev. Samuel Marsden was familiar with the *Prince of Denmark*, having been a passenger on her on at least one previous occasion, in 1830.

The Rev. Samuel Marsden is an important and controversial figure in the histories of both Australia and New Zealand. Born in Yorkshire in 1764, he was ordained in 1793 and travelled to New South Wales in 1794. He became a chaplain in Parramatta, and was also a farmer and the owner of a considerable amount of land. Appointed a magistrate, he is now frequently referred to as 'the flogging parson', with a reputation for extreme cruelty and for a particular bias against Irish Catholics. On the credit side, he was also a successful breeder of sheep and is believed to have sent the first consignment of Australian wool to Britain.

He grew concerned about the activities of whalers, sealers and others who were allegedly forming a generally lawless society in the Bay of Islands in New Zealand, and he determined to establish a mission there to protect the Maoris from corruption and exploitation. In 1814, he sailed for the Bay of Islands in his own schooner, the *Active*, accompanied by John King, William Hall, and Thomas Kendall. It was on this initial visit to New Zealand that contact was made with Hongi Hika, who had returned to Australia with the missionaries in August 1814. When Hall, Kendall and King returned to the Bay of Islands later the same year, they established their mission station under Hongi Hika's protection. Hongi Hika's growing strength and influence was reinforced by the fact that he had brought back from Australia a large consignment of firearms for his warriors. Kendall was believed to have been heavily involved in dealing in arms and that activity, combined with his abandonment of his wife and alleged adultery with a Maori lady, led to his downfall and dismissal by Samuel Marsden in 1823.

Marsden is currently viewed with more sympathy in New Zealand than in Australia, particularly as his concern about the welfare of the Maori people appears to have been genuine. He is also believed to have been responsible for the introduction of both sheep farming and vine growing to New Zealand. His response to the plea for help regarding the importation of Maori heads in the *Prince of Denmark*, as can be seen from the following letter, was rapid, heartfelt and extremely effective[*].

Church Missionary House

Parramatta

18th April 1831

To Rev. D. Coates.

Dear Sir,

I lament to say that there are many Europeans now in New Zealand whose conduct is most scandalous. I had two interviews with Governor Darling last week on this subject, and have written to him today. Copies of my representation I purpose to forward to the society, unless some effectual measures can be adopted here to restrain the infamous acts of the Europeans. I have two chiefs with me now – one

---

[*] *(Quoted from:* Historical Records of New Zealand, Vol.1, *editor Robert McNab, [1908], Commons Attribution – share alike 3.0 N.Z. licence. Retrieved from The New Zealand Electronic Text Centre,* http://www.nzetc.org/tm/ scholarly/tei-McN01Hist-t1-b10-d59.html)

from the Bay of Islands, who is come at the request of the chiefs to seek redress; the other was taken away by force from the middle. I have no doubt but Governor Darling will do all in his power to afford the protection. Whether the law as it now stands will enable the Governor to do them justice appears a matter of doubt. You will have heard of the conduct of Captain Brind; he has been the cause of much bloodshed; many have been killed to the southward in consequence of what took place at the Bay of Islands, and the heads of the chiefs have been brought to Port Jackson by the Europeans for sale. When the chief who is with me went on board the *Prince of Denmark* he saw fourteen heads of chiefs upon the table in the cabin, and came and informed me. I waited on the Governor, stated the circumstance, and requested His Excellency to use every means to recover them, in order that they might be sent back to their friends. The chief knew the heads; they were his friends; when he retired he said, "Farewell my people, farewell my people". The circumstances to the southward are more fully explained in my statements to the Governor. I intend to call upon His Excellency again in a day or two. On my return from N. Zealand I recommended that a vessel commanded by a naval officer should visit the different places to which the Europeans resort, in order to check the conduct of the masters and crews who visit these islands. A copy of my letter I forwarded to your committee. In my present communication with the Governor I am of opinion that a resident should be stationed in New Zealand, with proper authority to notice the misconduct of the Europeans, and to whom the natives can appeal for redress. If no measures are taken the New Zealanders will redress their own wrongs, and take life for life, tho' they are most unwilling to injure the Europeans...

I remain *etc.*,

S. Marsden

Governor Darling was sufficiently moved by the Rev. Marsden's plea, to make an immediate response[*]:

Colonial Secretary's Office,

Sydney,

April 16th 1831

Whereas it has been reported to His Excellency the Governor, that the masters and crews of vessels trading between this Colony and New Zealand, are in the practice of purchasing and bringing from thence human heads, which are preserved in a manner peculiar to that country: and whereas there is strong reason to believe that such disgusting traffic tends greatly to increase the sacrifice of human life among savages, whose disregard of it is notorious, His Excellency is desirous of evincing his entire disapprobation of the practice above-mentioned, as well as his determination to check it by all the means in his power; and with

---

[*] *(Quoted from:* Moko; or Maori Tattooing, *[1896]. Commons Attribution – share alike 3.0 N.Z. licence. Retrieved from The New Zealand Electronic Text Centre, http://www.nzetc.org/tm/scholarly/tei-McN01Hist-t1-b10-d72.html)*

this view, His Excellency has been pleased to order, that the Officers of the Customs do strictly watch and report every instance which they may discover of an attempt to import into this Colony any dried or preserved human heads in future, with the names of all parties concerned in every such attempt. His Excellency trusts, that to put a total stop to this traffic it is necessary for him only thus to point out the almost certain and dreadful consequences, which may be expected to ensue from a continuance of it, and the scandal and prejudice which it cannot fail to raise against the name and character of British Traders, in a country with which it has now become highly important for the merchants and traders of this Colony, at least, to cultivate feelings of mutual goodwill: but if His Excellency should be disappointed in this reasonable expectation, he will feel it an imperative duty to take strong measures for totally suppressing the inhuman and very mischievous traffic in question.

His Excellency further trusts, that all persons who have in their possession human heads, recently brought from New Zealand, and particularly by the schooner *Prince of Denmark*, will immediately deliver them up for the purpose of being restored to the relations of the deceased parties to whom those heads belonged; this being the only possible reparation that can now be rendered, and application having been specially made to His Excellency for this purpose.

By His Excellency's Command,

Alexander McLeay

It is perhaps unsurprising that the *Prince of Denmark* left Sydney on 10 April 1831 (bound for New Zealand) before the governor's edict was issued. The *Sydney Gazette and New South Wales Advertiser* of 12 April 1831 reported that her cargo consisted of four kegs of tobacco, ten casks of gunpowder, three casks of muskets, 50 axes, five hundredweight of lead, one bale of blankets, and stores. If her captain was trying to evade controversy, a cargo of gunpowder, axes and muskets seems less than wise, but perhaps he felt that it might be prudent to defend himself and his crew from an angry Maori population. The same newspaper's issue of 19 July 1831 reported her return to Sydney in July with a much less controversial cargo of flax, skins and spars, but she also brought distressing news of the misfortunes of another vessel. The following report appeared in the *Sydney Gazette and New South Wales Advertiser* of 16 July 1831:

> The *Prince of Denmark* brings intelligence that the ship *Kains* which left this port on 6th June was off the heads about 50 miles east on Thursday, returning to Sydney, out of water; having lost two men overboard and had a topmast carried away in a heavy gale which she encountered on her passage to Launceston. Mr. Mathews, one of the passengers by the *Kains* came up in the *Prince of Denmark* and Messrs. Medley, Davis and Murphy, together with three steerage passengers were landed at Port Stephens by the ship's boat.

The *Sydney Monitor* of 17 August 1831 recorded that she sailed again for New Zealand on 14 August 1831 with a cargo of one hogshead of brandy, five kegs of tobacco, four boxes of tobacco pipes, 100 iron pots, four cases of hardware, six cases of muskets, 24 casks of gunpowder, three cases, two bales of slops, and stores. The *Sydney Gazette and New South Wales Advertiser* of 8 November 1831 noted that upon her return to Sydney, on 2 November 1831, she carried 20 tons of flax. On 22 November 1831, she left Sydney, bound for New Zealand under the command of Captain Jack. The *Sydney Herald* of 28 November 1831 recorded her cargo as 74 casks powder, 18 cases muskets, two kegs of flints, three boxes of pipes, 30 iron pots, one cask of hardware, one cask of tin ware, one hogshead of brandy, four kegs of tobacco, and stores.

An anonymous letter in the *Sydney Gazette and New South Wales Advertiser* from 'A misguided New Zealand Trader' was published on 15 December 1831, and included the following paragraph:

> The *Prince of Denmark* is the only one that seems to continue in the (flax) trade with a reckless determination. The last voyage took 4 months to bring up 20 tons. This would cause her to sink at least £300. She goes again to New Zealand.

The *Prince of Denmark* and Captain Jack returned to Sydney from New Zealand on 12 January 1832, carrying 55 tons of flax and two spars. Their return was noted in the *Sydney Gazette and New South Wales Advertiser* of 17 January 1832.

However, a second anonymous letter, this time to the *Hobart Courier* in February 1832 and probably from the same source, suggests that the *Prince of Denmark*'s involvement in the flax trade was merely a cover for the carrying out of a much more lucrative trade under the very noses of the customs officers:

> Sir,
>
> The flax trade with New Zealand and Sydney is rapidly on the wane; it has been carried on with ruinous consequences to those who have been any length of time in it. The only circumstances connected with that trade which at all appears to be a secret, is the amount of loss that each has sustained. It has long therefore been a matter of surprise to every one in Sydney why the *Prince of Denmark* schooner persisted in the trade, seeing the large sum of money she must sink every trip, particularly since the profitable trade in human heads has been put a stop to, by the very proper interference of Government. If that trade had not been put a stop to there would not have been a slave alive in New Zealand. Still it is currently said by many, and the owners of that vessel themselves always gave out that they were making money in the flax trade, and many believed it too, but the luckless adventurers who were thus induced to try it can tell a very different tale, or they soon found out that they would have been ruined had they continued in it. The inexplicable mystery is now explained – a mine of Platina has been discovered at New Zealand by that mysterious vessel the *Prince of Denmark*, and she has brought up a number of tons of that ore from time to time. This of course could not long escape the vigilance of the Custom house, but the owners of the vessel as yet have succeeded in keeping the place where it is found secret, and very properly too. The crude ore yields a large portion of metallica platina, and will realise a large sum in the London market. Some specimens have been jointly analysed by Drs. Malcolm and Boston, aided by J. Mac Laren

esq., all talented chemists in Sydney. They have declared it to contain platina 5,000, rhodium 2,075, palladium 0.400, iridium 0.025, osmium 0.030, iron and chrome 0.070 parts. Messrs. Wyre, McLaren and White have bought the schooner *Admiral Gifford* to carry down miners and machinery to work the ore. This discovery shows the propriety of these rich islands being placed under the protection of the British Government.

As few of your enterprising merchants have done much in the New Zealand trade, I have given them this hint, that the owners of their vessels may be on the look out when they visit these islands. It is said in Sydney that a respectable individual in this place is a partner in the lucky hit of the *Prince of Denmark*, or rather he ought to be so.

A Sydney Cit.

This peculiar letter, full of innuendo and casting hints of a mysterious past, would seem to be of a malicious nature. Its author was clearly alerting the authorities to an illicit trade, whilst at the same time spreading valuable information to competitors and thus dealing a double blow to the activities of the owners of the *Prince of Denmark*. There was some speculation at the time that one of the reasons for the decline in the flax trade was that the Maori people had been oversupplied with muskets and gunpowder and had no longer any great incentive to trade. It is perhaps true that a source of platina had been found and it is possible that large amounts of gunpowder could have been used in the quest to find sources of valuable minerals. Subsequent events, however, illustrate all too clearly that hopes of a prosperous trade in platina were not to be realised.

Nothing daunted, Captain Jack took the *Prince of Denmark* back to New Zealand, leaving Sydney on 8 May 1832. The *Australian* of 11 May 1832 noted his cargo as being four boxes of tobacco pipes, one bale of slops, one bale of blankets, one case of ironmongery, three kegs of tobacco, one hogshead of rum, and stores.

During this voyage, Captain Jack hired Mr. Barnet Burns as a flax trader for the sum of £3 per month. Barnet Burns was an English sailor who arrived in Sydney in 1828 on the *Nimrod*, and had then sailed for New Zealand in the brig *Elizabeth*, arriving there in 1830. He made a brief return to Sydney on the *Elizabeth* in 1831, but a conviction for gross assault may have precipitated his early departure for New Zealand on board the schooner *Darling*, which was then under the command of Captain Stewart. According to the *Sydney Gazette and New South Wales Advertiser* of 29 January 1831, a fellow crewman on the *Elizabeth* apparently insulted Barnet Burns by accusing him of being a convict, and Barnet Burns retaliated by 'leading him about the decks by his proboscis, like a pig by the snout'.

Barnet Burns was landed on the Mahia Peninsula, where he was among the first Europeans to settle. He became fluent in the Maori language and married the daughter of a local chief. During many adventures among warring Maori people, he was tattooed extensively, narrowly escaped being eaten, and eventually claimed to have attained the status of a chief.

In 1834, he abandoned his wife and family, sailing firstly for Sydney as a passenger

Mr. Barnet Burns (Courtesy of the Alexander Turnbull Library, Wellington, New Zealand)

on the *Bardaster*, and secondly for London as a crewman on the same vessel. In Britain, and later in France, he embarked on a new career as a showman and lecturer, appearing as a New Zealand Chief and performing Maori songs and dances. A contemporary account of one of his lectures in 1836 described it as:

> One incongruous jumble of impudence, of ignorance, of low wit, and bare-faced presumption.
>
> *Chichester Garland*, Volume 1, No. 1, June 1836, p.53*.

The following record of his contact with the *Prince of Denmark* appears in one of the various accounts of his own experiences that he published:

> About three weeks after we arrived, a vessel called the *Prince of Denmark*, came from Sydney, with all kinds of trade on board. The captain asked me, if I had been trading for any person lately. I told him, I had not: therefore, I engaged with him for the sum of three pounds a month, and no percentage on flax. He agreed with me to go about thirty miles further along the coast where my wife's brother lived, to a place called Youkawa, it being the most likely place at that time of the year for a good flax trade. The captain left me to take the trade ashore, and to proceed to Youkawa in a canoe, as I was not ready to start exactly at the

---

* (The foregoing information regarding Barnet Burns has been based to some extent on an entry in Wikipedia, Creative Commons Attribution/Share-Alike License 3.0. http://en.wikipedia.org/wiki/Barnet_Burns)

same time; so accordingly, he sailed for some other part of the coast. In the course of two days afterwards, I proceeded in a canoe with my wife and child, and her two brothers, together with slaves enough for the management of the canoe. When I arrived here, I found one white man trading for Captain Kent, who remained at one side of the river, which is a beautiful one, and I on the other; but still one tribe only divided, or at least, commanded by two brothers.

I remained here for some time; I dare say, nearly three years, during which time I was trading constantly for one person. I sent during this time about 107 tons of flax up to Sydney. The vessel had been sent to me three times; but hearing such bad news from New South Wales of the distress of England, I was determined then on never leaving New Zealand; and for that reason, I did all in my power to please the Natives.[*]

The *Prince of Denmark*'s next voyage to New Zealand departed from Sydney on 21 August 1832. The cargo on this occasion was described by the *Sydney Monitor* of 29 August 1832 as consisting of two bales of blankets, five cases of muskets, one cask of flints, 100 cases of gunpowder, one case of pipes, one case of ironmongery, one hogshead of rum, five kegs of tobacco, and stores.

Captain Jack and the *Prince of Denmark* were at Tauranga when the *Vittoria* struck rocks. Tools from the *Prince of Denmark* were used to help in the repair of the vessel. On 19 December 1832, she left New Zealand, bound for Sydney, under the command of Captain Jack. Her cargo consisted of 40 tons of flax and whalebone and the *Sydney Herald* of 3 January 1833 records her arrival at Sydney on 2 January 1833, where she landed three passengers: Thomas Abbot; Richard Horsley; and Charles Bailey. Later the same month, 60 tuns of sperm whale oil from the South Seas, per the *Prince of Denmark*, were sold in Sydney.

Some sources record that for a few of the *Prince of Denmark*'s voyages during the early 1830s, she was under the command of Captain Black. In the absence of any other information, the assumption has been made that the name 'Jack' has been either misread, or wrongly recorded as 'Black'.

On 7 March 1833, the Supreme Court of New South Wales considered the case of Henderson versus Jack. The case concerned 16 hundredweight of whalebone, worth £60 per ton, which had been brought to Sydney from New Zealand on the schooner *Prince of Denmark*. The whalebone was consigned to the plaintiff, Mr. Henderson, whose agents had been unable to obtain the goods from Captain Jack. The court decided in favour of the plaintiff and awarded him £48.

The *Sydney Herald* reported on 28 March 1833, that the *Prince of Denmark* had sailed from Sydney, bound for Hobart, under the command of Captain Henry Wishart, carrying general cargo and two passengers – Mr. Thomas Crampton and an unnamed New Zealander. She arrived at Hobart Town on 4 April 1833, where she landed a cargo of sundries. An advertisement in the *Hobart Town Courier* of 17 April 1833 announced:

---

[*] *(Quoted from:* A brief Narrative of the remarkable History of Barnet Burns, an English Sailor, *by Barnet Burns, [1835])*

> Just landed from the *Prince of Denmark*, and for sale, 50 logs of very superior cedar. Apply to John Kerr and Co., Liverpool Street.

Captain Henry Wishart is thought to be the same prominent and skilful whaler who had discovered and named Port Fairy in Victoria in 1828. He later became the first captain of the *Wallaby*, built in 1838. In 1839, the *Wallaby* was anchored in Sealer's Cove in Victoria while her crew pursued whales in the ship's boats. Captain Wishart was about to capture his 12th whale when it attacked the boat and overturned it. Captain Wishart rescued one drowning man before swimming for the shore, but suddenly cried out and disappeared below the surface. His body was later recovered, his legs showing the unmistakable signs of a shark attack. His remains were preserved in rum and returned to Hobart Town.

The case of Henderson versus Jack must have almost been the last straw for Captain Jack, for the *Prince of Denmark* was then put up for sale. The following notice appeared in the *Hobart Town Courier* on 26 April 1833:

> *Prince of Denmark*
> By Collicott and Macmichael
>
> At the old wharf on Monday next, the 29th instant, at 12 o'clock precisely without reserve, the fine fast sailing schooner *Prince of Denmark*, burthen per register 127 tons, coppered and copper fastened. The *Prince of Denmark* was built in one of his Majesty's dockyards, for a revenue cutter, and is the fastest sailer of any vessel in either colony. She is well found in stores, a list of which may be seen on application to Messrs. Hewitt, Gore and Co.
>
> Conditions 3 and 6 months on approved bills.

People familiar with Kirkcudbright will be surprised to learn that such a tiny town was the home of one of His Majesty's Dock Yards – it seems that auctioneers in the early 19th century were well versed in creative writing. We can, however, be grateful to the auctioneer concerned for providing another scrap of circumstantial evidence in support of the *Prince of Denmark*'s history as a revenue cutter.

She was bought by John Wallace Murdoch, a farmer from Sorell Creek, near New Norfolk, who registered her in Hobart Town (Registration No. 9), where she was to have a refit.

A few weeks later, the Rev. Henry Williams, who was in charge of the mission station at Paihia at the Bay of Islands, recorded the following entry in his journal[*]:

> Tuesday 21st May – Squally. Mr. Busby and I went to Kororarika by appointment

---

[*] (*Quoted from:* Journal of Henry Williams, senior missionary in New Zealand of the Church Missionary Society, *1826–1840, The New Zealand Electronic Text Centre, http://www.nzetc.org/tm/scholarly/tei-RogEarl-t1-body-d7.html*)

to see the chiefs. All very kind; they had prepared a feast of pigeons, pipis and kumara. While here the *Prince of Denmark*, schooner, arrived from Port Jackson and anchored at a short distance. As Mr. Busby's stores were on board, we went off to learn the news; found that Mr. Morgan and five Wesleyan missionaries were on board. Much perplexed to know how to act, but could do no other than ask all on shore until some preparation could be made, as from the flying reports received from Port Jackson deprived us of that pleasure we once enjoyed in receiving brother missionaries for a season.

The weather extremely bad, wind and rain, and with great difficulty we pulled on shore. All taken by surprise and every house filled, but little news from the Colony.

The Mr. Busby referred to in Henry Williams' journal was James Busby, originally from Edinburgh, who had arrived at the Bay of Islands in 1833 to take up his post as 'British Resident in New Zealand'. He held a meeting of Maori chiefs at Waitangi in 1834, to choose a national flag, which was later accepted by the Admiralty. New Zealand ships were then registered by Mr. Busby in the name of the independent tribes of New Zealand. When he heard of Baron de Thierry's intention to establish an independent state in Hokianga, he persuaded 34 Maori chiefs to sign a declaration of independence for New Zealand and to seek Crown protection. The declaration was acknowledged by the British Government and was seen both as being important in establishing Maori identity and in providing a reason for the eventual treaty of cession in 1840.

The Mr. Morgan referred to was John Morgan (*c*.1807–1865), a pioneering missionary who encouraged the Maori people to build roads and to invest in flourmills.

On 31 December 1833, the schooner *Joseph Weller* arrived in Sydney. She had been built by Mr. Cook and the party of shipwrights that had been landed at Port Pegasus from the *Prince of Denmark*, and was the first ship known to have been built on Stewart Island. When Mr. Cook and his party came ashore at Sydney, they were met by Captain Stewart, whose enthusiastic greeting was not reciprocated by the seven settlers. They were angry and felt let down by him, complaining that they had been left to fend for themselves without provisions. Captain Stewart claimed that he had been unable to return, due to his mounting debts and the enforced sale of the *Prince of Denmark* in 1827, but this explanation might reasonably have been heard with some scepticism after the elapse of so many years.

On 22 January 1834, the *Prince of Denmark* left Hobart Town, bound for Launceston under the command of Henry Wishart. She arrived at Launceston on 28 January and landed a general cargo which included sugar, tea, rum, tobacco and building stone. The *Sydney Gazette and New South Wales Advertiser* of 20 February 1834 reports that after picking up dispatches from the vessel *Mauritius* via the *Duke of Kent*, she sailed for Sydney on 8 February, arriving at Botany Bay on 18 February, and there landing passengers for Sydney to minimise the cost of harbour dues. She then left for Newcastle, to pick up a cargo of coal for Van Diemen's Land. On 9 March 1834, having picked up her cargo of coal and two passengers on 22 February, the *Prince of Denmark* left Sydney, bound for Hobart Town, under the command of Captain Wishart. The *Sydney Herald* of 10 March 1834 reported her cargo as consisting of 127 tons of coal, 530 cheeses, 14 casks of beef, 25 chests of tea, one case clock, and six cases of apparel. She arrived at Hobart Town on 19 March 1834 and sailed again for the South Seas on 10 April.

In December of 1834, John Wallace Murdoch went into partnership with Thomas Hewitt, who became owner of 22/64 of the shares in the vessel. Thomas Hewitt was the colonial agent for the London firm of John Gore and Co., who imported Australian produce such as wheat and wool. He was therefore a person well connected with all Van Diemen's Land's merchants and entrepreneurs. Even more significantly, Thomas Hewitt was a prominent backer of the whaling industry and had an interest in seeing the *Prince of Denmark* contribute to the success of that trade.

5 *A Curious and Rich Old Fellow*

Captain James Kelly of Hobart Town bought the *Prince of Denmark* in 1835 from John Wallace Murdoch and Thomas Hewitt for the sum of £500, but as will be seen later, Thomas Hewitt continued to have a stake in various joint ventures with Captain Kelly. Captain Kelly registered her in Hobart Town (Registration No. 11) and she was re-registered by him and Thomas Hewitt in 1841 (Registration No. 9).

Between the years 1819 and 1829, masters awaiting a pilot to take their ships up the Derwent River to Hobart Town were highly likely to have their vessels boarded by the memorable figure of Captain James Kelly. He was both harbourmaster and pilot throughout that period of time and lived in a farm near Kelly's Point (now Denne's Point) at the north end of Bruny Island. His farm commanded a fine view of the approaches to the mouth of the River Derwent and was the perfect place from which to observe all shipping movements up and down the river and to and from Hobart Town.

Captain Kelly has been described as a burly giant, whose trousers were said to have been large enough to hold five bushels of wheat, and who clambered aboard the vessels hove-to off Bruny Island with some difficulty. History has not recorded the circumstances in which the capacity of his trousers was determined. His difficulty in boarding vessels was contributed to by the fact that it was his practice to bring with him fresh eggs, milk and whatever vegetables and fruit were in season. The masters and crews of the ships he piloted quickly came to respect both his seamanship and his appreciation of their immediate needs. They would not have to stay in Hobart Town for long to realise that he was also to be respected as something of a local hero.

Born as James Devereaux, in Parramatta, Australia, in December 1791, he was reputedly the illegitimate child of Katherine Devereaux, an Irish convict from Dublin whose death sentence there had been commuted to transportation for life. While on the transport ship *Queen*, she is alleged to have had a liaison with the ship's cook, James Kelly, from which her child resulted.

In 1804, at the age of only 13, James, who had now adopted the surname Kelly, was apprenticed to the Sydney firm Kable and Underwood to learn the art of seafaring.

Henry Kable and James Underwood were former convicts who had combined forces to become leading shipbuilders, traders and seal hunters in Sydney, owning several ships including the *Contest, Endeavour, Marcia, Diana*, and *King George*. James Kelly had an eventful early career as an apprentice seaman, engaged in sealing between 1804 and 1807, then sailing to Fiji in search of sandalwood. In 1809, on completion of his apprenticeship, James Kelly signed on as a crewman on the *Governor Bligh*, which was captained by John Grono and owned by Andrew Thompson, the manager of Governor Bligh's farm. After a nine-month voyage to the south islands of New Zealand, they returned with a valuable cargo of 10,000 seal skins and a large quantity of red and white pine logs. James Kelly sailed to Calcutta in India on the *Marion* or *Mary Anne* in 1810, with a cargo of sea elephant oil, sandalwood, coal and timber; and again on the *Campbell Macquarie* in 1811, with a cargo of rice, wheat and sugar – this time becoming first officer. However, his next voyage on the *Campbell Macquarie* was disastrous, when the ship ran aground on the main island of the Macquarie group on 10 June 1812 and was completely destroyed. The crew were marooned on the island for 18 weeks, during which four men died. The survivors were not rescued until 3 October 1812, when the sealing vessel *Perseverance* arrived.

It was in late 1812, immediately after that eventful voyage, that Captain James Kelly received his first command: that of the sealer *Brothers*. He is believed to have been the first white person of Australian birth to become a master mariner and went on to command the *Mary and Sally* and the *Henrietta Packet*. Both of these ships were owned by Thomas Birch, an English surgeon turned ship-owner who had recently settled in Hobart Town. James Kelly then spent the six years from 1814–1820 commanding sealing ships owned by Thomas Birch. Hobart Town was now home to him, his wife Elizabeth and their growing family.

One of his most famous exploits was the circumnavigation of Van Diemen's Land in 1815 in an open whaleboat owned by Thomas Birch, in the course of which he is credited with the discovery of the natural harbour now known as Macquarie Harbour. Two years later, he was involved in hand-to-hand fighting with Maori people near Otago in New Zealand, following the killing of three of his crew on the *Sophia*. In 1818, he was engaged in searching the coast of east Van Diemen's Land for escaped convicts, and later the same year he personally foiled an attempt by convicts to steal the *Sophia* from the harbour at Port Jackson. In 1819, he was appointed to the posts of harbourmaster at Hobart Town and pilot to vessels navigating the River Derwent. He then became active in the transportation of convicts to Macquarie harbour and later to Maria Island. By 1826, he had realised the potential of the whaling trade and had formed the Derwent Whaling Club, an organisation that shared intelligence about the movement of whales among its members, who all profited from this cooperation. The following notice was quoted in a letter to the editor of the *Mercury* of 25 January 1866:

> Derwent Whaling Club (instituted in 1826) members: Captain James Kelly, Captain W. Wilson, W. A. Bethune Esq. C. R. Nairne Esq. Eight dollars are to be

given to the first person who gives information of a whale being in the river. The produce of this club is divided into 7 shares: 5 go to the members, the sixth to charitable purposes, and the seventh to the native youth who displays the greatest expertness as headsman.

Men involved in the sealing and whaling trade were seen generally as being at the outer edges of respectability. They lived a rough and dangerous life, mingling sometimes with desperate men such as escaped convicts and bushrangers and at other times with aboriginal people and Pacific Islanders, with whom their relationships were not always amicable or honourable. However, men like Captain Kelly were able to use their considerable skills and talents to bring home valuable cargoes, reward their crews with decent wages, and buy for themselves and their families a lifestyle that sometimes seemed at variance with their perceived backgrounds. Nevertheless, Captain Kelly could not be seen as innocent of the kind of deeds and actions associated with his trade. In the 1820s, he was charged with severely mistreating one of his convict servants, William Jones, and was also accused of assaulting John Wilson, a customs officer. His reputed amorous propensities resulted in him appearing in court in 1839 to answer a case brought against him for a criminal conversation with the plaintiff's wife, and for assault. Substantial damages were awarded against him, but the assault was not proved. Captain Kelly, apparently not a man to let sleeping dogs lie, then brought a series of counter charges against the plaintiff and others. The eventual outcome was that he was found liable for damages to two people against whom he had raised actions, which were judged to be malicious prosecutions. None of these events seem to have had any adverse effect on his status and popularity. In some quarters, his reputation might even have been enhanced.

These were exciting times in Hobart, and the many larger-than-life characters that peopled the waterfront seem to have thrived on competition and been happy to gamble their money – and sometimes their lives – to enhance both their fortunes and their reputations. The following letter published in the *Hobart Town Courier* of 14 August 1835 captures the spirit of the times:

> Sir,
>
> A challenge having appeared in one of the journals of Tuesday last, from the owner of the *Prince of Denmark* offering to sail that vessel against the Government schooner *Eliza* for £500, I beg to state that the first offer was for £100 which was immediately accepted, and if I were also to take the match at £500 he would probably rise to £1000. I am still ready to accept his challenge for £100. I may add that the *Prince of Denmark* was also a Government vessel being originally built as a revenue cutter and a noted fast sailer. Still I anticipate to beat her with the *Eliza*, providing I can have the liberty to sail her.
>
> I am William McDonald, *Britomart*.

It sounds as if Mr. McDonald and the *Eliza* were in a bit of a jam. Honour prompted him to accept the challenge, but he seemed all too well aware that the *Prince of Denmark* was a faster vessel. For £100, he was prepared to gamble that his professional skills and perhaps a lucky wind shift could help him to win the day. Any larger sum however was apparently going to be at considerable risk. The circumstantial evidence of the *Prince of Denmark*'s reputation for speed and her history as a revenue cutter are worthy of note.

The income and benefits that Captain Kelly derived from sealing, whaling, and from his roles as harbourmaster and pilot, was used to purchase or charter a growing number of ships, and to acquire a considerable amount of good arable land on Bruny Island. The produce and the livestock he then gained from his land found a ready market in the masters of the vessels he piloted up and down river to and from Hobart Town, and also enabled him to cut out any middle men in supplying provisions for his own vessels.

As the whaling industry grew, Captain Kelly resigned both as harbourmaster and as pilot and concentrated on the management of a growing fleet of vessels. He formed partnerships at various times, such as Kelly and Lucas, Kelly and Hewitt, and Kelly and Bethune, among many others, for specific business ventures. The ships he either owned outright or in which he had a financial interest included the *Australian*, the *Clarence*, the *Hetty*, the *Mary and Sally*, the *Prince Leopold*, the *Venus*, the *Amity*, the *Mary and Elizabeth*, the *Mary Ann* or *Marianne*, the *Cheviot*, and the *Dogo*, but the ship with which his name is most often remembered is the schooner *Prince of Denmark*. Captain Kelly was a man of some importance in the early history of the European settlement of Van Diemen's Land in general and of Hobart Town in particular. During the period in which the whale trade prospered, he had bought 3,100 acres of land on Bruny Island, diversified into farming sheep, cattle, pigs, geese and fowls, and had built substantial dwellings for himself and other members of his family. He was a man of considerable standing in Hobart Town, elected one of the first directors of the Derwent and Tamar Fire Marine and Life Assurance Co., he was a prominent member of St David's Church, and a contributor to the cost of building Hobart Town's Theatre Royal. The following extract from a letter written by Captain E. M. Chaffers, Master of HMS *Beagle*, is evidence of the respect in which he was held[*]:

HMS *Beagle*

May 14th 1836.

Dear Kelly,

According to promise I embrace the opportunity of dropping you a line, trusting it will meet you and your family in good health as I am happy to say we are all on board the little barque. Those specimens of metal you gave me Mr. Dassom examined with the blowpipe and found to be nothing more than Lon [*sic*] Pyrites and of no value in point of a mine. After we left V.D.L. a quick run took us to

---

[*] (*Extract from a transcription in* Kelly Papers *from the collection of W. L. Crowther, Tasmanian Archive and Heritage Office*)

King Georges Sound, a place something better than reports make it and that no doubt in a few years will be of some note, just before we arrived Governor Stirling with a party had arrived from Swan River over land and returned the same way, in this route they discovered an excellent tract of land about midway, fit for grazing or cultivation, this is an excellent discovery and of course will raise the land in estimation. There was another party to start soon after from the Swan in an Easterly direction. The good people on the West Coast I think will find out what sort of country they are in, that is if enterprise will do it.

Princess Royal Harbour may be made an excellent port with trifling expense and there are many resources of trade within its reach that no one has thought of yet, or if they have, they do not take advantage of it.

Sir R. Spencer proves the most active man in the place and his snug little farm speaks a great deal, no one else near the harbor have undertaken farming, in fact there does not appear to be any emulation among the people, they want someone like yourself to show them how to make money and improve the country. From what I hear a whaling establishment would answer for the first as the fish come into shallow water in Princess Royal Harbour in the season and are very numerous in the sound, but no one has thought about it yet – in fact no one knows about it…

Like many people who have risen from humble origins to positions of wealth, power and respectability, Captain Kelly clearly enjoyed his new status and relished the fact that his friends and acquaintances included people such as Captain E. M. Chaffers and Sir John and Lady Franklin. Sadly, his domestic life was shattered by the loss of five of

HMS Beagle (*Courtesy of Edinburgh Napier University*)

his children between 1817 and 1831, closely followed by the death of his wife Elizabeth in 1831, a few days short of her 34th birthday. His household had five convict servants, at least one of whom served the Kelly family faithfully for 31 years. In 1833, he commissioned a portrait of his daughter Elizabeth from the artist and naturalist Thomas J. Lempriere, and his daughters Sophia and Mary Ann received piano lessons from Joseph Reichenberg, an Italian-born British Army 40th Regiment Bandmaster who was a mainstay of music-making in Hobart Town. His sister-in-law Mary Griffiths eventually married Sir John Jamieson, one of the wealthiest men in New South Wales; and two of his sons – Edward and Thomas – were sent to Bath Grammar School in England. A letter from Edward to his father survives and further illustrates the Kelly family's pride in their rising status and general popularity[*]:

20th April 1841

Tottenham Green

My Dear Father,

It is with great pleasure I write to inform you that the *Marianne*, Captain Hayle arrived in the London Docks on the 29th ultimo, all safe and sound. I have received yours and Mary Ann's kind letters which gave me great pleasure to hear that you are all well. I am glad to say that Thomas and I are also well.

In your letter I read that you had transferred us from the care of Mr. Jno. Gore to the care of Mr. Charles Gore, a change I did not expect but on the whole a change I assure you that Tom and I were glad to find. We have just returned from Mr. Bennett's after spending eight days with his family, during which time Tom and I were as comfortable as we could wish to be, and I have no doubt you will write to Mr. B. and thank him, as also Mrs. B. for her kindness to us. I have given Mary Ann the particulars of how our time was occupied.

We had not returned to school above 2 hours when we were much delighted to receive a letter and packet of newspapers by the Post, they were from Mary Ann per *Emu*. The papers afford us inexpressible delight to read the accounts of Tasman's 3rd Regatta. I perceive that you are again occupied as one of the committee and I doubt not, as usual, you had enough to do.

The *Prince of Denmark* was moored off the Pavillion Point, Mary Ann's letter tells me and I understand that you had a tent moored on shore, like the fashionable folks. I was much delighted to read in the papers also that after Sir Jno. Franklin had retreated from the field you were left to officiate in distributing the latter prizes and I understand that your speeches were excellent, but owing to the shouts of Bravo Kelly Hurrah Huzza *etc. etc.* some of them were scarcely audible.

I suppose we may soon expect the *Cheviot*, Capt. Young... We are much obliged to you for having been so kind as to increase our weekly pocket money 2/-... I

---

[*] (*Extract from a transcription in* Kelly Papers *from the collection of W. L. Crowther, Tasmanian Archive and Heritage Office*)

Sir John Franklin (Courtesy of Library and Archives Canada)

was much surprised to hear when Captain Hayle told me it was your intention to sell the Brig *Marianne* and I doubt not but she will realize a good price...

Your affectionate son, Edward Kelly

One of Hobart Town's greatest social and sporting occasions was the Grand Van Diemen's Land Regatta, which was founded in 1839 by the famous naval officer and later explorer, Sir John Franklin, who was then the lieutenant governor of Van Diemen's Land. Captain James Kelly was a member of the first management committee, and later its chairman.

Lady Franklin wrote to a friend, describing the first regatta and referring to a song entitled *The Blue Song**:

> It was written by Kelly the whaler, a curious and rich old fellow who was the chief manager of the boats. I understand he sports a carriage on which he has for a crest a hand grasping a harpoon with the motto *Olium*.

---

* *(Letter extract taken from the* Sydney Morning Herald *of 8 April 1939)*

Captain Kelly presented his walking stick, a fine example of the art of scrimshaw, to the Lady Franklin Museum in Hobart. It is now part of the Beattie Collection, and is held in the Queen Victoria Museum and Art Gallery in Launceston. It is made of carved whalebone, metal and whale's tooth, and the design incorporates a clenched fist at the top, reminiscent of the crest described by Lady Franklin. The museum in Launceston also houses Captain Kelly's accordion, confirming his interest in music.

By the early 1840s, the wanton destruction of whales had begun to seriously reduce the world's stocks of the species with disastrous consequences for the businesses of men such as Captain Kelly. As recession began to bite, he tried to sell off some of his ships in London, but was unable either to get a fair price for them or to gain a return cargo. On top of his growing financial woes, his eldest son James, whilst a member of the crew of the whaler *William IV*, was killed by a blow from a whale's tail on 16 August 1841. Captain Kelly was made bankrupt in September 1842, and less than a month later, his son Thomas, newly returned from school in Bath, died of hypothermia after his whaleboat capsized on the Derwent River as he sailed towards Bruny Island. Thomas Raine, a seaman, and the son of Captain Thomas Raine, a previous owner of the *Prince of Denmark*, died in the same incident. Despite personal tragedy and financial ruin, Captain Kelly survived until 1859, when he collapsed and died of a stroke. He had remained highly regarded throughout Van Diemen's Land and was credited with establishing a hugely successful industry in which, although he lost almost everything, he paved the way for others to make their fortunes.

He is still honoured today in the modern city of Hobart by the existence of the names Kelly Street, Kelly's Lane and Kelly's Steps, and his name was also given to several features on the charts of Macquarie Harbour, Port Davey, Bruny Island and the D'Entrecasteaux Channel.

Kelly Street, Hobart Town (Courtesy of Wikimedia Commons)

6   The Ship's Logs

Original logs, now held in the care of the Archives Office of Tasmania, provide the most authoritative information available regarding the day-to-day working of the *Prince of Denmark* by her various captains, officers and crew-members. The surviving logs cover several different voyages and periods of fitting out in 1835, 1836 and 1837, and one voyage spanning 1851 and 1852. Despite the many disparaging comments made elsewhere about the character of sealers and whalers, the logs of the *Prince of Denmark* have been kept meticulously in accordance with the best traditions of seafaring. For the most part, they consist of the routine recording of wind direction and strength, notes of the sail handling decisions taken, observations of latitude and longitude, observations of features of land sighted, observations of other shipping, records of the occasional ill-health and ill-discipline of the crew, and records of cargo loaded and discharged.

Reading between the lines, however, some emotion and evidence of both human strengths and frailties can be detected. The captain's joy and satisfaction each time a whale is caught is expressed in a little sketch of a whale's tail in the margin. His pride in his vessel is notable when he makes a point of recording that when in port on a Sunday, the decks are scrubbed and the ensign and burgee are hoisted. He also records, with obvious satisfaction, his little schooner's ability to keep pace with a much larger and theoretically faster barque on a voyage from Two Fold Bay to Hobart Town. Occasionally, there are telling glimpses of the captain's worries, fears and frustrations, as foul weather, defecting crew, groundings, 'uncivil' natives, lack of provisions and widespread sickness take their toll.

In transcribing the logs from the hand-written originals, I have omitted much of the routine data about wind strength, direction, and the ship's course, as they add little

FACING: *A typical page from the log of* Prince of Denmark (*Courtesy of the Archives Office of Tasmania, Australia*). *The legibility varies according to the steadiness of the vessel, and that of the log-keeper's hand. The ink has also suffered from the effects of sunlight and water (both salt and fresh), making transcription a long and slow process.*

Log On Board The Schooner Prune

Date	Winds	Remarks In Board
		fresh gales and Cloudy with
Sunday 23d	N.W.	Showers of Rain Boat out And People Imploy : as yesterday
Monday 24th	S.W.	Fresh Breezes and Cloudy, with Passing Showers of Rain unbent H. topsail to repair 3 Boats out & Crew and Shore Hands Imploy'd Cleaning Bone
Tuesday 25th	N.W.	Moderate Breezes and Cloudy All Boats out Myself repairing the topsail
Wednesday 26th 9 whales to day 15 to 20 Sun	Nble	Moderate Breezes and Cloudy A.M. Mr Chase got one whale P.M. Mons freele a whale got them Both home Myself Repairing the topsail and on Sundry Jobs about the rigging Recd from Fitchey vessel 1 Cask of Pork one 1 Bag of Sugar
Thursday 27th 4 whales got to day 11 Sun	N.W.	Moderat and fine 3 Boats out cut In two whales took the Blubber on Shore and lighted the works

to the narrative. I have, however, quoted the captain's remarks sections in full, changing only some of his spelling, and occasionally adding punctuation to make his account easier to follow. A few words have proved indecipherable, and those I have left blank. As might be expected, the entries in the shore logs are much more legible than those made in times of stress and foul weather. In the glossary, as well as explaining the meaning of nautical terms, I have endeavoured to provide information that explains some of the complicated procedures that may be indicated in the log by a single word or phrase.

The many references to sail handling provide valuable new information about the *Prince of Denmark*'s rig and clarify those matters that have caused confusion in the past. Although she was rigged generally as a conventional schooner, her captain consistently refers to her carrying a fore-topsail and a fore-topgallant sail, rather than the more usual lower and upper fore-topsails. This can be explained by the fact that the log also makes several mentions of her having a fore-topgallant mast in addition to her fore-topmast. In other words, her forward mast was in three sections, like that of a brig, rather than in two sections, like that of a schooner. It follows that the upper square sails on her foremast are described as if they were those of a brig, rather than those of a schooner. Today, she would perhaps be most accurately described as a schooner/brigantine. The men who sailed in her, however, were in no doubt that she was a schooner.

An undated sketch of a ship appears in the log for May 1836, accompanied by the words 'Thomas Gay in the month of May'. The log also records that Mr. Gray commenced work on 20 May 1836. Several sources refer to the *Prince of Denmark* having had a captain at this time whose name was Gray, but there was also a whaling captain called Thomas Gay who commanded the *Offley* in 1850.

At first glance, the sketch is little more than a doodle with no features that identify it as an image of any particular vessel. On closer study, the letters 'HK' can be clearly seen on the mainsail. Significantly, she is rigged as a conventional schooner, but the foremast is very clearly drawn as being in three separate sections (a mainmast, topmast, and topgallant mast). Other details of her rig are consistent with the information in the log. Regarding the 'HK' letters, James Kelly bought the *Prince of Denmark* from Thomas Hewitt, and subsequently went into partnership with him for several individual ventures. It would seem highly likely therefore that the letters 'H' and 'K' on the mainsail signify Hewitt and Kelly. This little sketch is very probably the only known image of the *Prince of Denmark*, and one of only two images of any of the 58 commercial sailing ships known to have been built in Kirkcudbright between 1789 and 1859.

The logs of a trading voyage to the Isles of the Navigators in 1835–1836, and a whaling voyage to New Zealand in 1851–1852, are of particular interest and are incorporated in chapters 9 and 12, with a commentary, which it is hoped will explain their significance to readers unfamiliar with the workings of a sailing ship. Further to this, logs covering six periods of time and describing maintenance, fitting out, and a variety of passages are reproduced as appendices.

Sketch of the schooner Prince of Denmark *by Thomas Gay (Courtesy of the Archives Office of Tasmania, Australia)*

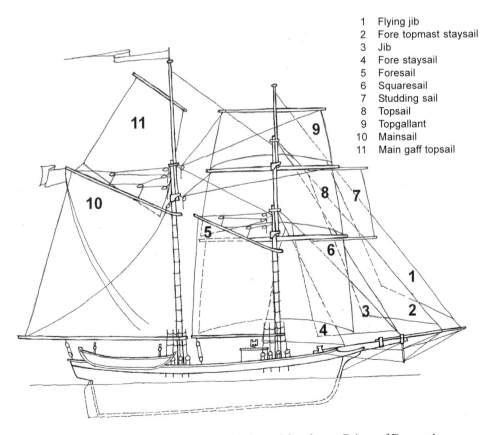

1   Flying jib
2   Fore topmast staysail
3   Jib
4   Fore staysail
5   Foresail
6   Squaresail
7   Studding sail
8   Topsail
9   Topgallant
10 Mainsail
11 Main gaff topsail

Diagram illustrating the rig and probable form of the schooner Prince of Denmark

7 The Whale Trade

Commercial whaling today is viewed by most civilised societies as utterly deplorable. The driving of several of the largest creatures inhabiting this planet to near extinction is indefensible, particularly so when the products derived from whaling are all now replaceable with more environmentally-friendly items. The people who were involved either in whale hunting or in using the products of whaling in the early 19th century had no access to the kind of data we now take for granted and little knowledge or understanding of the extent of the problem they were creating for future generations. To judge them by 21st-century standards would be unfairly harsh, and would recognise neither their enterprise nor their courage.

Between June and September every year, very large numbers of humpback whales and southern right whales would migrate northwards from Antarctic waters to their winter feeding and breeding grounds off Australia. The waters around Van Diemen's Land were an area in which they congregated and where many gave birth to their young. In the late 1820s and early 1830s, they were so plentiful that it was considered dangerous to cross the estuary of the River Derwent in a small boat.

The first whale known to have been caught in the River Derwent was in 1804, by Jorgen Jorgenson, who was then mate of the British whaling vessel *Alexander*; and the first whaling station in Van Diemen's Land was established at Ralphs Bay, on the eastern side of the River Derwent, shortly afterwards in 1806.

Jorgen Jorgenson was no ordinary harpooner. Born in Copenhagen in 1780, the son of a clockmaker to the Danish Crown, he went to sea apprenticed to a British collier and later sailed to Australia on a whaler, arriving at Port Jackson in 1800. He then joined the crew of the *Lady Nelson* and participated in exploration and the founding of settlements at Risdon Cove in 1803 and Sullivan's Cove in 1804. His return to Denmark via Cape Horn in 1807 coincided with the Napoleonic War, and after a prolonged British attack on Copenhagen, he was commissioned to command a Danish warship, the *Admiral Juul*. Captured by the British, he became a prisoner of war. While engaged as an interpreter on a British trading mission to Iceland, he and others became incensed by what they considered to be the unjust rule of Iceland by the Danish Government. They carried out a bloodless coup and Jorgenson became the ruler of Iceland. In 1809, after eight weeks in power, he was arrested by the British and returned to London. Fluent in French, German, Danish and English, as well as understanding Latin, he was then engaged as a British spy, observing the Battle of Waterloo in that capacity. A career as a playwright and author came to an end when debts, drunkenness, gambling and theft led to his being sentenced to death. This sentence was commuted to transportation to Van Diemen's Land in 1826. On obtaining his ticket-of-leave, he undertook exploration work for the Van Diemen's Land Company and later became a police constable. Marriage to a drunken and dissolute Irish convict set him back on the road to ruin, and he died in hospital in January of 1841.

By the late 1820s, there was a huge demand for a variety of products derived from whales. Whale oil was used as a fuel for lamps and as an ingredient of candle wax. It was also used in the manufacture of margarine, soap and in the oiling of wool. Spermaceti, a wax found chiefly in the head cavities of the sperm whale, was an ingredient in cosmetics, candles and lubricants, and was also used in the dressing of fabrics and in the production of ointments. Ambergris, a waxy substance found in the digestive system of the sperm whale, was used in the manufacture of perfume and as flavouring for food, and was also dried and used to make beads and jewellery. Baleen, or whalebone, much valued for being light, flexible and strong, was used for the manufacture of many items that are nowadays made of plastics. Typical uses were as the spokes of parasols, hoops in dressmaking, ribs in stays and corsets, and whips for horse riding. The appearance of elegant ladies in the photographs, taken in Adelaide, Australia and Burntisland, Scotland, may owe much to the skilful deployment of whalebone.

Throughout the 1820s and 1830s, the whaling industry was a major source of income for Australia. Approximately 60 shore whaling stations were established on the coast of Van Diemen's Land, each providing employment for about 30 men. The owners of the shore whaling stations were often prominent merchants and entrepreneurs, many of whom were also active in sealing, timber operations, farming and shipping.

Lady with crinoline and child at Adelaide

Ladies with parasols at Burntisland, Scotland

The requirements of a shore-based station were that it should be a good anchorage, and as close as possible to waters in which whales congregated. It also needed to have room to accommodate a slipway for the launching of whaleboats, a platform for flensing or cutting the blubber from the carcases, a try-works for reducing the blubber to oil, a site for huts in which the men would live, and an assortment of storage buildings.

Three or four whaleboats would have been based at each station, hauled up onto the shore when not in use. Each would have been clinker-built and of about 26ft in length, propelled by five oarsmen with a boatsteerer at the helm and a harpooner in the bows. Whenever whales were sighted, the boats would be launched in pursuit, frequently in desperate competition with the crews of other nearby whaling stations. The aim was to harpoon the whale as soon as possible after it surfaced, it being unable to immediately dive, having not had time to replenish its supply of oxygen. Ideally, the boat would be brought so close to the whale that the harpoon could be pushed into its body, rather than thrown at it. The danger of the activity combined with the richness of the prize and the determination to beat the rival crews gave plenty of opportunity for daring and bravado to override conventional prudent seamanship.

Whenever a boat or boats got sufficiently close to a whale, the harpooner would strike and hope that his harpoon would hold or remain fast in the whale's back. The whaleboat and its crew would then be towed by the whale until it became exhausted, enabling the harpoon line to be shortened up and the boat brought alongside the whale for the crew to kill it with their lances. Lances were much longer than harpoons, designed to kill the whale by causing injuries which flooded its lungs with blood.

Cutting in her last right whale (Courtesy of NOAA National Marine Fisheries Service USA)

Whalers knew that they had won the battle when the whale's spouting became tinged with red. One flick of the whale's tail would be sufficient to kill a man or to shatter the whaleboat, throwing its crew into the water. When the harpoons of two or more rival parties held fast in the body of the same whale, the convention was that the owners of the first two harpoons to hold fast shared the whale in equal parts.

A long battle to exhaust a harpooned whale could result in the whaleboat and its crew being towed at high speed for a considerable distance. When the whale was finally defeated and slain, the crew was then faced with the daunting task of towing its carcase back to the shore. Towing a whale weighing several tons and perhaps up to 60ft in length was no easy matter for five oarsmen who were most likely already exhausted from the pursuit. When wind, tide, or sea conditions made the tow impossible, carcases were anchored and buoyed for later collection, but that was an undesirable and very risky strategy. Many valuable carcases left in such circumstances were either lost in adverse weather conditions or stolen by disreputable opportunists.

When a whale's carcase had been successfully towed either alongside the hull of a whaler or to the slipway of a shore station, the work of 'cutting-in' could commence. 'Cutting-in' is the process of removing the thick layer of fat under the whale's skin. The work was done by men standing on a timber staging slung over the ship's side, or, in the case of a shore station, built over the carcase. To begin removing the blubber, an insertion was made near to the whale's tail and a hook fastened through the whale's skin. The hook was attached by a tackle, either to the ship's mast or to sheer-legs on shore. Cuts

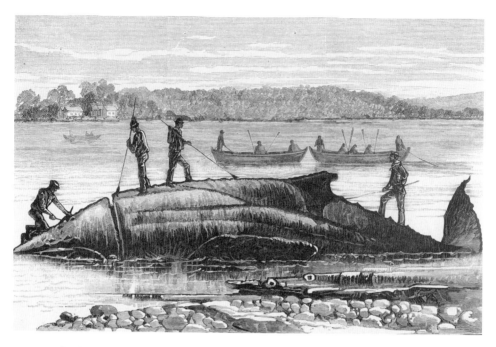

Cutting up a stranded whale (Courtesy of the State Library of Victoria, Australia)

were then made in the whale's skin in rings, spiralling from its tail towards its head, using cutting spades mounted on poles that were 15 or 20ft long. As pressure was exerted from the tackle, a strip of skin and blubber became detached and the carcase revolved, enabling the spiralling cut to be gradually extended. The detached strip of blubber was then cut into smaller pieces, in preparation for being boiled down to produce oil.

Whether on board ship or on a shore station, a try-works was used to boil down the blubber. This consisted of two or more large cast-iron or copper pots, built into a brick or stone base, forming a ventilated hearth and held together with iron brackets. When the try-works was lit for the first time, a wood fire was used to start the process. Once sufficient heat had been generated, scraps of blubber became combustible and the process was self-sustaining until the last scrap was consumed.

Captain James Kelly either owned or managed five whaling stations between 1824 and 1854, and the partnership of Kelly and Lucas had a station at Adventure Bay on Bruny Island between 1829 and 1841. In the 1829 season alone, they caught 44 whales. Ruins of the Adventure Bay Whaling Station still exist and consist of 12 stone structures, which have recently been the subject of archaeological investigations. Similar whaling stations existed at Recherche Bay and at Southport.

Despite the generally low esteem in which whalers seem to have been held, some contemporary reports refer to them as being extremely hospitable and their roughly built dwellings being surprisingly clean and orderly. Whalers' huts usually had thatched roofs and were normally built of timber, clad in wattles and clay. The dominant feature of the interior was a large brick or stone fireplace, and a hearth that was often surrounded by aboriginal people, cooking utensils and dogs. Whales' vertebrae were used as stools, and curtained bunks lined the sides. A table and benches occupied most of the floor space, and barrels for storage of salt meat, flour and water stood against the walls. Window openings were unglazed, but could be closed with wooden shutters. The rafters were used for storage of coils of rope and a profusion of other whaling and nautical equipment.

The foregoing description is based on a contemporary account given by Edward Markham, who visited the station at Recherche Bay. Mr. Markham recorded his pleasure at tasting a slice of damper (bread baked in the wood ashes without yeast), and his amusement at the men's dinner, which included doughboys boiled in the try-pots. He remarked, perhaps somewhat diplomatically, that the difference between whale oil and olive oil could not be perceived.

In 1835, during her first year of ownership by Captain Kelly, the *Prince of Denmark* made a voyage to Two Fold Bay in South Australia carrying cattle and sheep. On 6 July 1835, the following report appeared in the *Sydney Herald*:

> *Prince George*, Revenue Cutter, from Jervis Bay on Friday last, reports the arrival of the whaling schooner *Prince of Denmark* at that place, June 21st, with 300 barrels of sperm oil, out from Hobart Town six months, afterwards in Two Fold Bay, with four whales on board.

She then became engaged in supporting whaling activities at various shore stations, including those at Two Fold Bay, Portland Bay and Recherche Bay. This work consisted of acting as a mother-ship to these outposts, bringing livestock and other provisions from Captain Kelly's farm, supplying empty casks, loading full casks of oil for delivery to Hobart Town, and occasionally taking sick or injured crewmen home for medical attention.

8 Below Decks

When operating as a merchant vessel, the *Prince of Denmark* would have normally sailed with a crew that consisted of her master and perhaps six men. Her master and her mate would have been accommodated in austere but practical cabins below deck, at the stern of the vessel, accessed by a companionway forward of the steering position. The crew would have lived in the fo'c'sle below deck and in the bows of the vessel. Their accommodation would have been extremely basic and would have consisted of shelf-like bunks, probably stacked in three tiers, on either side of the vessel. This accommodation would have been accessed via a companionway immediately aft of the windlass. The crew's quarters would have been subject to the most violent motion in the ship and would have also probably been very wet. These were the conditions that were normal on sailing ships of all sizes in the early 19th century. The galley, where all food was prepared and cooked, would have been tiny and was probably in the form of a deckhouse close abaft the main mast. Its cooking range would have been wood-fired.

When operating as a whaler or as a sealer, the *Prince of Denmark*'s typical crew consisted of her master and anywhere from 17 to 21 men. It seems likely that her master and perhaps four officers would have shared the accommodation at the stern; the master with his own cabin and two officers sharing each of two other small two-berth cabins. The remaining men must have lived in the discomfort of the extremely overcrowded fo'c'sle. In one respect at least, the crews of whalers had an advantage over their comrades in merchant ships – whaling ships were nearly always a blaze of lights due to the ready availability of top quality lamp oil.

Surviving crew lists show that the ship's company included Scotsmen, Irishmen, Englishmen, Frenchmen, Prussians, Chinese, Americans, Portuguese, Germans, Australians, New Zealanders and South Sea Islanders. Taking into account language difficulties and varying social habits, one imagines that the camaraderie that normally exists among seafarers must, on occasions, have been stretched to the limit. At sea, one watch would always have been on duty, though not necessarily on deck. It would be inconceivable that all of the ship's company were below deck at any one time, so it would have been normal for bunks to be occupied by different people at different times.

On many occasions, up to nine passengers were also carried, usually on the homeward passage. These passengers, often identified only by nicknames, were rather vaguely described as South Sea Islanders. Most people from South Sea Islands are thoroughly at home at sea and have a long tradition of making ocean passages in extremely small and frail vessels which offer little or no shelter from wind and weather. To this day, small motor and auxiliary sailing cargo vessels take deck passengers on voyages lasting several days, with very few creature comforts of any description. The *Prince of Denmark*'s deck passengers would have been tough, resilient, and able to look after themselves. They would also have been ready and willing to help to handle the ship and to learn any necessary new skills.

The *Prince of Denmark*, at only 65ft in length and 20ft in beam, was much smaller than most whalers – and was even small for a merchant schooner. To operate as a whaler, she must have carried at least three whaleboats, which were the fast rowing boats used to pursue whales, from which they were harpooned. Two of these boats would have been carried in davits, one on either side of the vessel, and the third was probably stored upside down between the foremast and the mainmast over the hatch to the cargo hold.

The try-works, an unwieldy and dangerous apparatus in which blubber was boiled to produce oil, was brick-built and secured to the deck by bolted iron brackets. It is difficult to envisage where it could have been sited on such a small vessel, but it is possible that it could have been located aft of the foremast. Smoke, sparks, and splashes of hot oil must have taken a heavy toll on the condition of both the sails and the sailors. The advantage of working from a shore-based whaling station to the crew of such a small vessel is obvious.

The hold of the *Prince of Denmark* must have been in the vicinity of 30ft in length, 18ft in maximum width, and 9ft in depth. Any storage spaces incorporated in either the fo'c'sle or the after cabin would have been inadequate to accommodate provisions for up to 28 men on a voyage lasting several months. It follows that a large amount of hold-space must have been taken up with casks of water, salt beef, salt pork *etc*. Whalers also had to carry a great amount of tools, equipment and rope, as well as the necessary materials for the manufacture and repair of barrels to carry oil. A sailing ship routinely held in stock: replacement blocks, rope, canvas, sails, spars, oars, paint, pitch, oakum, spun yarn, trunnels, nails, and a myriad of other items crucial to the carrying out of running repairs and maintenance.

The logs of the *Prince of Denmark*'s various whaling voyages record many instances when the ship's whaleboats were stoved in, usually by contact with a whale's tail, and several other instances when boats were totally destroyed. The ship's carpenter is mentioned several times for not only repairing boats that had been stoved in but also for building new boats on deck to replace those destroyed. The lists of material taken on board mention quantities of planking and describe the various lengths. It is hard to imagine how tightly packed the hold must have been, and even harder to see how the carpenter found space to build a boat on a working vessel, while underway, on a deck crowded with South Sea Islanders.

The utmost care must have been taken in planning the provisioning of the ship and ensuring that goods were properly stowed in the hold. As the voyage progressed, the necessary quantities of water, food, firewood and all consumables would naturally reduce and the space gained would, in theory, be taken up with barrels of oil, or other cargo. The balance was a delicate one.

9   *The Isles of the Navigators*

A voyage to any of the South Sea Islands conjures up in the minds of most people the usual images of waving palm trees, garlanded dancing girls, noble warriors, beautiful beaches and a life of ease surrounded by an abundance of tropical fruits. The activities of missionaries, both the well intentioned and the corrupt, might also feature in this preconception, along with a dash of cannibalism and the menace of exploitative traders.

In December 1835, the crew of the *Prince of Denmark* embarked on a voyage which was based on the less romantic but practical purpose of bringing back a valuable cargo of live hogs and salt pork, together with a sufficient supply of coconuts to feed the hogs for the duration of the homeward passage. To achieve this end, the crew of seamen was supplemented with coopers to make, repair and seal barrels, and butchers to slaughter the hogs and prepare the meat for salting down.

Whilst it was normal for coopers to be employed in a whaling vessel, the butchers must at times have been alarmed to find themselves in an environment so unfamiliar, uncomfortable and downright dangerous. The weather was to prove surprisingly rough and the task of slaughtering and butchering pigs at sea in such conditions must have been extremely unpleasant. In the course of the voyage, over 640 hogs were slaughtered, and over 90 were brought back to Hobart Town alive. The seamen cannot have relished the situation when they were ordered to assist the butchers in their work, and the butchers were unlikely to be of much reciprocal help to the seamen in the carrying out of their duty.

The name of the master for this voyage appears to be recorded in the log as Captain Youngson, but this could be an error, as other records refer to either a Captain James Young or a Captain John Young being master of the *Prince of Denmark* or other ships owned by Captain Kelly at this time. A Captain William Young was also both a whaler and a timber merchant, and owned land on Bruny Island. It is not impossible that there were four captains of such similar names in Captain Kelly's employment at the same time, but it is perhaps more likely that there have been errors in either the spelling or the transcriptions of their names over the years.

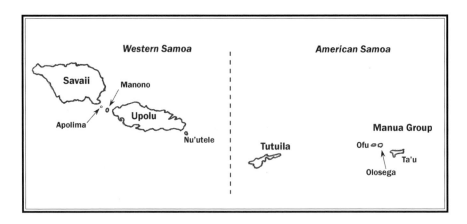

Sketch map of the Isles of the Navigators (Samoa)

In addition to maintaining discipline among his crew and the extra hands, Captain James Young had to ensure the safety of his ship and her company from the Samoan people. Captain Young was certainly well aware from personal experience, that the indigenous people of the Pacific had long memories, and occasionally held the crew of one ship responsible for both the real and the imagined misdeeds of their predecessors. The following vivid account of an earlier incident in Captain Young's career may be relevant to how he conducted himself in his dealings with the Samoan people[*]:

> The *Mary and Elizabeth*, under the command of W. Lovitt, sailed from Hobart Town on 12th April 1834. During the voyage she called in at Otago (New Zealand), and when there her boat, gear, and dead whales were seized and Captain Lovitt only escaped by a precipitate retreat. She then made for Cloudy Bay, where she was deserted by her crew and had to return to the Derwent, which she reached on 9th July. James Young was then put in command and she put to sea again on the 13th of the same month. She returned on 12th September and reported as follows: On the 10th August, in Admiralty Bay, lat. 41. 19. South, long. 175 East, the *Mary and Elizabeth*, having been drove in by stress of weather, several of the natives, amongst whom Captain Young recognised our old acquaintance, Tomawk, came alongside; Tomawk claimed acquaintance with Captain Young, and was received into the ship with his followers, one of whom he introduced as his brother, Waktoob, and others as his cousins (we suppose Highland cousins). Tomawk and his brother were invited into the cabin, and breakfasted with Captain Young—they appeared very friendly. Tomawk, on coming on board, said—'This brig belongs to Mr. Kelly.' Captain Young said, 'No, it belongs to Mr. Hewitt,' and endeavored to explain the nature of the charter. About an hour after breakfast, the weather clearing, Captain Young ordered his men to weigh the anchor, and requested Tomawk and his brother to sit on the companion, and to order their

---

[*] *(Quoted from:* The Old Whaling Days: A History of Southern New Zealand from 1830–1840, *by Robert McNab [1913]. Creative commons attribution – share alike 3.0 N.Z. licence. Retrieved from the New Zealand Electronic Text Centre,* http://www.nzetc.org/tm/scholarly/tei-McNOldW-t1-body-d1-d4-d5.html*)*

men into the canoes; they appeared to consent, and rose, as Captain Young thought, to comply with his request. Captain Young turned round to the head of the ship to give his orders to his own people, when the two chiefs, Tomawk and Waktoob, seized hold of him, and attempted to push him overboard; he resisted, and prevented their effecting their purpose, by entwining his arms in the main rigging; another New Zealander then struck him with a scrubbing brush on the hip, and brought him down on the deck; they then dragged him along the deck to the larboard pump, where they made him fast. Three of Captain Young's crew took to the rigging, the natives had knocked down the other three, and lashed them to the ring bolts—they then commenced plundering the ship, and took everything they could move, including charts, chronometers, ship's register, and other papers. At last they quarreled about a keg of tobacco, and fought with the ship's muskets, which happened to be loaded—two of them were killed, and Captain Young thinks that several more must have been wounded. When the natives began to fight amongst themselves, they left the ship, and took to their canoes, on which the men, who had fled to the foretop, came down, and released their commander and comrades. When the natives saw this, they gave up quarrelling, and made for the shore. One of the canoes was alongside, and Captain Young observed the chronometer in the bows of the canoe, and, stretching from his own deck, succeeded in rescuing it, though one of the natives made blows at him to prevent it. He then got up the anchor, and stood to sea, making for Cloudy Bay, where the *Marian* was whaling—he got within six miles of the station, and could distinctly see the smoke of the try-works, but the weather was such that he could not get into the Bay. After striving to accomplish this, from the 11th to the 27th of August, without any bedding, and hardly any clothing left them, Captain Young was compelled to run for Hobart Town, his crew being unable to stand the rigors of the season in their destitute condition.

Captain Young was evidently a man with considerable experience of all aspects of his profession. His navigation seems to have been impeccable, with all his landfalls being made when expected, and correctly identified. His tactics in taking chiefs or their families hostage until trade was successfully achieved, though apparently callous and provocative, were perhaps understandable given his past experience. What is more puzzling is his readiness to trade muskets, 'blunderbudgions', axes and bayonets to people of whom he was so wary.

The first section of the log records routine maintenance, some particular preparations that were made for what was going to be a long voyage through dangerous waters, and the loading of the necessary equipment and stores.

Tuesday 24 November 1835 The wind from the southeast with thick hazy weather throughout a.m. One carpenter employed from the shore repairing the copper on the masts and sundry jobs. People employed variously.

Wednesday 25 November The wind from the southwest with heavy rain a.m. People employed working in the hold. One carpenter from the shore employed in filling in the ports and sundries.

Thursday 26 November Strong gales from the S.S.W. with small rain. People employed variously. One carpenter from the shore employed at sundry jobs.

Friday 27 November Wind at southwest with frequent showers of rain. People employed reeving running rigging and carpenter employed from the shore at sundry jobs.

Saturday 28 November The wind from the southwest with clear weather. People employed bending the fore-topsail then washed the decks down. One hand employed painting the bulwarks.

Sunday 29 November The wind from the southwest. At 8.00 a.m. hoisted the colours then the people went ashore on liberty.

Monday 30 November The wind from the southward. At 6.00 a.m. took on board eight hides of fresh water and bent the foresail and top gallant sail and flying jib and gaff topsail then stowed them. One carpenter employed on sundry jobs. At 6.00 p.m. sent two hands ashore fill water.

Tuesday 1 December The wind from the S.W. and clear weather. Took on board 19 hides of water, 5½ pipes ditto, then stowed them in the hold. One carpenter from the shore at sundry jobs.

Wednesday 2 December. The wind from the westward and clear weather. Took on board ten tierces of water, four hides, five half pipes, and 56 bags of salt. One carpenter from the shore employed variously.

Thursday 3 December The wind from the westward and clear weather. Took on board two tierces, two hides, five half-pipes, two quarter pipes of water, 26 bags of salt. One carpenter employed from the shore.

Friday 4 December Hot sultry winds from the N.W. throughout with clear weather. Crew employed bringing off 75 bags of salt and sundry other jobs. A.m. unbent the jib and took it ashore to be altered. A.m. brought off a raft of fresh water. One carpenter employed from the shore sheathing the windlass and other jobs. Ditto weather.

Saturday 5 December Strong breezes from the northwest with fine weather. Crew employed fitting new fore lifts. Received on board three large iron pots. Midnight ditto weather.

Sunday 6 December Fresh breezes from the W.S.W. with fine weather. At 8.00 a.m. hoisted the colours and washed the decks down. At p.m. carried away our steering [stern?] moorings, swept, and got it up again and made it fast again. Clear throughout the day.

Monday 7 December Strong breezes and clear weather with heavy squalls. Received on board eight pipes of water, 12 pieces of —— 12ft long, and 15 pieces of ditto 15ft long, 140 planks 12ft long by 7in, and 14 kegs of powder and one brass howitzer. 3.30 p.m. the harbourmaster came on board and unmoored the ship and took her in the stream, took the *Australian* from alongside and took her to the *Brothers* of London with ballast.

Tuesday 8 December Strong breezes from the northwest throughout. Crew employed at sundry jobs. P.m. Mr. Kelly came on board ship and the crew and paid them their advance.

Wednesday 9 December Strong breezes from the S.W. most part with fine weather. Employed getting off sundry articles from the shore. Midnight calm.

Thursday 10 December Light breezes from the northward with hot sultry weather throughout. Employed getting off fresh water from the shore. Midnight calm.

Friday 11 December Strong breezes from the eastward most part with fine weather. Employed getting all snug for sea ——.

Saturday 12 December A fresh breeze from the eastward with fine weather. Employed at sundry jobs. Midnight ditto weather.

Sunday 13 December A strong breeze from the southwest throughout with clear weather. At noon the pilot came on board took charge and got under way. Wrought down the river. At 8.00 p.m. came to anchor off Brown's River with the small bower in 12 fathoms water and 50 fathoms of chain.

A shift of wind to the southwest was exactly what was needed to enable the *Prince of Denmark* to clear the southeastern shores of Van Diemen's Land and head to the open sea. The captain's relief at finally reaching the end of the fitting out period and ridding himself and his ship of the dust, dirt and shavings generated by the painters and carpenters can readily be imagined. His broaching of a keg of rum on the first day of the voyage was partly an indication of that relief, but partly also a way of rewarding and hence gaining the approval of the ship's company, of whom he was going to demand a huge amount of work in conditions of considerable danger and discomfort.

Monday 14 December A light breeze from the northwest and fine weather. At 4.00 a.m. got under way and made all sail. At noon the pilot left the ship the master went with him on shore. P.m. the master returned and made all sail to the eastward. The harbour log ends at noon and commences the sea log. Broached the cask rum.

Tuesday 15 December At noon Cape Pillar bore east just 6 leagues. Light airs and clear weather. At 4.00 took in the topgallant sail, carried away the fore-topsail sheet, lowered it down and reefed it. At 6.00 Cape Pillar bore N.W. by W. distance 6 leagues. Ship rolling much. At 6.00 p.m. let out the reef of the topsail, set the fore-topgallant sail. At 4.00 calm with heavy swell from the southward. Set the foresail and square sail. Out reef of the mainsail. Set the jib at 9 a.m. Set the fore-topmast sail. At noon hazy weather.

Wednesday 16 December p.m. commences with light airs and clear with a heavy sea from the southward. Watch employed sundry jobs. At 9.00 p.m. took in the topmast studding sail and square sail. At 1.00 a.m. the wind shifted to the northward. Tacked and stood to the eastward. At 4.00 a.m. the same continuing sea. At 10.00 a.m. broached a cask of beef. At noon fresh breezes and clear weather. Latitude by obs. 42.59 south.

Thursday 17 December p.m. commenced with fresh breezes and clear weather. People employed making mats for the boats. At 6.00 p.m. hoisted the boats up to the davit ends and secured them. At 11.00 p.m. strong breezes. Single reefed the topsail and mainsail. At 4.00 a.m. fresh breezes and cloudy weather. At 8.00 a.m. took in the fore-topgallant sail and flying jib. Strong gales and clear weather. At noon fresh breezes and ditto weather. Latitude obs. 42.52 south.

Friday 18 December p.m. commences with fresh breezes and clear weather. At 1.00 p.m. set the topgallant sail and flying jib and let out a reef of the mainsail. At midnight strong gale attended with small rain. Took in the topgallant sail and flying jib. At 4.00 a.m. fresh breezes attended with showers of rain. At 8.00 a.m. the strop of the main halyard block gave way. Fetched it down and put up a new one. At noon fresh breezes and hazy weather. Latitude obs. 42.27 south.

Saturday 19 December p.m. commences with fresh breezes and cloudy weather. At 7.00 p.m. set the fore-topmast studding sail. At 10.00 p.m. took in the fore-topmast studding sail. Midnight fresh breezes with heavy head sea. At 4.00 a.m. light wind and rainy weather. Set the fore-topmast studding sail. At 6.00 a.m. set the square sail and gaff topsail, let the reef out of the fore-topsail. At noon unbent the flying jib. Master and mate employed putting two cloths in it and the watch at sundry jobs. Latitude obs. 41.03 south.

Sunday 20 December p.m. commences with fresh breezes. At 4.00 p.m. ditto wind and weather. At 8.00 p.m. strong breezes and clear weather. At midnight ditto breezes and weather. Squared the yards. At 1.00 a.m. brailed up the foresail. At 8.00 a.m. fresh breezes and clear weather. Laid the yards right square. At 11.00 a.m. gybed ship. Fresh breezes and clear weather. The watch employed mending the flying jib. Latitude obs. 39.00 south.

Monday 21 December p.m. commences with light breezes and clear weather. At 8.00 p.m. light winds and ditto weather. At midnight light airs with heavy swell from the southwest. Lowered down the mainsail and square sail. At 4.00 a.m. ditto wind and weather. Set the foresail. At 7.00 a.m. set the mainsail and braced the yards. At noon light breezes and clear weather. People employed cleaning muskets and cutlasses. Latitude ob 38.27 south.

Tuesday 22 December p.m. commences with fresh breezes. At 6.00 p.m. took one reef of the mainsail and stowed the topgallant sail. Strong breezes. At 10.00 p.m. took in the second reef of the mainsail and single reefed the topsail. Strong gales and cloudy weather attended with showers of rain. Midnight ditto wind and weather. At 7.00 a.m. let out the reef of the foresail and unbent the flying jib to get it repaired, the watch employed at it. Noon latitude obs. 38.55 south.

Wednesday 23 December p.m. commences with strong gales and squally weather. At 7.00 p.m. took in the third reef in the mainsail. Midnight strong gales and rainy weather. At 4.00 a.m. ditto wind and weather. Carried away the forerunner bolt. Set it up to another. At 10.00 a.m. got up the fore staysail and bent it then let out the second reef of the mainsail and first ditto of the topsail and set the topsail. At noon light winds and hazy weather. Latitude obs. 38.23 south.

Thursday 24 December p.m. commences with light airs and hazy weather with an inclining swell from the northward. People employed repairing chafes on the rigging and sundry other jobs. At 8.00 p.m. light winds and thick hazy weather. Midnight fresh winds and ditto weather. At 7.30 a.m. set the fore-topmast studding sail. Light breezes. At noon light airs thick hazy weather. Watch employed variously. The carpenter employed putting in a bolt for the fore runner and sundry other jobs.

Friday 25 December p.m. commences with light winds and thick hazy weather. People employed variously. At 8.00 p.m. light winds and clear pleasant weather. Took in the studding sail from the larboard side and set it on the starboard ditto. Wind falling. Bound to the eastward. At 2.00 a.m. braced the yards up. Light breezes and clear weather. At 8.00 a.m. fine pleasant weather. Taking sights by the chronometer. The watch repairing topping lift. At noon ditto winds and weather. Latitude obs. 36.01 south.

Saturday 26 December p.m. commenced with light winds and fine pleasant weather. At 8.00 p.m. fresh breezes and hazy weather. At midnight ditto breezes with smooth water. At 2.00 a.m. tacked ship's head to the southward. At 4.00 a.m. tacked ship's head again to the N.E. Light wind and thick haze. At 5.00 a.m. saw ship on the weather bow running down on us. At 8.00 a.m. we spoke her. She had been one month from Sydney, had got 100 barrels of sperm oil. At 10.00 a.m. saw Cape Maria Van Diemen bearing N.E. by N. dist. 10 leagues. At noon the Three Kings bore N.N.W. dist. 15 leagues.

Sunday 27 December p.m. commences with light winds and hazy weather. Saw a ship on our lee beam standing to the N.E. At 4.00 p.m. the North Cape bore S.W. by S. dist. 10 leagues. Light winds and hazy weather. The North Cape of New Zealand bore S.E. distance 7 leagues from which we take a fresh departure. Midnight ditto winds and weather. At 3.00 a.m. took in the gaff topsail. Fresh breezes and clear weather. At 8.00 ditto winds and weather. At noon fresh breezes and ditto weather. Latitude obs. 33.34 south.

Monday 28 December p.m. commences with cloudy weather and fresh breezes attended with passing showers of rain. At midnight strong breezes. Took in the fore-topgallant sail. At 2.00 a.m. tacked ship's head to the S.E. Took in the flying jib and set the staysail. At 6.00 a.m. set the flying jib. At noon set the topgallant sail. Latitude obs. 32.02 south.

Tuesday 29 December p.m. commences with strong breezes and clear weather. Took one reef of the topsail. At 8.00 p.m. ditto breezes and weather with heavy sea from the northward. Midnight ditto wind and weather. At 4.00 a.m. fresh breezes attended with frequent showers of rain. At 6.00 a.m. fresh breezes with clear weather. At 10.00 a.m. took in the flying jib and fore-topgallant sail. At noon strong gales and clear weather attended with a heavy sea from the northward. Latitude obs. 30.09 south.

Wednesday 30 December p.m. commences with strong gales and cloudy weather. At 4.00 p.m. took in the second reef of the mainsail. At 8.00 p.m. ditto winds and weather. Midnight strong gales and cloudy weather. At 4.00 a.m. strong breezes and rainy weather attended with a heavy northerly swell. At 8.00 a.m. ditto winds and thick rainy weather. At noon ditto winds and heavy showers of rain.

Thursday 31 December p.m. commences with heavy gales and heavy showers of rain. Close reefed the fore-topsail and single reefed the foresail. At 8.00 p.m. more moderate still inclining to rain. Broached the last cask of beef. At 10.00 p.m. strong breezes with clear weather. At midnight, strong gales with very heavy squalls and showers of rain. Stowed the mainsail and jib. At 4.00 a.m. ditto winds and weather. At 8.00 more moderate. Set the mainsail. Let out one reef of the topsail, set the topgallant sail, jib and flying jib. Noon Latitude obs. 29.29 south.

Friday 1 January 1836 p.m. commences with light winds and fine clear weather. People employed variously. At 8.00 p.m. ditto winds and weather. At 10.00 p.m. set the fore-topmast studding sail and let out the reef of the fore-topsail. Midnight ditto winds and weather. At 2.00 a.m. light breezes attended with lightning and cloudy weather. At 4.00 a.m. calm and a heavy sea from the N.E. Lowered down the gaff topsail and mainsail and brailed up the foresail. At 7.30 a.m. set all the sail again. Broached the two kegs of peas. People employed —— and stowing them away again. Light airs and clear weather. Latitude obs. 28.54 south.

Saturday 2 January p.m. commences with light airs and calm with the same continuing sea. People employed stowing away the musket cases. At 9.00 p.m. light breezes from the N.E. with clear weather. Set all possible sail. Midnight ditto winds and weather. At 4.00 a.m. light airs and calm. Lowered down the mainsail and gaff topsail. At 6.00 a.m. unbent the mainsail to reduce it, being too large. The watch working at it. At noon ditto winds and weather. Latitude 28.51 south.

Sunday 3 January p.m. commences with light airs and clear weather. People employed altering the mainsail. At 6.00 p.m. ditto breezes. Got the mainsail bent again and set. At midnight smart winds and smooth water and clear weather. At 6.00 a.m. thick cloudy weather. Washed down the decks and pumped the ship out. At noon light winds and clear weather. Latitude obs. 28.23 south.

Monday 4 January p.m. commences with light breezes and clear weather. At 4.00 p.m. set the fore-topmast studding sail. At 8.00 p.m. light winds and pleasant weather. Took in the topmast studding sail. At midnight fresh breezes and cloudy. At 6.00 a.m. the watch employed splicing the topping lift it being stranded. At 9.30 a.m. took one reef in the topsail, took in the flying jib and gaff topsail and topgallant sail, took one reef in the mainsail. Strong gales attended with showers of rain. At noon latitude obs. 27.27 south.

Tuesday 5 January p.m. commences with strong gales and rainy weather. Close reefed the topsail and stowed the inner jib. At 3.00 p.m. heavy squalls with rain. Wind shifting round to the westward. All of a sudden lowered down the mainsail and stowed it. At midnight let out one reef of the topsail and set the topgallant sail and mainsail. At 7.00 a.m. set the jib. More moderate with rainy weather. At 10.00 a.m. took in the topgallant sail and mainsail, it being very squally. At noon set the mainsail and jib. Heavy breezes and thick heavy weather.

Wednesday 6 January p.m. commences with fresh breezes and cloudy weather. Let out one reef of the topsail and set the topgallant sail and flying jib. At 3.30 p.m. saw a ship on our weather beam standing to the southward. At 11.00 p.m. set the square sail. Midnight ditto winds and weather. At 3.30 a.m. set the topmast studding sail and gaff topsail. Fresh breezes and clear weather attended with a heavy swell from the southward. Lowered down the mainsail. At 8.00 light winds. People employed repairing chafes and sundry jobs. Cooper making barrels. At noon ditto weather. Latitude obs. 24.53 south.

Thursday 7 January p.m. commences with light winds and clear weather. The watch employed variously, the carpenter and cooper about their own jobs. At midnight light airs and clear weather. Set the top studding sail and square sail. At 3.00 a.m. took in the topmast studding sail and square sail. Set the jib, mainsail and gaff topsail. At 8.00 a.m. fine breezes and ditto weather. People employed about the rigging. At noon ditto wind and weather. Latitude obs. 23.32 south.

Friday 8 January p.m. commences with fresh breezes and clear weather. At 6.00 p.m. took one reef in the topsail and set the topmast studding sail. At 8.00 p.m. the wind drawing ahead, took in the topmast studding sail and braced up the yards. Took in the gaff topsail. Midnight ditto winds and weather. At 4.00 a.m. fresh breezes and cloudy weather inclining to rain. A.m. the watch employed cleaning muskets, the carpenter employed fitting up pigpens. At noon light winds and clear weather. Latitude obs. 22.50 south.

Saturday 9 January p.m. commences with light winds and clear weather. Heavy swell from the southward. At 8.00 p.m. light breezes with cloudy weather. At midnight light breezes and clear. At 2.30 a.m. tacked ship and stood to the S.E. At 6.00 a.m. got up the spare topsail and overhauled it ready for bending. At 8.00 a.m. unbent the topsail and fetched the other to the yard. At 11.00 a.m. tacked and stood to the northward. At noon the watch employed re-bending the new topsail. Latitude obs. 21.16 south.

Sunday 10 January p.m. commences with light winds and clear weather. The watch employed altering the new topsail, it being too large. At 8.00 ditto wind and weather. Midnight cloudy with calm weather. Brailed up the foresail and lowered down the mainsail. At 4.00 a.m. light air sprung up from the southward. At 8.00 a.m. ditto wind and weather. At noon calm and clear weather. Latitude by obs. 20.53 south.

Monday 11 January p.m. commences with light airs and calm. At 1.00 p.m. fresh breeze sprang up from the southward attended with showers of rain. Set the topmast studding sail and square sail. At 2.00 p.m. carried away the jaws of the main gaff. Unbent the mainsail to get a new jaw on it. At 3.00 took in the square sail and studding sail. At 7.00

p.m. set the flying jib and mainsail without the gaff. At 11.00 took in the flying jib and topgallant sail. Midnight squally weather with frequent showers of rain. At 8.00 a.m. set the topmast studding sail. At noon ditto winds and weather. Latitude obs. 19.39 south.

Tuesday 12 January p.m. commences with light winds and clear air. At 6.00 p.m. bent the mainsail and set it. Light breezes and clear weather. At midnight ditto winds and weather. At 3.00 a.m. saw Savage Island bearing N.E. At 10.00 a.m. the watch employed setting up the topmast and topgallant rigging and back stays. The south end of Savage Island bore E.S.E. distance 4 leagues. At noon light airs and calms. The watch employed making cartridges. Savage Island bore E. to S.E. distance 5 leagues. Latitude obs. 18.57 south.

The log records tersely without a hint of surprise, satisfaction or relief that in the vastness of the Pacific Ocean a landfall had been successfully made at the tiny island we now know as Niue. In the absence of sophisticated navigational equipment and comprehensive charts, the captain's dead reckoning had proved uncannily accurate and previous experience had presumably enabled him to correctly identify the land that had appeared to the northeast. The name Savage Island says quite a lot about its reputation at that time, and part of the captain's skill lay in bringing his ship close enough to shore to make an accurate identification, while still being far enough away, and with enough wind and sea room to escape if a fleet of war canoes put out from the shore. The fact that the watch was put to the task of preparing cartridges as soon as land was sighted is indicative of the tension that would have been felt on board. Thanks to the careful preparations made before sailing, a month after leaving home, there was no pressure to send a party ashore for water or fresh food and no need to carry out any repairs.

Wednesday 13 January p.m. commences with light winds and clear weather. At 6.00 p.m. Savage Island bore S.E. by S. distance 6 leagues. At midnight light airs and calm. At 3.00 a.m. tacked ship's head to the N.E. At 8.00 a.m. light winds and clear weather. At 10.00 a.m. saw a whaler on the lee bow, southward. At noon he bore down on us and hailed us. The captain went on board with —— to see if he could give him anything for it. Latitude obs. 18.21 south.

Thursday 14 January p.m. commences with light airs and calm. Spoke the ship *Meridian*, whaler of and from Edgartown with 600 barrels of sperm whale oil, 14 months out. Captain Youngson went on board and the captain of her came on board here. At 5.00 p.m. put the captain of her on board. Received two gallons of sperm oil from her. At 6.00 p.m. made all possible sail for the eastward. Midnight ditto winds and weather. At 2.00 a.m. the wind shifted round to the south with heavy showers of rain. At 8.00 a.m. light airs and clear weather. At noon latitude obs. 18.06 south.

Friday 15 January p.m. commenced with light airs and smooth water. At 3.00 p.m. lowered down the mainsail and brailed up the foresail. At 8.00 p.m. hauled down the jib and clewed up the topgallant sail. Calm from 2.00 until 3.00 a.m. Received a breeze from the westward with cloudy weather, made all sail. At noon light airs and clear. The carpenter finished with the pens. Latitude obs 17.57 south. At noon served out the last piece of beef, there being no more on board.

Saturday 16 January p.m. commences with light airs. At 2.00 p.m. tacked ship's head to the eastward. At 7.00 p.m. tacked ship's head to the northward. Light winds and cloudy.

At midnight heavy breezes from the N.E. with clear weather. At 4.00 a.m. ditto winds and weather. At 8.00 a.m. tacked and stood for the S.E. Tacking ship to the best advantage as the winds are so variable. At noon clear weather and light airs with fresh breezes and frequent showers of rain. Latitude obs.17.13 south.

Sunday 17 January p.m. unbent the flying jib and repaired it. At 4.00 p.m. bent it again. Light airs and cloudy. Midnight fresh breezes and ditto weather. At 2.00 a.m. tacked ship's head to the northward and eastward. Light winds with passing showers of rain. At 8.00 a.m. light breezes and cloudy weather attended with squalls and showers of rain. At noon fresh breezes with showers of rain and squalls. The wind very variable.

Monday 18 January p.m. commences with fresh breezes and squally weather attended with frequent showers. At 7.00 p.m. took in the flying jib and topgallant sail and gaff topsail, double reefed the topsail and mainsail it looking very wild like to the N. At midnight tacked and stood to the northward. At 2.00 a.m. tacked ship's head to the northward. Light winds and cloudy weather. At 6.00 a.m. made all possible sail to the northward. Rainy weather attended with showers of rain. At noon fresh breezes and clear. People employed making boarding nettings. Latitude obs. 15.27 south.

Tuesday 19 January p.m. commences with clear weather. At 3.00 p.m. took in the topgallant sail. Took one reef topsail. At 5.00 p.m. very heavy squalls. Hauled down the mainsail and clewed the topsail down. At 6.00 set them again double reefed. At 8.00 tacked and stood for the southward and westward. At 11.30 p.m. the ship was taken aback with a heavy squall and carried away the main boom. At 6.00 a.m. the carpenter commenced fishing it. More moderate with a heavy sea from the N.W. At 10.00 a.m. tacked ship's head to the N.E. and set the foresail and close reefed topsail and staysail. At noon very heavy squalls with rain and thick weather.

Wednesday 20 January p.m. commences with fresh gales and heavy rain attended with the same continuing sea. At 8.00 p.m. wore ship's head to the S.W. More moderate but still looking wild like. At midnight ditto wind and weather. A.m. heavy rain and squalls. At 4.00 a.m. more moderate but still under low canvas. Ship labouring very much. At 6.00 wore ship and stood to the N.W. At noon calm at times and at others very heavy squalls with very heavy showers of rain. The carpenter employed about boom.

Thursday 21 January p.m. calm with heavy squalls at times. At 6.00 p.m. got the boom finished and shipped it in its place and bent the mainsail. Still under the topsail, foresail and staysail. At 8.00 p.m. wore ship's head to the southward. Heavy squalls of wind and rain. Midnight heavy squalls and rain. A.m. continual rain the whole four hours with squalls. At 6.00 a.m. the watch employed repairing chafes. Ship labouring very heavy. Still under low canvas. At 8.00 a.m. more moderate. Set the jib. At noon heavy gales. Stowed the jib and reefed the foresail. Heavy squalls and rain.

Friday 22 January p.m. commences with moderate weather but still looking very wild like. Afraid to make sail for the squalls are so violent. At 6.00 p.m. more moderate with heavy showers of rain. At 8.00 p.m. wore ship's head to the northward. Midnight light winds and calm but still looking so wild, afraid to set sail on the ship. A.m. very heavy rain throughout the watch. At 6.00 a.m. ditto weather. Set the mainsail. At 10.00 a.m. wore ship's head to the N.W. Lowered down the mainsail. At noon ditto weather.

Saturday 23 January p.m. light breezes with constant rain. At 4.00 p.m. set the mainsail. At 6.00 p.m. tacked ship's head to the northward. At 10.00 p.m. tacked ship's head to the S.W. Light winds and dark cloudy weather. At 4.00 a.m. light winds and clear weather. At 6.00 light winds and clear weather. Let out all the reefs and made all possible sail. At noon fine pleasant weather. People employed about the rigging. Latitude obs. 15.10 south.

Sunday 24 January p.m. commences with strong breezes and clear weather. At 8.00 p.m. ditto winds and weather. Took in the flying jib and topgallant sail, one reef in the topsail, and ditto in the mainsail. At midnight strong breezes with cloudy weather. Tacked and stood to the N.E. Strong swell from west. At 6.00 a.m. tacked and stood to the westward. At 7.00 a.m. double reefed the topsail and mainsail. Strong gales with a heavy sea running from the westward. At noon heavy breezes and cloudy weather. Latitude obs. 15.03 south.

Monday 25 January p.m. commences with heavy gales and squally. Took in the jib and mainsail and topsail, reefed the foresail. At 6.00 p.m. heavy gales and showers of rain. Ship rolling and labouring much. Forereaching under the reefed foresail and staysail. At 7.00 p.m. set the topsail double reefed. At 9.00 p.m. very heavy squall, took in the topsail. Midnight ditto wind and weather. At 6.00 a.m. very heavy squalls with rain with a very heavy cross-running sea. Ship labouring very much. At 9.00 more moderate. Set the topsail. At noon wore ship's head to the northward. Lat 15.43 south.

Tuesday 26 January p.m. commences with moderate weather. Set the mainsail and topsail. At 2.00 p.m. unbent the topsail and bent the new one. At 7.00 p.m. lowered down the mainsail with a very heavy sea from the N.W. Midnight more moderate with cloudy weather, the sea falling fast. At 4.00 a.m. set the mainsail and topgallant sail and gaff topsail. At 6.00 a.m. made all possible sail to make land. At 7.00 a.m. saw the land bearing N.W. by W. just 10 leagues. At noon light airs and calm. The island of —— bearing from N.W. by W. to W. by N. distance 6 leagues. —— bearing from N.E. by E. to E.N.E. distance 10 or so leagues, being the Islands of the Navigators. Latitude obs. 14.27 south.

Wednesday 27 January First part light winds and calm. Midnight ditto winds and weather. At 4.00 a.m. made all sail and ran inshore. At noon strong breezes and squally weather. Stood close inshore and hoisted a signal for the canoes to come off at ——.

Thursday 28 January p.m. the canoes came off with two white men into them, a pig and some breadfruit one axe, one —— then the canoes left. Shortened sail and stood to the offing. At 6.00 p.m. the extent of the island bore N.N.W. to N.E. by N. distance about 4 or 5 leagues. Latter p.m. ditto winds and weather. This log contains only six hours to commence the trading log.

After a two-week passage from Savage Island, the *Prince of Denmark*'s captain had again brought his vessel safely to her intended landfall despite squally weather, gales and seas which had frequently caused her to labour heavily. Navigation would have been extremely difficult in those circumstances and would have depended much more on art than science. The ship's position could only be determined by plotting the compass course steered, estimating the vessel's speed and also estimating the amount she had drifted due to the effects of leeway and tide.

If there were Pacific islanders among the crew members, the captain would have known of their legendary skills as navigators and would have been able to compare his estimate of his vessel's position with their opinion of where they were. Their skills were based partly on an extremely well developed memory of the southern hemisphere's night sky, and partly on an uncanny understanding of tidal currents and wave patterns. They combined these two factors with others, such as knowledge of marine creatures, birds and flotsam to enable them to recognise areas of ocean as surely as rural people would recognise a landscape.

Thursday 28 January (Trading log) First part light breezes and clear air. At 6.00 a.m. the canoes came off with trade. At noon we finished and run down to another place of the island. At 2.00 p.m. canoes came off. At 6.00 finished trading. Shortened sail and stood to the offing until morning. Disposed of four muskets and six bayonets and six axes. Latter part wind and weather ditto.

Friday 29 January First part light winds and pleasant weather. At 2.00 p.m. tacked ship's head in shore. At 8.00 a.m. commenced trading. Trade for this day was one musket, six axes, some pipes for coconuts. At 3.00 p.m. sent our own boat ashore for mortar and stones for to build up the pots, with two white men belonging to the shore and three of our own men. At 6.00 our boat came off. Discharged her then hoisted her up. Made all possible sail to another place of the island. The extent of the islands bore from E. to S.W. by S. distance 3 leagues. 24 yds. of calico for sundry necessaries for the ship's use. To the white men, 6 yds. of calico, 2 lbs. of tobacco and two-dozen pipes for their trouble.

Saturday 30 January First part strong breezes and squally with showers of rain. Took in the topsail and flying jib. At 4.00 stood in towards the island. Light winds and clear weather. At 6.00 commenced building up the pots. Middle part ditto winds and weather. Two canoes came off but they had nothing to trade. Crew under arms to protect the ship. Stood to the offing and tried to get round the north part of the island but the current being so strong we could not get round. The extent of the island S. by W. to S.E. dist 4 leagues. At 10.00 p.m. bore up and ran to the south part of the island. Latter part ditto winds and weather. Sun obscure.

Sunday 31 January First part light winds and calm. At 8.00 a.m. commenced killing. Light winds and pleasant weather. At 5.00 p.m. sent our own boat ashore to see about trade for a blunderbuss but it being Sunday they would not trade. Killed for that day 46 pigs. At 6.00 p.m. commenced salting down. Shortened sail and stood to the offing. The extent of the island bore from N.N.W. to N.W. distance 3 leagues. Latter part ditto wind and weather.

Monday 1 February First part light winds and clear weather. At 4.00 a.m. tacked and stood towards the island. At — a.m. the canoes came off. When finished with them run down to another place of the island. Trade for that day two new muskets and one old ditto, one blunderbudgion, 6 yds. of calico. At 6.00 finished trading then bore away for the island of Opolu. At 7.00 p.m. the extent of the island bore from N. by N.E. distance 3 leagues. Latter part ditto winds and weather.

Tuesday 2 February First part light winds and pleasant weather. At 5.00 a.m. called all hands. The butchers to commence packing. The one employed getting casks out of the hold and pumping of water. At 8.00 a.m. the butchers commenced slaughtering. Killed for this day 64 pigs. At 6.00 p.m. finished. The extent of the land bearing N. by E. to W. by N. Wind at N.W. tacked ship's head to the N.E. At 8.00 p.m. commenced cutting up and salting. Latter part ditto wind and weather.

Wednesday 3 February First part light winds and clear weather. At 2.00 a.m. finished salting. Ditto winds and weather. Middle part strong breezes and rainy weather. P.m. the crew employed helping the butcher to repack the meat. Strong gales and rainy weather. Lowered down the mainsail and stowed it. At 6.00 p.m. the extent of the land of Upolu bearing from W. by S. to W. by N. distance 4 leagues. Tutuila bearing E.S.E. directly. Latter part ditto winds and weather.

Thursday 4 February First part strong breezes and rainy weather with heavy cross-sea. At 9.00 a.m. commenced packing the meat into the casks, some of the pieces being spoilt. P.m., some of the canoes came off then they went ashore to fetch off their trade in the morning. At 6.00 p.m. stood to the offing, the extent of the land bearing from S.W. to W.N.W. distance 3 leagues. Latter part ditto winds and weather.

The illustration below depicts the shore at Apia on the island of Upolu in 1842. The buildings shown are typical of the architecture of Samoa, round-ended and open-sided to suit the climate. Apia, now the capital of Western Samoa is almost certainly one of the places where the *Prince of Denmark's* crew carried out their trading only six years earlier. Two visiting vessels are shown anchored off the beach, just as the *Prince of Denmark's* crew would have done.

Friday 5 February First part strong breezes and thick rainy weather. Wind from W. by S. to E. by E. At 6.00 a.m. tacked ship's head inshore. Middle part fresh breezes with all possible sail set toward the island. No canoes came off. For this day stowed down eight hogs, 14 beef tierces. At 6.00 p.m. shortened sail. Head to the N.W. the extent of the land bearing from W.N.W. to W.S.W. distance 3 leagues. Latter part ditto winds and weather.

Saturday 6 February First part light winds and clear weather. Wind from N.E. to S.W.. At 2.00 a.m. tacked ship's head towards the land. Light winds and variable. At 8.00 a.m. the canoes came off to trade. Trade with the canoes for this day was one musket and seven axes and some calico. At 11.00 a.m. sent our own boat ashore with some white men belonging to the island and the two New Zealanders. At 7.00 p.m. they came off with two very large pigs, one musket, one axe, 6 yds. of prints and 8 yds. of calico, one cleaver, one bottle of powder, two-dozen of pipes, 2 lbs. of tobacco. Latter part ditto winds and weather.

Sunday 7 February First part light winds and clear weather. Tacking on and off shore. Middle part light winds and rainy weather. Killed this day 12 pigs. At 1.00 p.m. sent our own boat ashore with two white men and their chief. At 3.00 p.m. one canoe came off with trade of a musket. Thomas Latten went ashore. At 5.00 p.m. our own boat came on board then hoisted her up shortened sail and stood to the offing. The extent of the land

Grand Place d'Apia, Ile Opoulou (Courtesy of Treasures of the NOAA Library USA)

bearing from S. by E. to W.S.W. distance 3 leagues. Latter part strong breezes and rainy weather.

Monday 8 February First part strong gales and rainy weather. Close reefed the topsail and stowed the mainsail and jib. At 6.00 a.m. wore ship's head inshore. More moderate. Set all possible sail towards the island. At 8.00 a.m. turned the meat over in the press. Killed one pig being rather badly. Middle part strong gales and hours of rain. Took in the topgallant sail and flying jib. Latter part strong gales and very heavy squalls of rain. Lying to under the foresail, and close reefed the topsail and staysail. Ship labouring very heavy.

Tuesday 9 February First part strong gales and heavy squalls. Ship labouring very much. Heavy seas. Middle part ditto winds and weather. Stowed away eight beef tierces, two hides. Latter part more moderate.

Wednesday 10 February First part light winds and clear weather. At 2.00 a.m. wore ship's head in shore. At 10.00 a.m. went into the ship harbour to fish our bowsprit but there being 28 fathoms of water close to the land we did not bring up. Traded one musket and a few charges of powder. Butchers employed killing and salting and killed 24 hogs. Latter part at 6.00 p.m. the extent of the land bearing S.S.E. to W.S.W. distance 3 leagues. The island of Savaii bearing from W. by S. to W. by N. distance 8 leagues. Latter part light winds with all possible sail set towards the island of Savaii.

Thursday 11 February First part fresh breezes and cloudy weather. At 2.00 a.m. took in the topgallant sail. At 8.00 a.m. commenced killing. Killed 12 hogs. At 2.00 p.m. commenced cutting up and salting down. At 6.00 p.m. the island of Savaii bearing S.W. by S. distance 6 leagues. Latter part light winds and calms with the same continuing sea from the N.W. Winds from W. to N.W. Latitude by obs. 13.04 south.

Friday 12 February First part light airs and calm with the same swell. Ship rolling very heavy. At 8.00 a.m. commenced packing. Packed two hides. Middle part strong breezes and clear weather. At 2.00 p.m. tacked off the Island of Savaii but no canoes came off. At 6.00 p.m. the extent of the island bearing from S.S.E. to W.S.W. distance 3 leagues. Shortened sail and stood to the offing. Latter part strong gales and rainy weather. Wind at N.W.

Saturday 13 February The first part strong gales and heavy rain. At 2.00 a.m. tacked ship's head in shore. At 8.00 a.m. bore away for the lee part of the island, there being too much sea for their canoes to come off. At 11.00 a.m. there was one canoe came off with one white man. To it we sent our own boat ashore and kept the chief on board. At 5.00 p.m. the canoe came off. Traded two muskets and 5 fathoms of calico. The extent of the island bearing from S. to W.S.W. distance 3 leagues. Middle and latter part light winds and heavy rains. Kept the chief on board all night and the white man. Winds from N.W. by E.

Sunday 14 February. First part light winds and pleasant weather. At 11.00 p.m. tacked ship's head in shore. At 6.00 a.m. called all hands. Sent the boat ashore and the butchers and the rest of the crew to commence killing. Kept the chief on board. At 12.00 the boat came off with trade of two muskets and one carbine. At 1.00 the boat went ashore again. Kept the chief's sons on board. The chief went ashore to get more trade. Killed this day 12 hogs. At 5.00 p.m. the boat came off with another two muskets trade and one cleaver, 3 fathoms of blue calico. The trade for this day is 48 hogs, four ——. The extent of the island bearing from W.S.W. to S.S.W. distance 2 leagues. Middle part ditto winds and weather which from north and west.

Monday 15 February The first part strong breezes with showers of rain. At 2.00 tacked ship and stood in shore. At 7.00 a.m. sent the boat on shore and a great number of canoes came off. Still keeping the chief's sons on board. At 12.00 the boat came off with two muskets of trade being 20 pigs. Traded with the canoes on board, 3 fathoms of blue calico, 2 fathoms of white ditto, 2 fathoms of prints and a number of pipes for mats and coconuts. The chief and his wife came off to see the ship. Killed this day 26 hogs. At 7.00 p.m. the boat came off with trade for two muskets and six bayonets. Latter part ditto winds and weather.

Tuesday 16 February The first part smart breezes and cloudy weather. At 6.00 a.m. called all hands and the butchers to commence killing. Killed 30 pigs. At 10.00 a.m. the people employed in cutting up and salting them down. The vessel under easy sail, the wind from E.N.E. to W. At 6.00 p.m. the island of Savaii bearing S.S.W. distance 8 leagues.

Wednesday 17 February The first part clear weather with light breezes. At 6.00 called all hands up to help kill. Killed 14 large pigs. At 9.00 a.m. the butchers employed packing the meat into the casks. The people employed in the hold breaking out and stowing down the meat that is salted. At noon the butchers cutting up and salting the pork. At 3.00 p.m. the missionary boat came on board and several canoes and left at 5.00 p.m. At 6.00 the island bore S.E. by S.W. distance 6 leagues.

Thursday 18 February First part calm weather and light airs. At daylight called all hands, the butchers to commence killing and the seamen to lend a hand. Killed 30 hogs. At 9.00 a.m. the boat went ashore to trade. The butchers salting and packing. Traded this day six muskets, four bayonets and 4 fathoms of calico and 1 fathom of ditto. The extent of the land bearing from S.E. to W.N.W. Ship tacking off and in under easy canvas. Wind from W.N.W. to E.S.E.

Friday 19 February First part light winds and pleasant weather. At daylight called all hands, the butchers to commence killing and the seamen assisting. Killed 30 hogs then began to pack and stow down the casks. The boat trade this day four muskets, ten bayonets. At 8.00 p.m. hoisted a light for the boat she not then came off. Trade seven bayonets, 4 fathoms of calico for two hogs. Middle and latter parts ditto winds and weather.

Saturday 20 February First part light winds and clear weather. At daylight called all hands to kill and salt down. Killed 37 hogs. Traded on board the ship two muskets being 21 hogs. Gave 10 yds. of calico, one shirt, two pairs of axes, one bottle of powder, two-dozen of pipes, half a bar of soap, six flints to one white man being on board the ship eight days to lend a hand in the boat. Middle part ditto winds and weather. The winds from N.W. to E.S.E. Latter part light winds and rainy weather.

Sunday 21 February First part light winds and rainy weather. At daylight called all hands to commence killing and salting. Killed 32 hogs. Middle part light winds and clear weather. No trade today. Latter part light winds and rainy.

Monday 22 February First part light winds and showers of rain. At daylight called all hands to commence killing and packing. At 8.00 a.m. began to —— out the hold and stowed down six hides and four beef tierces. At 1.00 p.m. the captain went ashore to see the hogs traded. Traded one musket ashore and one ditto on board. At 4.00 p.m. the boat came off. Middle part light winds. The extent of the land bearing from W.S.W. to S.S.E. distance 2 leagues.

Tuesday 23 February First part light winds and clear weather. At daylight called all hands to commence killing and packing and sent the boat ashore. Killed 29 hogs. At

2.00 p.m. the boat came off and the chief's wife, then sent the boat ashore again to another place for the trade of a blunderbudgion, but did not come off this night the hogs not being made fast. Kept a light at the masthead all night. Middle part light airs and variable. Latter part ditto winds and weather.

Wednesday 24 February First part light airs and variable. At 6.00 a.m. called all hands to commence killing and salting. Killed 26 hogs. At 1.00 p.m. the boat came off being ashore all night, the hogs not being ready, and was used very well with the natives. Traded the blunderbudgion, eight bayonets and some powder. Middle and latter part ditto winds and weather.

Thursday 25 February First part fresh breezes and rainy weather with all possible sail plying to windward, there being so strong a current running to the westward. Wind from E.S.E. to N.E. At daylight called all hands to commence killing and packing. Killed 23 hogs. At 8.00 a.m. the boat went ashore for to trade. Traded three muskets, eight bayonets, 3.5 fathoms of calico. Middle and latter part light winds and variable.

Friday 26 February First part fresh breezes and clear weather. At 6.00 a.m. called all hands to commence killing and packing. Killed 25 hogs. At 8.00 a.m. the boat went ashore to trade. Traded two muskets, four axes, five bayonets. Middle part light winds and rainy weather. The extent of the land bearing from S. to S.W. distance 4 leagues. Latter part light winds and cloudy weather.

Saturday 27 February First part smart breezes and clear weather. At 6.00 a.m. called all hands to commence killing and salting. At 8.00 a.m. the boat went ashore with a white man belonging to the island being on board seven days. Gave him 10 yds. of yellow calico, 12 pipes, one bayonet, two ——, one bottle of powder, half a bar of soap when the boat came off. Made all sail to the eastward to another part of the island. Stowed down ten hogs, two beef tierces, a quarter-pipe of pork, traded six bayonets. Middle part strong breezes and clear weather. At 6.00 p.m. the extent of the island bearing from S. by W. to W.S.W. distance 6 leagues. Latter part light winds and clear weather.

Sunday 28 February First part light winds and clear air. At 6.00 a.m. saw a ship to the northward standing in shore. At noon the captain of her came on board, it being the *Champion* of Edgartown. Bewarth the master having 1,500 barrels of sperm whale, 26 months out from America. At 3.00 p.m. sent our own boat ashore to see if there was any trade. The carpenter of the ship purchased two muskets. Traded three bayonets. Middle part light winds and clear weather. Traded one musket. At 6.00 p.m. the island of Savaii bearing S.S.E. to W.S.W. distance 4 leagues. Latter part cloudy weather.

Monday 29 February First part fresh breezes and rainy weather. At 10.00 a.m. sent the boat ashore to trade. Traded two muskets. Traded on board 2 fathoms of white calico, 2 fathoms of —— and 2 fathoms of —— ditto. At 6.00 p.m. the extent of the land bearing from W.N.W. to E.S.E. distance 2 leagues. Middle and latter part light winds and clear weather.

Tuesday 1 March First part fresh breezes and clear weather. At daylight called all hands to commence killing and salting. Killed 22 hogs then sent two boats ashore to trade. Traded four muskets. Traded on board three muskets. Bought one double and single block for 1 fathom of white calico. At 6.00 p.m. the extent of the land bearing from E.N.E. to W.N.W. distance 3 leagues. Middle and latter parts fresh breeze and rainy weather.

Wednesday 2 March First part strong breeze and rainy weather. At 2.00 a.m. lighted the fires but it raining so heavy the fires was drowned out so we could not kill today. At 8.00 a.m. sent the boat ashore to the island of Apolima. Traded one musket. At 6.00 p.m.

the island of Apolima bore N. by E. distance 4 leagues. Wind from W.N.W. to E.S.E. Middle and latter parts light winds and clear weather.

Thursday 3 March First part light winds and clear weather. At 5.00 a.m. called all hands to commence killing and salting. Killed 53. At —— a.m. sent the boat ashore to trade. Traded musket. Traded on board two muskets for 14 hogs and some further ——, —— fathoms of yellow calico and some pipes. Took six muskets out of the cases. Middle and latter parts strong gales and heavy rains.

Friday 4 March First part fresh breezes and rainy weather. At daylight called all hands to commence killing and salting. Killed 24 hogs. Traded 1 fathom of white calico for a piece of —— ——. At 1.00 p.m. sent the boat ashore to trade. Traded two muskets. At 6.00 p.m. the extent of the land bearing from W.N.W. to N.N.E. distance 3 leagues. Middle and latter part light winds and cloudy.

Saturday 5 March First part light winds and cloudy. At 6.00 a.m. called all hands to send the boat ashore. Traded two muskets. Traded on board three muskets. Wind from E.S.E. to N.W. Middle part light winds and clear. Latter part light winds and pleasant weather.

Sunday 6 March First part light winds and clear weather. At daylight called all hands to commence killing and salting. Killed 25 hogs. At 11.00 a.m. the canoes came off. Traded for shells and coconuts three ——, some pipes some charges of powder, one-dozen of pipes, for one piece of turtle shell, one old musket, four new ditto, for 22 hogs. At 6.00 p.m. the extent of the land bearing from E. to W.N.W. distance 3 leagues. Middle and latter parts light winds and clear weather.

Monday 7 March First part light winds and clear weather. At 5.00 a.m. sent the boat ashore to trade. Traded on board six old muskets, one new ditto, for five mats. 4 yds. of calico, eight bayonets, one wood axe, one butcher's cleaver, one shirt for a white mat. At 6.00 p.m. the extent of the land bearing from E. to W. by N. distance 4 leagues. Middle and latter parts light winds and clear weather.

Tuesday 8 March First part light winds and clear weather. At daylight called all hands to commence killing. Killed 45 hogs. At 9.00 a.m. commenced stowing the hold. Stowed down ten hogs, two —tures of pork, one beef tierce of lard. At noon three canoes came off. Traded two muskets. Two hands repairing the topsail. Middle and latter parts light winds and clear weather. Winds from S.E. to N.E.

Wednesday 9 March First part light winds and cloudy weather. At 6.00 a.m. made all sail towards the island. At 11.00 a.m. the captain went ashore to trade for yams. Fetched off seven hogs. At 6.00 p.m. the boat came off. One musket. Kept two chiefs on board the time the boat was ashore, the natives not being so civil at this place. Middle and latter part fresh breezes and rainy weather.

Thursday 10 March First part strong breezes and cloudy weather. At 6.00 a.m. sent the boat ashore for wood. Got two boatloads of wood off but the natives being so uncivil we did not send the boat ashore at that place again. Traded two bayonets, one wood axe. Traded on board four wood axes, one boat axe[?], one bayonet for yams, one musket. At 6.00 p.m. the extent of the land bearing from W. to N.E. distance 4 leagues. Wind from S.W. to N.W. Middle and latter parts light winds and pleasant weather.

Friday 11 March First part fresh breezes and variable. At 6.00 a.m. sent the boat ashore for yams. Traded two muskets. Paid to John Parker two muskets, —— one red shirt, one pair of trousers, 2 lbs. of tobacco, 10 yds. of calico, one bayonet, one checked shirt, being the amount of his wages in trade, being on board one month and six days. Thomas Lathen[?] came on board but not fit for duty. At 1.00 p.m. squared away for Tutuila,

Opolu, bearing W.N.W. distance 3 leagues. At 7.00 p.m. shortened sail and hauled by the wind. Tutuila bearing from S.E. to E. distance 5 leagues. Wind from S.W. to N.W. Middle and latter parts light winds and cloudy weather.

Saturday 12 March First part light winds and clear weather. At 6.00 a.m. called all hands then commenced starting water. Started eight hydes [*sic*] and took them ashore and filled them and towed them off and started six of them. At 1.00 p.m. sent the boat ashore for coconuts, fetched 400 of ditto. At 6.00 p.m. the extent of the island Tutuila bearing from N.W. to N.E. distance 3 leagues. Broached one cask of pork. Middle and latter parts light winds and clear weather.

The illustration opposite shows the fine natural harbour at Pago Pago on the island of Tutuila. Pago Pago (pronounced Pango Pango) is now the capital of American Samoa. As the best natural harbour on the island, it would almost certainly have been one of the places visited by the *Prince of Denmark* and the illustration shows a brig of roughly the same size as the *Prince of Denmark* sailing across the harbour.

Sunday 13 March First part light winds and clear weather. At 8.00 a.m. the captain went ashore and fetched off eight large hogs for one musket and 100 coconuts and some breadfruit plants. At 3.00 p.m. the boat went ashore again and fetched off 400 coconuts. At 6.00 p.m. very heavy squalls and rain. Swung ship head to the offing, the extent of the island bearing N.W. by N. to E. distance 2 leagues. Latitude by obs. 12.26 south. Latter part strong gales with heavy squalls of rain. Wind from E. to S.E.

Monday 14 March First part strong gales and heavy squalls. At 3.00 a.m. hauled down the jib and clewed down the topsail with very heavy squalls and rain. At 6.00 more moderate. Made all possible sail towards the island. At noon the island bore N. by E. distance 6 leagues. Light winds and rainy weather. At 6.00 p.m. the extent of the land bearing from N.E. to E. by N. distance 11 leagues. Light winds and rainy weather. Latter part light winds and clear weather. Island from E.S.E. to E.N.E. Latitude by obs. 14.19 south.

Tuesday 15 March First part light winds and clear weather. At 6.00 a.m. made all sail toward the island. At noon strong gales and showers of rain. At 6.00 p.m. double reefed the mainsail, single reefed the topsail. Strong gales and squalls with heavy rain. Latter part ditto winds and weather.

Wednesday 16 March First part strong gales and rainy weather. At 8.00 a.m. sent the boat ashore to trade for coconuts. Fetched off this day one boatload of wood, two ditto of coconuts, being 800 nuts. The canoes fetched off 1,000 nuts being trade for six bayonets. Middle and latter part light winds and clear weather.

Thursday 17 March First part light airs and clear weather. At 6.00 a.m. sent the boat ashore for a raft of water, but fetched off 400 nuts first, the tide not assisting to fill the casks. At noon went ashore again. Raining very heavy and wild like with a heavy sea from the S.W. Put the raft in tow but was obliged to go in again, there being too much sea on the bar. Lost one hogshead in the surf and broke oars. At high water tried again and got out with much difficulty. Sent the other boat in to help them off. At 8.00 p.m. the boats came off with the raft. Got it on board and stowed in the hold then hoisted the casks up. The canoes came off with 800 nuts for six bayonets. Latter part light winds and clear weather.

Friday 18 March First part light airs and clear weather. At 9.00 a.m. the canoes came off with breadfruit and coconuts. Traded seven bayonets, five fathoms of blue calico and five of yellow ditto. Paid to William Pain one musket, one grinding stone, one piece of

Pago Pago Harbour, Tutuila

print, one pair of shoes, one pair of trousers, 1 lb. of tobacco, some flints, two-dozen of pipes, one bottle of powder for the wood, one bottle of ditto for the water, 16 yds. of green narrow calico. This log contains 12 hours to end the trading log.

Towards Hobart Town, Saturday 19 March At noon the west end of Tutuila bearing N.W. distance 7 leagues, in latitude 14.20 south and longitude 170.20 west, from which I take my departure. At 4.00 p.m. set the square sail and topmast studding sail having 89 live hogs on board. Midnight light airs and thick rainy weather. At 6.00 a.m. set the square sail. Light breezes and variable. The watch employed breaking nuts for the hogs. At 10.00 a.m. set other studding sail. At noon sun obscured.

The captain and his crew must have been very pleased with the results of their four months of hard work. Navigation had been impeccable, negotiations with local people had gone well, caution, and presumably fair trading, having given no opportunity for animosity to arise. Contacts had been established both with local chiefs and with the mysterious 'white men' who had chosen to live in splendid isolation. They may have been seamen who had been tempted by the lure of the 'Pacific way', or missionaries who were more interested in stamping it out. Some of them might even have been fugitives from Australia's penal colonies who were merely anxious to disappear.

The living conditions that the captain and crew were to endure for the passage home were unsavoury to such an extent that the luxury of returning home would compensate for any sadness felt at leaving behind the beautiful Isles of the Navigators. The extra numbers of butchers and coopers would make the forecastle even more crowded than usual, and the hold must have been tightly packed with coconuts and with casks of salt pork. Worst of all, the live cargo of over 90 live hogs jammed into pens on deck would have been smelly, noisy and would have generated extra work from feeding them and cleaning out their pens. The handling of sails and the constant maintenance necessary to keep the *Prince of Denmark* under control and seaworthy cannot have been easy.

Sunday 20 March p.m. fresh breezes with heavy rain. Hoisted the boats up to the davit ends and lashed them. At 7.00 p.m. took in the topmast studding sail. Light airs and rainy weather. At 10.00 p.m. the main throat halyards gave way. Rove them again and set the mainsail. Midnight heavy rains and squalls. Looking wild like. At 4.00 a.m. squared the yards and set the square sail. Smart breezes and showers of rain. At 6.00 a.m. set the topmost studding sail. Carried away the flying jib stay. Got it spliced and set up in its place again. At noon fresh breezes and showers of rain. Latitude obs. 16.51 south.

Monday 21 March p.m. fresh breezes and showers of rain. At 2.00 p.m. took in the gaff topsail. Lost the logline. At 6.00 p.m. strong breezes and showers. At 8.00 p.m. took in the topmast studding sail. Strong breezes and squally. Midnight ditto winds and weather. At 1.00 a.m. set the foresail and ——. Strong breezes but clear weather. At 4.00 a.m. heavy squalls of wind and rain. At 8.00 a.m. strong breezes and clear. At noon ditto wind with passing showers of rain. Latitude obs. 19.38 south.

Tuesday 22 March p.m. strong breezes and rainy weather. At 6.00 p.m. braced forward the yards. At 8.00 p.m. light breezes and showers of rain and heavy southerly sea. At midnight heavy squalls of wind. At 4.00 a.m. took in the topmast studding sail and square sail. Fresh breezes with rain. At 8.00 a.m. commenced to fish the bowsprit. Seamen and carpenter employed at it. At noon light winds and hazy weather. Latitude by obs. 21.41 south.

Wednesday 23 March p.m. light breezes with dark cloudy weather. People employed variously. At midnight light winds cloudy weather. At 2.00 a.m. light airs and clear weather. At 4.00 a.m. ditto winds and weather. At 6.00 a.m. squared the yards and set the square sail and topmast studding sail. Light winds and inclining to rain. People employed at various jobs, the carpenter employed sheathing the windlass. At noon light winds and hazy weather. Latitude by obs. 22.48 south.

Thursday 24 March p.m. light airs and thick hazy weather inclining to rain. At 6.00 p.m. ditto wind with a heavy swell from the S.E. Lowered down the mainsail. At 8.00 p.m. ditto winds and heavy rain. At midnight light airs with clear weather. At 4.00 a.m. fine pleasant breezes and clear weather. At 8.00 ditto winds and weather, the watch employed repairing the foot of the mainsail. At noon light breezes and clear weather with the same continuing swell. Ship rolling heavily. The hogs knocking about very much. Latitude obs. 23.45 south.

Friday 25 March p.m. fresh breezes and clear weather. At 4.00 p.m. finished repairing the mainsail then bent it again. At 8.00 p.m. ditto winds and cloudy weather inclining to rain. Ship rolling about much. At midnight strong breezes and cloudy with a heavy cross-sea. At 4.00 a.m. set the mainsail and hauled the ship by the wind. At 10.00 took in the square sail and studding sail. At noon strong breezes and clear weather. Latitude by obs. 25.47 south.

Saturday 26 March p.m. strong breezes and cloudy weather with the same continuing sea. Killed one hog, it being badly, but it was not fit for use. At 6.00 p.m. reefed the topsail and mainsail. Stowed the topgallant sail and flying jib. Strong breezes and squally and looking wild like. Midnight cloudy with small rain. At 4.00 a.m. strong breezes and clear weather. At 8.00 a.m. cloudy with small rain. At noon strong breezes and cloudy but clear at times. The watch employed fitting a boom guy and fore sheets. Latitude obs. 27.17 south.

Sunday 27 March p.m. light winds and clear weather. Tacked ship's head to the S.W. and set the topgallant sail and flying jib. At 4.00 p.m. fresh breezes with clear weather. At 8.00 p.m. ditto wind and weather. At midnight light breezes and cloudy. At 4.00 a.m. light breezes and clear weather. At 6.00 a.m. let out the reef [in] the topsail and mainsail and set the topgallant sail and flying jib. Light winds and clear weather. Killed two small pigs for the ship's use. Broached one hog of pork. At noon light winds and clear. Latitude obs. 26.29 south.

Monday 28 March p.m. light winds and fine pleasant weather. At 4.00 p.m. fresh breezes with small rain. At 8.00 p.m. light breezes and cloudy weather. Midnight light airs and ditto weather. A.m. light breezes and clear weather. At 8.00 a.m. light airs and cloudy weather. People employed at sundry jobs. Rove new topsail braces then set the topmast studding sail and square sail. Pleasant breezes with an increasing swell from the E.S.E. At noon ditto winds and weather. Latitude obs. 27.04 south.

Tuesday 29 March p.m. light airs and clear weather with the same inclining swell from the E.S.E. At 4.00 p.m. fresh breezes with clear weather. At 8.00 p.m. light airs and fine pleasant weather. Midnight ditto wind and weather. At 8.00 a.m. light airs and clear weather. Saw some sperm whales. Noon ditto wind and weather. The watch employed repairing the foresail, and the butcher employed about the hogs. Three men off duty badly ——. Latitude obs. 27.39 south.

Wednesday 30 March p.m. light airs and pleasant weather. At 8.00 p.m. calms with the same continuing sea from the E.S.E. and fine pleasant weather. Midnight ditto weather. At 4.00 a.m. ditto. At 8.00 a.m. light airs and clear weather, the watch employed setting up the bobstays and —— guys and repairing the square sail. At noon light breezes and clear weather. Latitude obs. 27.55 south.

Thursday 31 March p.m. fresh breezes and cloudy weather. The butchers attending the hogs. At 4.00 p.m. light breezes and clear throughout. At midnight fresh breezes and cloudy weather. At 4.00 a.m. ditto winds and weather. At 8.00 a.m. strong gales and cloudy with rain at times. Took in the topgallant sail and flying jib, reefed the topsail and mainsail. At 10.00 a.m. strong gales and squalls. Took in the second reef of the mainsail. At noon strong breezes with a heavy cross-sea. Latitude obs. 29.35 south.

Friday 1 April p.m. strong gales and cloudy. Ship straining much with a heavy cross-sea running. The captain taken very bad and obliged to go to bed. Muligan badly, also four of the seamen badly. At 4.00 p.m. tacked ship's head to the westward. At 8.00 p.m. more moderate with a heavy head sea. At midnight strong breezes and cloudy. At 4.00 a.m. strong gales and squally with a heavy sea from the S.W. Afraid to make sail, the squalls being so violent. At 8.00 a.m. let the reefs out of the mainsail and set the topgallant sail and jib. At noon more moderate. Latitude obs. 29.07 south.

Saturday 2 April p.m. fresh breezes with clear weather. 4.00 p.m. ditto winds and weather. At 8.00 p.m. light breezes and cloudy. At midnight fresh breezes and cloudy. At 4.00 a.m. light breezes with passing showers of rain and an inclining sea from the S.E. At 6.00 a.m. strong breezes attended with squalls. Took a reef in the mainsail and hauled down the topgallant sail then set it again. At noon strong gales with clear weather. The captain got better again. Muligan keeping at his duty but rather badly. Latitude obs. 29.38 south.

For a significant number of the officers and crew to succumb to illness during squally and unsettled weather must have been acutely uncomfortable and alarming. No details are given of the nature of the illness, but it is most likely to have been caused by food poisoning, contracted from either the food and water procured on shore, or from that in the ship's stores. Either could have suffered from prolonged exposure to high temperatures. The forecastle – crowded, damp, poorly ventilated and subject to violent motion – would not be a pleasant place for either the sick or the healthy crewmen.

The business of handling the ship had to continue, and the urgent need for sail changes must have taxed the officers and their short-handed crew to their limits.

Sunday 3 April p.m. strong gales and squally weather. At 2.00 p.m. took in the outer jib and the second reef of the mainsail. Strong gales with clear weather. At 10.00 p.m. ditto winds and weather. At midnight ditto winds and weather. At 2.00 a.m. let the reefs out of the mainsail and set the square sail and topmast studding sail and gaff topsail. Pleasant breezes and clear weather. At 8.00 a.m. light breezes and ditto weather. At noon light winds and clear weather. Squared the yards. A heavy sea from the S.E. Ship rolling very heavy. Killed two small hogs for the ship's use. Latitude obs. 30.40 south.

Monday 4 April p.m. light airs and clear weather. At 4.00 p.m. ditto winds and weather. At 8.00 p.m. light winds and clear weather. Made all possible sail. At midnight fresh breezes and ditto weather. At 6.00 a.m. strong breezes and squally with showers of rain. Took in the studding sail and square sail. At 8.00 a.m. strong gales and squally. Took in the outer jib and topgallant sail. Took one reef in the topsail and in the mainsail. The watch employed in mending the topgallant sail, put 14 yds. of no. four canvas into it. At noon more moderate. Made all sail again. Latitude obs. 31.58.

Tuesday 5 April p.m. fresh breezes and cloudy with passing showers of rain. At p.m. light winds and cloudy with a heavy sea from the S.W. Midnight strong breezes and clear weather. At 4.00 a.m. fresh breezes and ditto weather. At noon ditto winds and weather. The butcher employed about the hogs, the seamen about sundry jobs. Harravere[?] and Latten[?] and Alexander still not fit for duty. Latitude obs. 31.47 south.

Wednesday 6 April p.m. first part strong breezes with clear weather. At 4.00 p.m. ditto wind and weather. At 8.00 p.m. the wind hauled round to the S.E. with cloudy weather. Set the fore-topmast studding sail. At 10.00 p.m. set the square sail. At midnight fresh breezes and cloudy inclining to rain. Let out the reef of the mainsail. A.m. ditto wind with passing showers. At 8.00 a.m. strong breezes and cloudy weather inclining to rain with a heavy sea from the southward. At noon the watch repairing the gaff topsail. Latitude obs. 32.37 south.

Thursday 7 April p.m. fresh breezes and cloudy with showers of rain. At 8.00 a.m. strong breezes and heavy weather. Lowered down the mainsail. A heavy cross-sea running. Midnight strong gales and squally. At 6.00 a.m. strong gales and squally. Split the square sail then took it in. At 8.00 a.m. heavy gales. Called all hands to bring the ship to. Set the foresail then clewed up the topsail and stowed it, then hove her to under the reefed foresail. At noon ditto weather but a very heavy sea. Sun obscured.

Friday 8 April p.m. strong gales and very heavy squalls of wind and rain. Ship labouring much. At 6.00 p.m. more moderate. Set the single reefed topsail then bore away. At 10.00 p.m. strong gales and violent squalls. Shipped a very heavy sea. At midnight heavy gales. Clued up the topsail and rounded the ship's head to the S.E. Shipped more heavy seas. At 4.00 a.m. ditto wind and weather. At noon ditto wind and weather. Carried away the plate of the topmast backstay. Got a tackle on it and got it secured again. Sun obscured.

Saturday 9 April p.m. strong gales and heavy squalls of wind and rain. Ship making little way. At 4.00 p.m. more moderate. Set the topsail single reefed but still afraid to run. Midnight, heavy gales. Took in the topsail again. At 8.00 a.m. ditto winds and weather. At noon heavy gales and squalls. Latitude by obs. 34.29 south.

Sunday 10 April p.m. strong gales and heavy squalls. Housed the main topmast and sent the topgallant yard down. At 6.00 p.m. set the topsail close reefed, then wore ship's head to the N.W. More moderate but still too much sea to run. At 8.00 p.m. let one reef out of the topsail and set the jib then kept her away before the wind. Midnight more moderate and clear weather. At 4.00 a.m. light breezes and clear weather. At 8.00 a.m. wore ship's head to the westward. Killed one hog, it being rather badly through being knocked about so much in the gale. At noon ditto winds and weather. Latitude by obs. 35.28.

Monday 11 April p.m. light airs and clear weather. Sent up the topgallant yard and set the topmast studding sail and square sail. At 4.00 p.m. fresh breezes and cloudy weather. At 8.00 p.m. ditto wind and weather. Set the mainsail. Alexander, Hurral, and Herrow better and fit for duty again. At midnight ditto wind and weather. At 4.00 a.m. strong breezes and dark cloudy weather. Lightning very heavy from the S.W. At noon ditto wind and clear weather. The watch employed starting water into the large casks for the hogs. Latitude obs. 36.06.

Tuesday 12 April p.m. fresh breezes and clear weather. The watch employed making covers for the round houses. At 2.00 p.m. set the topmast studding sail. Fresh breezes and clear weather. At 6.00 p.m. ditto breezes and cloudy. At midnight light breezes and cloudy. The second mate taken very bad. Not fit for his duty. At 4.00 a.m. ditto wind and weather. At 8.00 a.m. the second mate rather better, able to be on deck. At noon pleasant breezes and clear weather. The people employed about the rigging and making mainsail tiers. Latitude obs. 36.41.

Wednesday 13 April p.m. pleasant breezes and clear weather. The watch employed repairing the gaff topsail. At 6.00 p.m. fresh breezes and cloudy weather. Midnight light winds and variable. At 4.00 a.m. pleasant breezes and clear weather. At 8.00 a.m. fresh breezes and cloudy weather. The second mate able to do his duty again. At noon pleasant breezes and clear weather. The watch employed variously. Three hands rather badly. Latitude obs. 37.35 south.

Thursday 14 April p.m. light breezes with clear weather. At 8.00 p.m. light breezes from the eastward with a clear sky. At midnight smart breezes and cloudy weather. Gybed ship, the wind inclining to come from the northward. At 4.00 a.m. strong breezes with cloudy weather. At 8.00 a.m. fresh breezes and cloudy weather. Braced forward the yards, the wind inclining to northward more. At noon strong breezes and cloudy weather. The watch employed variously. Latitude by obs. 38.32 south.

Friday 15 April p.m. strong breezes and cloudy weather. At 4.00 p.m. took in the topmast staysail and topgallant sail. Reefed the mainsail and topsail and stowed the outer jib. Strong breezes and looking very wild like attended with showers of rain. At 8.00 p.m. strong gales and heavy squalls wind and rain. Put two sows in the hold being very bad. At midnight more moderate. Set the topgallant sail and flying jib. At 4.00 a.m. pleasant breezes and clear weather. Let the reefs out of the mainsail and topsail. At noon ditto winds and weather. Latitude obs. 39.17 south.

Saturday 16 April p.m. fresh breezes with clear weather. At 4.00 p.m. ditto winds and weather. At 7.00 p.m. strong breezes and heavy squalls. Took in the topgallant sail and reefed the topsail and mainsail and stowed the flying jib. At midnight strong gales and heavy squalls. Took in the 2nd reef of the mainsail. At 4.00 a.m. more moderate but still looking wildlike. One sow had three piglets. At 8.00 a.m. strong breezes and heavy squalls of wind and rain with a heavy sea from the west. At noon ditto winds and weather. Latitude obs. 40.42.

Sunday 17 April p.m. strong gales and heavy squalls of wind and rain. At 4.00 p.m. very heavy squalls. Close reefed the topsail and reefed the jib. At 6.00 took in the topsail and hove her to with her head to the westward. Midnight ditto winds and weather. At 2.00 a.m. more moderate. Set the topsail and jib and kept her fore reaching. At 8.00 a.m. heavy gales. Ship labouring very much. One hog died. We hove it overboard, not being fit for use. At noon ditto wind and weather. The hogs in a very bad condition, ship rolling about so much. Latitude obs. 40.47 south.

Monday 18 April p.m. strong gales from the southward and westward with dark cloudy weather. Ship under close-reefed topsail and mainsail. At 4.00 p.m. more moderate but a heavy sea running. At 6.00 p.m. let out one reef of the mainsail and outer jib, the wind inclining to easter. At 8.00 fresh breezes and cloudy. At midnight light winds and ditto weather. At 8.00 a.m. light airs and variable. One sow had seven pigs. Killed a hare for the ship's use. At noon light airs from the northward. Latitude observed 40.21 south.

Tuesday 19 April p.m. light airs and pleasant weather. Set the topmast studding sail and square sail. At 6.00 p.m. fresh breezes and clear weather. At midnight light airs and ditto weather. Wind from the westward. Took in the studding sail and square sail. At 4.00 a.m. light winds and clear weather, the wind inclining to southerly. At 8.00 a.m. saw the land of Van Diemen, St Patrick's Head bearing W.S.W. distance 18 leagues. Light airs and calm sea. Calm throughout the latter part. At noon the watch employed cleaning the muskets. Calm weather. Latitude obs. 41.09 south.

Wednesday 20 April p.m. light airs and cloudy weather. Running along the land. St. Patrick's Head bearing S.Westerly distance 6 leagues. At 8.00 p.m. ditto winds and weather. At midnight light winds and cloudy weather. At 8.00 a.m. ditto winds and clear weather. St. Patrick's head bearing W. by N. 6 leagues. At noon calms and light airs at times from S.W. to S.S.E. Latitude obs. 41.47. The watch employed repairing the square sail, the butcher about the hogs.

Thursday 21 April p.m. light airs and calm. Maria Island bearing S.S.W. distance 12 leagues. At 6.00 p.m. light airs from the N.E. Set the studding sail and square sail. At 8.00 p.m. calm. Lowered down the mainsail with an inclining sea from the eastward. Ship rolling about much. At midnight ditto weather. At 6.00 a.m. the Schoutens bearing S.S.W. distance 5 leagues. St. Patrick's Head bearing N.N.W. distance about 10 leagues. At noon light airs and calm airs from the S.E. to N. Wine Glass Bay bearing west, distance 3 leagues. The watch employed fitting a new truss rope[?] and truss[?] it being ——.

Friday 22 April p.m. light airs from the southward with dark cloudy weather. The Schoutens bearing W.S.W. distance 3 leagues, the ship standing to the offing. At 4.00 p.m. the wind at S.S.E. Tacked and stood inshore. At 6.00 p.m. light airs from the southward. Tacked ship's head to the eastward. At 2.00 a.m. tacked ship's head to the southward. At 8.00 a.m. the Schoutens bore W.N.W. distance 5 leagues. Maria Island bearing S.W. distance 4 leagues. Light winds and variable with cloudy weather. Wind from S.S.E. to E.S.E. flying about. At noon light airs and calm weather, Maria Island bore W. by S. distance 2 leagues. Tacked ship's head to the eastward. Killed one hog being rather badly. The watch employed variously. The butchers about the hogs.

Saturday 23 April p.m. light breezes and cloudy weather. Standing to the offing. Lowered down the mainsail and repaired some of the seams that was split rocking about so much. At midnight calm with cloudy weather and a heavy swell from the eastward. Lowered down the mainsail and jibs and brailed up the foresail. At 2.00 a.m. a light breeze sprang up from the S.S.E. Made all sail again. Latter part fresh breeze. Standing to the E.S.E. Wind at S.E. Cape Pillar bore S.W. distance 6 leagues. The people employed variously. This 24 hrs. has been bright round the compass but light until the latter part.

Sunday 24 April p.m. fresh breezes and showers of small rain. Tacked ship's head inshore, the wind from the southward. At 4.00 p.m. Cape Pillar bore S. by W. distance 6 leagues. Tacked ship's head to the southward and eastward. Midnight fresh breezes attended with showers of small rain. Wind at south. Tacked ship's head to the W.S.W. At 8.00 a.m. Cape Pillar bore W.S.W. distance 5 leagues. Tacking to the best advantage to get round the Pillar. At noon light winds and variable from S.S.W. to S. A strong current running to the northward and eastward, and a very heavy swell from the eastward.

Monday 25 April p.m. light winds and clear weather. Plying to the best advantage towards and against a strong current running to the N.E. Cape Pillar bearing west. distance west 3 leagues. At 6.00 p.m. Cape Raoul bore W.N.W. distance 5 leagues. Light airs from the southward with thick hazy weather. Midnight calm. Lowered down the mainsail but there came away a very heavy squall from the S.W. Single reefed the mainsail and topsail. At 2.00 Cape Raoul bore north 6 leagues. At 6.00 a.m. set the square sail and studding sail running up the river. At 8.00 a.m. came to with the small bower in Sullivan's Cove then the Harbour Master came on board and got the ship under way again and took her further in shore and moored her with the two anchors. Latter part light winds and clear weather. This log contains 36 hours to end the sea log.

This five-month voyage would seem to have been extremely successful. Careful planning, inspirational navigation, scrupulous control of trading and extremely hard work by the crew had resulted in a deck cargo of live pigs and a hold filled with valuable barrels of salt pork being brought safely home, despite some harsh weather conditions. The fact that all of this had been achieved with the captain still able to return a quantity of trading goods to storage in Hobart Town implies that bargaining conditions had been good. The *Hobart Town Courier* of 29 April 1836 reported the arrival of the *Prince of Denmark* under the command of Captain Young, from the Isles of the Navigators, with 20 tons of pork and 98 live pigs.

10 *Kelly's Boom Years*

This chapter summarises descriptions in the ship's log of the *Prince of Denmark*'s activities during six periods of time between April 1836 and November 1837. A transcription of the log of each of these periods is reproduced in full in appendices I–VI.

After the return of the *Prince of Denmark* from the Isles of the Navigators in April 1836, she spent a period of nearly three months lying alongside the new wharf at Sullivan's Cove in Hobart Town, being unloaded, scrubbed, repaired and fitted out for a return to whaling. For some of the early part of that period, the live hogs remained in their pens on deck, presumably awaiting sale or transfer to Captain Kelly's farm. When the captain kindly covered them up with sails to protect them from the weather, they rewarded him by tearing the sails to pieces. It must have been a relief when they were finally disposed of, the ship scrubbed out, the pens dismantled, the sails repaired and the decks restored to order. The hold was also emptied and the various trading goods that were no longer required were returned to Captain Kelly's store.

A few weeks later, the *Colonial Times* of Hobart carried the following advertisement:

> Wanted – For the schooner *Prince of Denmark*, a competent sober person, to take charge as master; reference will be required. For particulars, apply to the owner.
> James Kelly, Macquarie Street, near the old wharf, 19th May 1836.

An entry in the log for 20 May 1836 records that Mr. Gray commenced work. Mr. Gray is presumed to have been the same person as the Thomas Gay responsible for the sketch of the *Prince of Denmark* (page 63) and was duly appointed as the new master.

On 26 May and on 30 May 1836 there are references to shortening the foremast and the mainmast. This does not quite come into the category of normal maintenance and implies that Captain Kelly considered his vessel's rig to be too tall for the squally weather that had caused her to labour so much on the passage home from the Isles of the Navigators. The large sail area necessary to drive her to reach her maximum potential speed as a revenue cutter had perhaps become a liability.

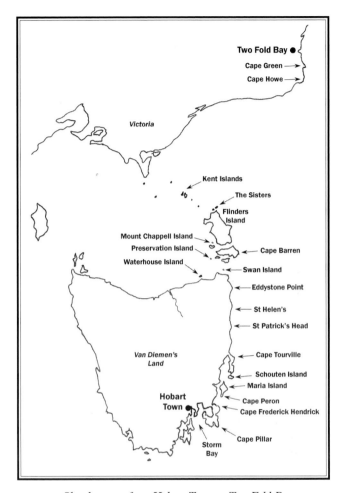

Sketch map – from Hobart Town to Two Fold Bay

A week was spent in late June heaving the ship down to permit maintenance to the underside of her hull. Heaving down is a laborious and difficult operation that required great skill, teamwork and vigilance. While the ship was moored alongside the wharf, all ballast and any other loose items would have to be removed from the hull, to cause her to float as highly in the water as possible.

Tackles would then have been rigged from the mastheads to firmly embedded anchors on the shore. Teams of men would then haul on these tackles to cause the vessel to gradually lean further and further over towards the shore, taking great care to ensure that the strain was spread as equally as possible to each mast. If the topsides of the ship had been exposed for long to excessive sunshine, it might have been necessary to caulk them before the process began to prevent a sudden ingress of water. With skill and care, the ship could be hove down until she lay on her beam-ends with her keel just exposed. Work could then begin on scraping and scrubbing away any accumulation of weed and other marine life, and on repairing any areas of damage to the copper

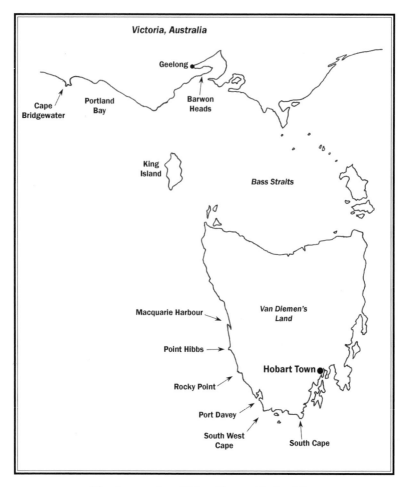

Sketch map – from Hobart Town to Portland Bay

sheeting or to the planking itself. The painting on page V of the colour section shows a vessel hove down in Australian waters and her crew working close to her keel.

On completion of her refit, the *Prince of Denmark* left Sullivan's Cove in Hobart Town on 23 July 1836, under the command of Captain Kelly, for a voyage to one of the whaling stations at Two Fold Bay in southeast Victoria, near to the site of the modern town of Eden. She made her way up the east side of Van Diemen's Land, but after only two days was forced to anchor in Fortescue Bay, due to adverse weather conditions. Fortescue Bay was close to the penal colony at Port Arthur and any vessel anchored in the vicinity was a temptation to desperate prisoners who had little to lose by making a bid for freedom. Captain Kelly's early experience in Sydney of an attack on one of his vessels by prisoners had clearly made him particularly cautious, as on 25 July, while stormbound, he armed the watch with loaded muskets.

Cape Howe, close to Two Fold Bay, was sighted on 5 July, and Captain Kelly went ashore to examine a river a few miles to its southwest. This trip ashore emphasises the fact that men like Captain Kelly were not only businessmen or merchant traders, but also pioneers and explorers, constantly looking for new anchorages and unexploited natural resources, noting coastal features and seeking new opportunities to establish whaling stations and settlements.

The next few days were spent at Two Fold Bay unloading empty casks to be filled with oil, and taking on board casks of salted beef and casks of water. On 11 August 1836, the *Prince of Denmark* left Two Fold Bay in sight of the barque *Brougham*, and both vessels set their courses southwards for Van Diemen's Land. Five days later, the *Prince of Denmark* arrived at Sullivan's Cove, having kept the *Brougham* in sight at all times and even succeeded at one stage in leaving her astern. The log records all sails having being set to advantage, including the square sail and studding sail, and the impression is given that Captain Kelly was keen to pace his little schooner with her newly shortened masts against the larger and theoretically much faster barque. He must have been very pleased with the result.

From 18 August until 3 November 1836, the *Prince of Denmark* was fully employed in the vicinity of Recherche Bay, supporting the shore whaling stations, catching whales, and shipping casks of oil back to Sullivan's Cove. Recherche Bay is situated on the west side of the D'Entrecasteaux Channel; one of the approaches to the port of Hobart Town, which lies at the head of the estuary of the River Derwent. Cutting in of the whale carcases took place alongside the *Prince of Denmark*, but the blubber was then brought to the shore station for trying-out.

The *Prince of Denmark* came close to disaster on 8 October 1836, when she ran aground on the 'Denmark' rock during a violent hailstorm in squally weather. She was re-floated within a few minutes, but damage may have occurred then which was to result in later problems.

After unloading her cargo of casks of oil at Sullivan's Cove in November, another lengthy period of maintenance began which lasted until early March. It would seem that leaks must have been evident: the process of heaving down began again to permit further repairs to the hull's copper cladding and also re-caulking of some of the planking next to the keel. The false keel was found to have considerable damage which had probably been caused by the grounding on the 'Denmark' rock.

On Friday 10 March 1837, with all repairs and maintenance complete, the freshly painted *Prince of Denmark* sailed past Recherche Bay on her way south through the D'Entrecasteaux Channel to the open sea. She was bound for Portland Bay in Victoria, South Australia, and was therefore heading up the west side of Van Diemen's Land. That coast is an inhospitable one, providing no havens that are safe to enter during strong westerly winds.

In fresh winds and squally weather, it was quickly found out that despite all the time and effort spent on refurbishment, the vessel was leaking heavily, requiring the crew to spend long hours every day manning the pumps. Either the cause of these leaks had not been found, or perhaps the process of heaving down had strained the hull and created a new problem. A slightly worrying situation for the captain was then made worse on the morning of 15 March 1837, when he realised that the distance he estimated he had travelled northwards was greater than the charted distance to the Australian mainland. Tension eased when after a very cautious approach in poor visibility, the coast was glimpsed, identified, and the ship's true position determined.

One crewmember – Stilman White – seems to have been a thorn in the flesh of authority, both during the fitting out period and at sea. He features twice in the log for being absent without leave, before being discharged. Despite his discharge, he must have had some redeeming qualities, as he was hired again only a few days later. He had not, however, changed his ways, and was again logged for being absent without leave.

A gentleman of the same unusual name, spelt in exactly the same way, was convicted of theft – simple grand larceny at the Old Bailey, in London on 23 October 1828. He was sentenced to transportation for seven years. Earlier the same month, he had stolen a watch, a seal, two watch keys and two other keys from James Dods, who was a steward on the *Lord Melville*, which was then lying off Irongate Wharf at the Tower of London. Stilman White was 24 years of age. Harsh as his sentence may seem, he was a lucky young man, as in the same court only a few days earlier, three 16-year-old youths had been sentenced to death for the theft of a few pairs of scissors. (Facts quoted from Old Bailey Proceedings Online [www.oldbaileyonline.org, version 7.0, 19 May 2012], October 1828, trial of STILMAN WHITE[t18281023-156])

However, evidence of the fact that Stilman White was by no means all bad is given in the following extract from the *Hobart Town Courier* of 9 August 1833:

> On the recommendation of the Port Officer, a Ticket of leave has been granted to Stilman White, for rescuing a soldier with an infant child who fell overboard when a detachment of the 21st Fusiliers were being disembarked from the bark *Funchal*.

A ticket-of-leave was a form of parole, which provided freedom within a defined district and allowed a prisoner to seek employment, marry, or bring family from home, and own property. The holder of a ticket-of-leave was not, however, allowed to carry firearms or to board a ship. Stilman White, despite having a ticket-of-leave, would only have been able to find employment on a ship during 1836 after the completion of his full sentence of seven years. True to form, Stilman White was in trouble again in January of 1834, and was sentenced to have his ticket-of-leave suspended for three days, during which he was to be imprisoned and kept to hard labour on the tread-wheel. All this was for leaving town without a pass, travelling to the Huon River and absenting himself from muster and church for four weeks. Just eight months later, he left town without a pass again, receiving in consequence a further suspension of his ticket-of-leave and being sentenced to three months labour on the Sorell rivulet road party.

The *Prince of Denmark* made a safe arrival at Portland Bay on 16 March 1837, and after a few days spent unloading cargo and taking on ballast, departure was made on 22 March for the return passage to Hobart Town. Only three days later, she was safely back at anchor in Hobart Town. The following advertisement appeared in the *Colonial Times* of Hobart Town:

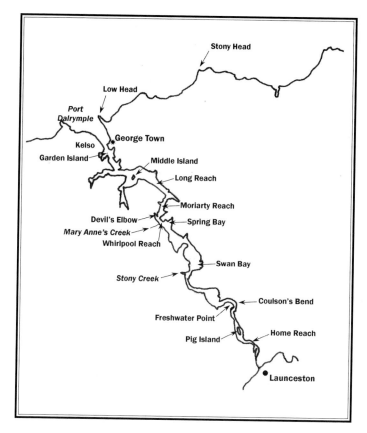

Sketch map of Launceston and the Tamar River

For Launceston, The Fine Fast-sailing Schooner *Prince of Denmark* will sail for the above port, on Thursday next. For freight apply to Hewitt, Gore and Co., 22nd May 1837.

Her next voyage from Hobart Town to Launceston and back, between June and August of 1837, seems to have been fraught with difficulties and misfortunes. From the very outset, the ship was again leaking and required to be pumped every hour. Later, it was necessary to pump her continuously, which must have been both intensely worrying and exhausting for everyone on board. The weather was bad, the seas heavy, and damage to the sails was widespread. Running aground on the way up-river to Launceston whilst a pilot was aboard, would not have helped the master's frame-of-mind.

Sleet and snow on the return passage and damage to the main boom by a passing vessel at Sullivan's Cove can only have added to a general air of misfortune. The lowest point came on 18 July 1837, when the mate, William Fletcher, having undergone and survived all the difficulties and dangers of the voyage, was drowned in the relative safety of the harbour at Sullivan's Cove.

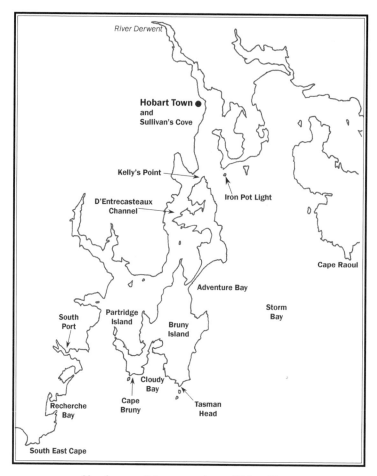

Sketch map of the approaches to Hobart Town

The only good news was that the carpenter's efforts at Launceston to carry out additional caulking and to make repairs close to the rudder did seem to have cured the leaks, as no reports were made of pumping operations on the homeward voyage.

From August until October 1837, the *Prince of Denmark* was engaged in what seem to have been highly successful whaling operations at Southport and Recherche Bay. The number of other vessels named in the log and the several references to 'opposition parties' and named individuals such as Griffiths and John Petchy, give some impression of the intense whaling activity that was taking place at this time. John Petchy, like Captain James Kelly, was a prominent whaler, farmer, ship-owner and merchant, and had three whaling stations at Recherche Bay. He and several of his crew were drowned at Hobart Town Regatta in 1850 when their vessel capsized.

The log for this period of time wastes no words on elaborate descriptions of the various activities, but nevertheless, it gives a clear picture of the contrasts between waiting for fair weather, waiting for whales to appear, scrambling to catch them in competition with others, towing them home, cutting-in, trying-out and stowing away the barrels of oil for shipping to Hobart Town. An impression of the diversity of the skills whalers needed is also given by the accounts of gathering materials for the repair or construction of huts for the shore stations, some of which were for the crews of other ships owned by Captain Kelly.

It has been reported that in the late 1830s, the *Prince of Denmark*, like other ships owned by Captain Kelly, made two successful trading voyages to London. It is presumed that these voyages would have been made chiefly to take top-quality whale oil and baleen directly to the London market, but it is possible that a broad range of other goods such as wool, furs and timber was also carried. Few details of her activities between 1837 and 1840 have been found, other than the fact that she was present at the Tasman Regatta at Hobart Town in 1840. Perhaps two prolonged visits to London would account for some of the missing years.

During 1840, Captain Kelly ran into serious financial difficulty and, like many other businessmen in Hobart, he must have struggled to comprehend the extent of the recession that suddenly overwhelmed him and his way of life. His desperate attempts to raise capital by selling some of his ships in London proved unsuccessful, and on Tuesday 8 December 1840, the following advertisement appeared in the *Hobart Courier*:

> Schooner *Prince of Denmark*
>
> W. T. Macmichael will sell by auction at the new wharf on Monday the 14th instant at 12 o'clock precisely, and without the least reserve, that well-built and fast-sailing schooner *Prince of Denmark*, 127 tons burthen, with all her standing and running rigging, cables, anchors, *etc.*, as she now lies off the new wharf.
>
> This vessel is well adapted for the trade to the neighbouring colonies, coal mines or whaling, and being well found in stores, can be sent to sea at a trifling expense.

Somehow, Captain Kelly must have persuaded his creditors to hold off pursuit of the money they were owed, as it seems that he succeeded in retaining ownership of the vessel which had served him so well. At the end of August 1841, the *Prince of Denmark* sailed from Hobart Town for Sydney via Two Fold Bay, still owned by Captain Kelly and Thomas Hewitt – but under the command of Captain Smith, carrying a cargo of sundries. On 29 September 1841, she returned to Hobart Town in ballast, sailing again on 22 December on a sealing voyage.

11 *The End of Shore Whaling*

The activities of shore whaling stations were now in terminal decline, but ship-based whaling continued to be viable – although it involved ever-longer passages and a great deal more time spent on searches for increasingly elusive whales. The *Prince of Denmark* was still regarded as a whaling vessel at this time, but clearly had to be versatile and able to take advantage of any opportunities that arose to generate income, from carrying either passengers or cargo. On one occasion during 1842, her crew of only nine men caught a valuable sperm whale while on passage from Portland Bay to Hobart Town, but later lost its head during rough weather in Recherche Bay. This would have been the cause of much distress to the crew, as well as to the whale, as the head of the sperm whale is the chief source of spermaceti, the most valuable of all the whaling industry's products. As Captain Kelly laboured under the stress of his financial difficulties, it seems that some of his crewmen tried to take advantage of the situation. The *Hobart Courier* of 4 March 1842 reported that:

> Several seamen belonging to the schooner *Prince of Denmark* were charged by Mr. Kelly, the owner of that vessel, with neglect of duty, two of whom were committed to the house of correction, the others reprimanded and discharged.

The *Prince of Denmark* was reported by the *Colonial Times* of 3 May 1842 to have arrived at Hobart Town from the Auckland Islands on 25 April 1842, under the command of Captain W. Smith, with a cargo of empty casks. She sailed again on 27 May 1842, under the command of Captain David Robert Comyn. Captain Comyn was based in Hobart Town, and though nothing is known of his early years, he later became master of (firstly) the *Adelaide* of Hobart Town, and (secondly) the *Priam*. The *Priam*, owned by Henry Reed of London, was a brand-new ship when Captain Comyn took charge of her, and she sailed on 21 May 1852 on her maiden voyage from Plymouth, bound for Portland, with 277 passengers on board. She arrived safely on 25 August, despite an outbreak of measles on board. Captain Comyn was commended by his passengers for his untiring energy, and for his attention to their health, welfare and comfort.

The *Hobart Courier* of 3 June 1842 reported that the goods recently exported on the *Prince of Denmark* consisted of:

> 50 cases Geneva, 2 cases black oil, 20m. shingles, 4 bales gunny bags, 20 do. Gunnies,
> 1 package pens, for D. McPherson; 275 chests tea, 250 half chests tea, 2 cases, for
> Kerr and Co.; 1 piano, for Dr. Maddox; 5 casks black oil, for J. T. Waterhouse.

Dr. George Maddox, the recipient of the piano, was the assistant colonial surgeon at Launceston. In October 1842, three female occupants of the Launceston House of Correction were charged with his attempted murder, sentenced to death, and later reprieved.

The *Prince of Denmark*, still under Captain Comyn's command, left Launceston for Hobart Town on 22 June 1842, arriving safely on 29 June. The *Hobart Courier* of 1 July 1842 reported her cargo as consisting of:

> 12 cases oil, for W. M. Orr: 1 cask hardware, for the Union Bank: 2 do. Nails for
> J. W. Peppers: 59 tins oil for W. M. Orr, 52 casks beef, 26 cases pickles, 2 cases
> merchandise, for S. Levy: 9 boxes soap, 1 box boas, 1 do. Candles, for A. Morrison:
> 328 bags oats for W. T. Macmichael: 62 do., for J. Shadwick: 57 do., and 1 case
> sundries for T. W. Seagar: 164 bags oats, on order.

On 23 July 1842, the *Prince of Denmark* arrived at Adelaide from Hobart Town, under the command of Captain Comyn, carrying two passengers – Mr. F. Archer and Mr. Coglin. On 19 August 1842, the *Hobart Courier* reported that she was back at Hobart, having sailed from Portland Bay with general cargo, including 543 bags of rice, 195 bags of sugar, and passengers: Mr. Russel; Mr. Archer; Mr. and Mrs. Frost and three children; Mr. Smith; and Master Conolley.

The *Colonial Times* of Hobart Town published the following advertisement on Tuesday 23 August 1842:

> For Adelaide, South Australia – the fast-sailing schooner *Prince of Denmark*, 120
> tons, D. R. Comyn, Master, now ready for receiving cargo will sail on 27th ins.
> For freight or passage, apply on board, or to Duncan McPherson, New Wharf,
> 22nd August 1842.

When Captain Comyn took command of the *Prince of Denmark*, recession was beginning to bite and the following extract from the *Hobart Times* of 26 August 1842 illustrates that coastal traders were struggling against rising costs:

> Extortion – We regret to learn that the extortionate charges at Adelaide render it
> impossible for coasting vessels to trade to that port. The charge for the *Prince of*
> *Denmark* just arrived thence, was within a few shillings of £30!

Four months later, controversy over the matter of extortionate charges was brought to a conclusion by the firm resolve of the governor, as reported in the *Nelson Examiner and New Zealand Chronicle* of 24 December 1842:

> The heavy port dues at Adelaide are materially affecting the trade of that place. A correspondence has taken place between the supercargo of the *Prince of Denmark*, schooner, of 128 tons (but carrying only 90) and the local government, relative to the charge of £29-13s. on that vessel. The Governor declined making any exception in this case as the act has been passed a sufficient time to allow shipowners to acquaint themselves with its provisions.

Following the devastating losses suffered by Captain James Kelly, most of his goods, money and personal property were assigned to his chief creditors Thomas Brown and William Knight, who became owners of the *Prince of Denmark* in September 1842. Their new vessel appeared as No. 23 in the Hobart Town register of shipping. They also acquired land at Woodcutters Point on Bruny Island in 1843, and built a hut there out of turf, to accommodate shepherds looking after their livestock. The remains of their hut have recently been excavated and the site is now included in the Tasmanian Heritage Register.

The *Prince of Denmark* sailed on under the command of Captain Comyn, and despite the excessive harbour dues, she made a further passage to Adelaide. *The Southern Australian* of 16 September 1842 reported her arrival there two days earlier from Hobart Town, with four passengers – Mr. Calvert, Mr. Grant, Mr. Cock, and Mr. Tonkin. According to the *Hobart Courier* of 14 October 1842, she returned on 5 October 1842, carrying sheep, sundries and three passengers – Mr. Panthorn, Mrs. Gregory, and a child. Two further passages between Hobart Town and Portland Bay were then made.

Her last recorded passage while under the ownership of Thomas Brown and William Knight was in January 1843, and the *Colonial Times* of 24 January reported that she sailed from Portland Bay to Hobart Town with a cargo of 400 sheep and one passenger: Mr. Winter. Despite being engaged mainly in carrying cargo, her resourceful crew still seized every opportunity that presented itself to resume whaling. In December of 1842, they caught a whale that tried out at four and a half tuns, realising between £200–300.

The following article in the *Launceston Examiner* of 4 January 1843 gives a fine example of the versatility of the crew:

> Whaling – we are glad to hear that the *Prince of Denmark*, Captain Smith, has taken another sperm whale off Port Davey on Tuesday last by one of the boat's crew. The produce of the first will, it is said be upwards of £500, and the quantity of oil will be about 7 tuns. The *Prince of Denmark* is the property of Messrs. Garret and Watson. This vessel is employed in bringing stock from Port Albert, and it is manned by whalers, who allow no chance to them of capturing the "leviathan monsters of the deep".

The bush telegraph must have been very accurate, as it was not until February of 1843 that ownership of the vessel officially changed to that of Alfred Garrett and George

Watson of Hobart Town: she appeared as No. 5 on the Hobart Town Register of shipping. The change of ownership coincided with a return to full time whaling, and she arrived empty at Hobart Town in late February, after landing some of her crew at Macquarie Island. Alfred Garrett was a local director of the Union Bank of Australia at Hobart Town. Like Captain James Kelly, he had links with the Derwent and Tamar Insurance Co. George Watson was a well-known Hobart Town whaler, noted for being the helmsman in a race in February of 1838 between the crew of the American whaler *Statesman* and a local crew. The race, which was won by the local crew, was over a 6-mile course, and was for a prize of £10. George Watson is reported to have harpooned the last whale to be caught in the Derwent River, on 23 June 1856. His brother John was a prominent shipbuilder in Hobart Town.

Alfred Garrett's period of ownership of the *Prince of Denmark* was to be a very brief one, for on 29 April 1843, his shares were bought by John Watson; the Watson brothers becoming joint owners. The new owners appointed Michael Connor II, as captain of the *Prince of Denmark* and the *Hobart Courier* of 5 May 1843 reported that she had sailed from Hobart Town for Portland Bay with stores, two days earlier.

Michael Connor II was born in Sydney in 1801 and moved to Hobart in about 1825. He became mate of Captain James Kelly's *Mary and Elizabeth* in 1832, and later commanded various whaling vessels owned by Captain Kelly's friend and rival, Thomas Lucas. He married Lucas' daughter Elizabeth in 1835, and they set up home together in Kelly Street, in Hobart.

The *Prince of Denmark* resumed whaling under his command, and the *Launceston Examiner* of 16 September 1843 reported that a cargo of oil and bone was landed at Hobart Town from Portland Bay whaling station on 10 September.

A reminder of the hazards of navigation was given in the *Launceston Examiner* of 25 October 1843:

> The schooner *Shamrock* and the *Prince of Denmark* whilst beating up the river came into violent collision. The *Shamrock* received considerable injury.

Whether by good luck, skilful handling, or robust construction, the *Prince of Denmark* survived a potential disaster.

In April and May of 1844, Governor George Grey (later Sir George Grey) led an expedition to the southeast of South Australia. Little was known about this area at the time, and such information as existed had been gleaned chiefly from the reports of men who had driven stock across the land. The governor was accompanied by Thomas Burr, the deputy surveyor general, and George French Angas, artist to the expedition. An entry in Thomas Burr's journal reads as follows:

> *1st May 1844.* To the south we saw Rivoli Bay with two vessels riding at anchor, while immediately between us and Rivoli Bay and to the west there was a lake (Lake George) only separated from another lake (Lake Eliza), which terminated in Guichen Bay, by a narrow strip of land. These lakes had not previously been seen, and were named by the Governor.

Sir George Edward Grey (Courtesy of Auckland Libraries, New Zealand)

3rd May 1844. Up at break of day. The Governor walked over to the beach at Rivoli Bay; the party consisted of seven persons. On arriving we signalised and were heard by the whalers. We walked towards the nearest point of land from the vessels, and on coming near were met by a party of sailors who had been sent to see who we were. The surprise of the whalers was great; they considered we must be a party from some ship that had been wrecked; on hearing that the Governor was with us, their politeness was great; they took us in one of the boats to an island on the northwest point of the bay which is covered with penguins. From this island I took many bearings to distant points situated to the southeast. The whalers had a station (two huts) on shore, and had dug a well, in which there was good water. The vessels in Rivoli Bay were the *Isabella* and the *Prince of Denmark*, schooners from Hobart Town.*

Thomas Burr's description of his party's reception by the whalers is at variance with what one might expect from a band of men free from the restraints of civilised society, engaged in a business which could be reasonably described as dangerous, barbaric and thoroughly unsavoury. Rough as the whalers may have been, they were sufficiently astute to recognise the value of creating a favourable impression on their distinguished visitor and his party.

---

* *(Quoted from:* Thomas Burr's journal, *in the* R.G.S. of London Journal, *Volume 15, p.171 [1845]. Courtesy of The Royal Geographical Society and the Institute of British Geographers, and Wiley-Blackwell, Publishers)*

Mr George French Angas (Courtesy of The Mitchell Library, State Library of New South Wales, Australia)

Only a few weeks later, the crews of the *Prince of Denmark* and the *Isabella* found themselves in a perilous position, when their anchor cables parted during heavy weather. The *Isabella* was driven on to the shore, where she was completely wrecked. The *Prince of Denmark*'s qualities as a fast ship probably saved her from disaster, as she was able to make sail and claw her way off shore until the weather eased. The *Shipping Gazette and Sydney General Trade List* of 24 August 1844 reported the incident:

> The brig *Dorset*, upon her arrival at Adelaide, reported the following wreck, having been boarded by some of the crew belonging to the vessel: "The schooner *Isabella*, of Hobart Town, Hayes, master, was wrecked on 23rd June in a bay a little to the NW of Cape Buffon, in lat. 35° 37' south, long. 140° 12' east, where she was lying whaling in company with the *Prince of Denmark* of Hobart Town. The *Isabella* parted from her cables during a heavy westerly gale and drove immediately on shore. The *Prince of Denmark* also parted after the gale had subsided, but was got under weigh and kept so until the sea went down sufficiently to allow them to pick their anchors up. The *Isabella* is a complete wreck, but the crew had saved everything moveable, and were living on shore. They had mated with those of the *Prince of Denmark*, but both vessels had only procured three

fish, one of which had yielded by their account sixteen tuns. They had seen many whales, but the weather had been so boisterous they could not capture them. They expected to leave for Hobart Town on or about the 20th August. The natives on this unfrequented part of the coast were very sociable, but much addicted to thieving.

Despite the difficulties described above, the *Sydney Morning Herald* of 25 October 1844 reported that the *Prince of Denmark*, four weeks out from Hobart Town, had arrived at Boyd Town on 6 October 1844, with 80 barrels of black oil, and sailed again for the whaling grounds five days later. Her next voyage also seemed to have been successful, as the *Launceston Examiner* of 4 December 1844 announced that:

> The *Prince of Denmark* has arrived at Hobart Town with 16 tuns sperm, 8 tuns black oil and 5 cwt. bone after an absence of 2 months.

Five months later, the *Colonial Times* of 20 May 1845 gave the following announcement of another change in her circumstances:

> The only 'Polacca rigged' vessel that has ever we believe been seen in these colonies is the old clipper the *Prince of Denmark* belonging to Mr. George Watson. She is intended for the whaling business, and we have no doubt will sustain her old character for success. May she well prosper, say we.

On 30 May 1845, George Watson officially became her sole owner (Registration No. 17 at Hobart Town), and she continued her whaling activities under the command of a new captain, Robert Heays.

The following extract from the *Cornwall Chronicle* of 7 June 1845 gives a fine description of an exciting incident in the *Prince of Denmark*'s career, and also seems to convey something of the affection in which the elderly vessel was now held:

> Whale killed in the harbour – this morning in consequence of a notice in our avant courier the *Trumpeter*, by which Mr. Watson announced his intention kindly to keep the whale, killed by his party the day before in Sullivan's Cove, till 12 o'clock this day, the new wharf was thronged with crowds of people of both sexes, flocking towards the *Prince of Denmark* to view this monster of the deep; and there it was floating by the side of the little schooner – a large leviathan – even in its death sleep. The fish is but a small black one, and is expected to produce about 4 tuns of oil, and a proportionate quantity of bone. The following are briefly the particulars of its capture: about 3 o'clock p.m., Mr. Watson, who was on board the *Prince of Denmark*, was informed there was a whale near the buoy off the domain – two boats were immediately sent in pursuit and in about ten minutes were both fast to her; the whale line in one of them being new, became foul and she was dragged by the whale under water, but without receiving any damage or any other harm occurring save a good ducking. The other boat however, headed by Captain Heays, stuck close to her, and, after a beautiful run up and down the river, the victory was achieved in about an hour after she was

struck, and she was towed alongside the *Prince of Denmark* where she is being cut in and tried out; she is about forty feet long. This is a good beginning for the *Prince of Denmark*, which starts next Saturday on a whaling voyage.

Throughout that year, she made a number of successful whaling voyages, sailing firstly from Hobart Town and later from Sydney. The first of these voyages began on 12 June 1845, and the *Hobart Courier* of 22 April 1846 reported her return to Hobart Town from the South Seas. In September of 1846, she sailed for a South Seas whaling voyage with a crew of 19 men, whose names are recorded in a document held by the Archives Office of Tasmania:

> —— Campbell, —— James, George Foreman, —— Randolph, Henry Robinson, Chas. Creswell, —— Maddocks, Chas. Selby, J. Gale, Lawrence Mills, William Ahern, —— ——, —— ——,—— —— Johnston, —— ——, James Jims, —— James.
> Master, Robert Heays.

The *Colonial Times* of 21 September 1847 published the following enthusiastic account of the outcome of the voyage:

> The *Prince of Denmark* – this fine whaling brig, the property of Mr. G. Watson, arrived on Sunday after an absence of upwards of five months, with nearly thirty tuns sperm oil; thus having fished during the last twelve months about 60 tuns of that valuable commodity. This is doing well – would that all our colonial whalers were equally lucky.

On the 4 July 1848, the *Colonial Times* of Hobart Town gave a further joyous report:

> We are happy to say that our colonial whaling brig *Prince of Denmark* was telegraphed this morning going into Fortescue Bay, with two sperm whales alongside. We trust this wholesale work will continue.

Perhaps it did, because the *Prince of Denmark* landed 235 barrels of sperm whale oil at Recherche Bay during 1848. She also escaped disaster in July of the same year, when her anchor and cable were lost in a gale at Port Davey. Despite some success and good fortune, her captain and crew both faced difficulties, as is evident from the following report published in the *Launceston Examiner* on 20 February 1850:

> Melbourne – The whaling brig Prince of Denmark, 70 tons, Heays, sailed on Wednesday but returned to port on Thursday, several of the men having refused to work. The necessary warrants for the apprehension of the insubordinate seamen were obtained and despatched by the police boat.

In September of 1850, she arrived at Hobart Town from another whaling voyage to the South Seas, again under the command of Captain Robert Heays. Her crew list, taken from a document held by the Archives Office of Tasmania, was as follows:

> Bull, James Maccassey, James Newbel[?], H. Wright, C. Daley, James Mullins, John Nettale[?], I. Royall, W. Silvan, John Dunn, James Towers[?], C. Robertson, J. Russell, S. Parker, W. Curry, W. Johnson, C. Gray, G. Taktall, J. Miller.

The voyage did not seem to start well, as indicated by the following report taken from the *New Zealander* of 30 November 1850:

> The Whaling brig *Prince of Denmark*, Captain Hayes, of Hobart Town, is eight weeks out from that port; a clean ship. She has been cruising chiefly off the east coast, and reports having struck two humpback whales, but was unable to secure either. Off Hawke's Bay, struck a large sperm whale which they were on the point of securing, when an accident happening to the lines, the prize got clear away: from the size of the animal it was calculated to yield about ten or eleven tuns of oil, which at the current rate in Hobart Town, would have been worth £600 in all. The *Prince of Denmark* called here to convey Mr. Waterhouse of Hobart Town, on a voyage to the Feejees, but that gentleman having gone a passenger by the *John Wesley* she will now return to the whaling grounds off our coast.

The Mr. Waterhouse referred to is probably the Rev. Joseph Waterhouse, whose father, the Rev. John Waterhouse had been appointed in 1839 as superintendent of Wesleyan Missions in Australia and Polynesia. The *John Wesley* was a new vessel owned by the Wesleyan Mission, and would almost certainly have provided accommodation more suitable for a missionary than that offered by the *Prince of Denmark*.

The reference to the *Prince of Denmark* being a clean ship shows that in the eight weeks of her voyage, she had not caught any whales. Successful whalers could be identified from far away by smoke from the try-works, by the smell of the process, or from the fact that masts, sails, rigging and crew would all have been coated with oily soot stains. At £600, the value of the sperm whale that escaped would have been several times greater than the value of the vessel. Perhaps success came later in the voyage, for in December 1850, the *New Zealander* reported Captain Heays sailing again:

> The whaling brig *Prince of Denmark* of Hobart Town sailed on Thursday for the whaling grounds, calling first at the great barrier for firewood. Captain Hayes intends cruising chiefly off the east coast, from the North Cape to Cook's Straits.

This voyage was to be a long one. The *Prince of Denmark* sailed from Hobart Town on 1 October 1850 for the South Seas and was not heard of again until she was spoken to on 3 March 1851 by the schooner *Wellington*, at latitude 44.31 south, longitude 172.40 east (a little to the east of Dunedin in the south island of New Zealand). Captain Heays reported that he was carrying 25 tuns of sperm whale oil. The *Hobart Courier* of 9 September 1851 reported her return two days earlier, when she landed 130 barrels of oil. On 13 September 1851, the *Hobart Courier* advertised the sale of 12 tuns of sperm oil from the *Prince of Denmark*, to be sold 'by order of trustees of G. Watson's estate'.

In April of 1851, George Watson had been forced to assign all his estates and effects to William Rout and Richard Cleburne, merchants in Hobart Town, and on 20 September 1851, the following advertisement appeared in the *Hobart Town Courier*:

> The Whaling Brig *Prince of Denmark*
>
> by Mr. T. Y. Lowes, on Tuesday 23rd instant
>
> at 12 o'clock at the Franklin Wharf,
>
> By order of the Derwent and Tamar Insurance Co.
>
> To be sold without the least reserve,
>
> The clipper brig *Prince of Denmark*, 70 tons burthen, with all her try-works, boats, casks and gear as equipped for whaling. She is remarkably well found, and was doubled and coppered about three years ago. Also a first rate chronometer, by a celebrated maker.
>
> Terms in next advertisement
>
> An inventory of her stores *etc.* may be seen at the auctioneers.

On 7 October of 1851, Richard Cleburne became the owner of the *Prince of Denmark*, and registered her at Hobart Town (Registration No. 52).

12 *A Troubled Voyage*

Richard Cleburne, the new owner of the *Prince of Denmark* had arrived in Hobart Town from his native Ireland some 30 years earlier, and had established a considerable diversity of businesses there. Initially a merchant trader, he had some involvement in the import of American tobacco during 1832, which led to speculation and gossip that he had a hand in smuggling. At about the same time, he acquired 1,500 acres of land on the bank of the River Derwent and built himself a substantial mansion. He then began direct trading between Hobart Town and Melbourne in a ship called the *Blossom*, the construction of which he had commissioned.

Between 1840 and 1843, he was a director of the Colonial Bank, and at the same time (like Captain James Kelly), he was involved with the Derwent and Tamar Insurance Co. In 1848, he tried unsuccessfully to lease land for coal-mining purposes at Schouten Island, and in 1849, he expanded his already established soap, salt and candle business in the harbour area of Hobart Town. The Exhibition of Industry of all Nations (the Great Exhibition of 1851) in the Crystal Palace, London, included an exhibit of a box of soap made by Richard Cleburne, which was considered superior in quality to the best English soap imported to Van Diemen's Land at the time. He was a prominent opponent

Mr. Richard Cleburne (Courtesy of the Allport Library and Museum of Fine Arts, Tasmanian Archive and Heritage Office, Australia)

of convict transportation, a Hobart City Commissioner, and in October of 1851, he was elected to the legislative council representing Huon, retaining his seat until 1864, the year of his death.

The log of the *Prince of Denmark*'s first whaling voyage to New Zealand under the ownership of Richard Cleburne began on Wednesday 8 October 1851, when the she made her way down the River Derwent from Hobart Town. Light and changeable winds initially made for slow progress, then freshening winds increasing to gale force obliged the captain to anchor off Partridge Island and to keep the crew busy with repairs and maintenance. It was not until 25 October 1851 that the *Prince of Denmark* was finally clear of the southeastern tip of Van Diemen's Land and could be steered directly for Cook Straits.

Wednesday 8 October 1851 a.m. got under way with a light breeze at southeast, marked till dark. Making little progress at dusk. Brought up about two miles from where we left at noon. Midnight, calms.

Thursday 9 October At daylight got under way and sailed down the river with a light breeze at N.W. At noon the sea breeze set in. Stood in to D'Entrecasteaux channel. At sunset, calms. At dusk let go the anchor in 13 fathoms. Midnight calms.

Friday 10 October At daylight, calms. Hove short and set the sails. At 8.00 a.m. a light breeze from the north. Steered down the channel. At noon, calms. At 2.00 p.m. a light breeze from N.E., which carried us within a mile of Partridge Isle, when the wind shifted to S.S.W. and blowed fresh. At 5.00 p.m. came to anchor and sent on shore such things as was to be left there and got a boat, and pulling oars and one steer oar. At 8.00 set anchor watch. Midnight hard breezes from S.S.W.

Saturday 11 October At daylight got under way with a moderate breeze from S.S.W. At 8.00 the breeze increasing. At 9.00 a fresh gale at S.S.E. Put back and at 10.00 came to anchor where we left at daylight. Middle and latter part hard gale.

Sunday 12 October Hard gales throughout the 24 hours.

Monday 13 October At daylight got under way with a fresh breeze from S.S.W. At 2.00 p.m. off South Port. At dusk came to anchor in Recherche Bay in 12 fathoms. At 8.00 set anchor watch for the night.

Tuesday 14 October At daylight got under way with a light breeze from the west and worked further in the bay. A.m. sent the boat on shore for repairs. People employed variously about the rigging. Latter part fresh breezes. At 8.00 set anchor watch.

Wednesday 15 October Light winds and variable. Carpenter repairing boat. P.m. got two tuns of water. At 8.00 set anchor watch.

Thursday 16 October Fresh breezes with light showers of rain. People variously employed. Boat finished and got on board not painted. At 8.00 set anchor watch.

Friday 17 October Strong breezes through the 24 hours. Employed painting boat and other sundry jobs.

Saturday 18 October Hard gales throughout the 24 hours.

Sunday 19 October Weather more moderate but all appearance of bad weather.

Monday 20 October At daylight got under way with a light breeze from the N.E. and steered to the S.W. At noon passed the South Cape. At 2.00 p.m. a sudden shift of wind to the west. Tacked ship and ran to the N.E. At 10.00 the wind shifted again to the N.E. Wore ship and steered S.W. At midnight, off the Whale's Head about 6 miles offshore. Light airs and cloudy.

Tuesday 21 October First part of this day light airs and cloudy weather. At noon a sudden shift of wind to the S.W. Squared the yards and ran to the N.E. Latter part hard breezes with rain. At sunset shortened sail for the night.

Wednesday 22 October First part of this day fresh breezes with light mizzling rain. Steering N.E. by E. At noon passed Cape Pillar. Latter part moderate. Saw a schooner standing inshore. At sunset shortened sail.

Thursday 23 October Light breezes with fine weather. Saw several vessels standing to the south. The wind hauled to the S.W. and then to S.E. and E.

Friday 24 October First and middle of this day light breezes with thick hazy weather and rain at times. Latter part fresh breezes and clear weather. Stood to the E.S.E.

Saturday 25 October Throughout this day, steady breezes and clear weather. Steering east by north for Cook Straits. Saw finbacks.

Navigation from Van Diemen's Land to Cook Straits was relatively straightforward. No particular hazards such as reefs or island groups were on a direct line between the two places and, most importantly, the line of 40 degrees of latitude ran directly from the northern tip of Van Diemen's Land to the middle of the approach to Cook Straits, which separate the north and south islands of New Zealand. When visibility was good and the wind was fair, the captain would be able to steer a course along the line of 40 degrees of latitude using his noon observation by quadrant to keep the sun at a constant angle.

The purpose of the voyage, however, was to catch whales. Crews on all forms of fishing vessels rely heavily on the skill, experience and judgement of the captain to make the voyage lucrative. No catch means no wages. It matters not that the captain may simply have been unlucky. A crew already frustrated by a long passage with a slow start would not take well to either the lack of success at catching the two black whales sighted or to the numerous sightings of finbacks. Finback whales were considered such fast and powerful swimmers that they would defeat all attempts to catch them.

Sunday 26 October First part of this day fresh breezes and clear weather. Steering N. by E. for New Zealand. Saw finbacks. Latitude 42.12 longitude 154.02 east.

Monday 27 October First part of this day fresh breezes, all sail set. Middle and latter part light breezes. Saw finbacks in great numbers. Latitude 42.21 Longitude155.30.

Tuesday 28 October Light breezes with thick foggy weather throughout the day. Latitude by ac. 42.03½ longitude 157.28.

Wednesday 29 October First part of this day light airs and cloudy weather. Middle and latter part hard breezes with light mizzling rain. Latitude 43.00 longitude 159.15.

Thursday 30 October Hard breezes with constant rain at sun set. Close reefed the topsails and hauled up the foresail. At 10.00 the fore-topsail sheet parted. Clewed it up and set the foresail. Latitude by ac. 43.20. Longitude by ac 162.10.

Kirkcudbright's

Prince of Denmark

Colour section

The Rev. Thomas Kendall, and the Maori chiefs Hongi Hika and Waikato (Courtesy of the Alexander Turnbull Library, Wellington, New Zealand)

The Rev. Samuel Marsden (Courtesy of the Alexander Turnbull Library, Wellington, New Zealand)

Mr. James Busby, 1832 (Courtesy of the Alexander Turnbull Library, Wellington, New Zealand)

Captain James Kelly (Courtesy of the Queen Victoria Museum and Art Gallery, Launceston, Tasmania, Australia)

III

Panel 3 of Panorama of Hobart c.1825 Courtesy of the Mitchell Library, State Library of New South Wales, Australia

The Success hove down to the Couizer (Courtesy of the Mitchell Library, State Library of New South Wales, Australia)

Cape Pillar the entrance of the River Derwent (Courtesy of the State Library of Victoria, Australia)

Whalebone at Prince of Denmark *wreck site (Courtesy of Fortune de Mer, New Caledonia)*

Examining try-pots at Prince of Denmark *wreck site (Courtesy of Fortune de Mer, New Caledonia)*

Friday 31 October First part of this day hard breeze. Middle and later part light breeze. Hauled to the west. Hauled the ship's head up N.E. by E. Saw finbacks. Latitude by ac. 43.25 Longitude by ac. 164.40.

Saturday 1 November Throughout this day light breezes and rain with light mizzling rain. At 6.00 p.m. lowered after a black whale. Could not get fast. At dark the boats returned on board. Latitude 43.20 Longitude 165.13.

Sunday 2 November Throughout this day hard breezes from N.E. with thick hazy weather and rain. Latitude by ac. 43.36 longitude by ac. 165.30.

Monday 3 November Hard breezes with thick hazy weather throughout the 24 hours, with light mizzling rain. Latitude by ac. 43.36. Longitude by ac. 165.40.

Tuesday 4 November Weather the same as yesterday. At 4.00 a.m. wear ship to the N.W. At 8.00 again wear ship to the eastward. Saw fin back all day. At sunset again wear ship to the N.W. Latitude by ac. 43.40 Longitude by ac. 167.02.

Wednesday 5 November First part of this day hard breezes and thick hazy weather with rain. At 2.00 a.m. took in the fore-topsail. The yard parted about 5ft from the hounds while the men was stowing the sail. At daylight sent the fore-topsail yard down and fixed it. At 6.00 p.m. sent it up and bent the sail. Middle and later part calms. Latitude and Longitude the same as yesterday.

Thursday 6 November Calms throughout the 24 hours. p.m. lowered after a black whale. Could not get fast. Latitude 44.04 Longitude 167.08.

Friday 7 November Moderate breezes and smooth water throughout 24 hours. All sail set, steering N.E. by N. The snow-topped mountains in sight to the S.E. Latitude 43.44 Longitude 168.04.

Less than two weeks after clearing Van Diemen's Land, the sight of the mountains of the South Island of New Zealand would be welcome. The captain could now follow the coast in a northeasterly direction until Cook Straits opened up, but would be careful to keep a sufficient distance off shore to give himself plenty sea-room in case a westerly gale arose.

Saturday 8 November Light breezes and fine pleasant weather throughout the 24 hours. Steering N.E. by N. P.m. got two porpoises. Latitude 42.55 Longitude 169.06.

Sunday 9 November Light breezes and fine weather throughout the 24 hours. All sail set, steering N.E. Latitude 42.25 longitude 170.51. p.m.

Monday 10 November Weather the same as yesterday. At 8.00 p.m. passed Cape Foul Weather at the distance of 5 or 6 miles, and steered N.½E. to round Rocky Point.

Tuesday 11 November First part of this day, light breezes. Middle and later part, fresh breezes. At 9.00 a.m. passed Cape Farewell and at 6.00 p.m. passed Cape Stephens then steered E.S.E. by compass.

Wednesday 12 November First part of this day, fresh breezes. At 7.00 held abreast of Port Nicholson. At 11.00 p.m. past Cape Palliser. Light breezes and strong puffs at times. Got five porpoises during the day.

Thursday 13 November Moderate breezes and fine weather throughout the day. At noon, passed Castle Point about 5 miles offshore. At sunset, off Chalky Cliffs.

Friday 14 November First part of this day moderate. Middle and latter part hard gale from S.W. At 8.00 a.m. passed Cape Kidnapper and stood into Hawks Bay. At 11 came to an anchor in 7 fathoms in the S.E. end of Hawks Bay.

Saturday 15 November Hard breezes with a heavy swell setting in the bay. A.m. got under way and run further up the bay. At 2.00 p.m. came to an anchor at the —— in five fathoms. Smooth water. Went on shore to get a spar for a topsail yard. Two of the men run away from the boat.

Sunday 16 November More moderate. Applied to the magistrate to get the two men that run away. He succeeded getting them for which he charged two pounds and ten shillings for one man that was disorderly on shore.

Monday 17 November Fine weather throughout. At sunset got the spar on board. It was then calm.

Tuesday 18 November At daylight hove short and set the sails. Found two men missing and supposed to go in a boat that came off in the evening. I was obliged to go on shore after them and succeeded in getting them by the help of the natives. At 11.00 a.m. got under way and stood out of the bay.

It does not appear that the captain was in command of a happy ship's company. It is bad enough that two men had deserted within a few hours of landing in New Zealand, worse that either the same two or another two men deserted three days later, and perhaps worst of all that the *Prince of Denmark* had then to continue her voyage with an unknown number of reluctant and embittered crewmen aboard.

Wednesday 19 November Light breezes and fine weather throughout the 24 hours. P.m. saw humpback. Went in chase of them but could not get fast. Sunset, shortened sail in the middle of Hawks Bay.

Thursday 20 November Light breezes with constant rain. Saw humpback. Did not lower after them, being in deep water.

Friday 21 November Light breezes and fine weather. Stood into the N.E. corner of the bay. Some of the shore party's boats came off and informed us there had been one school of whales in the bay. Bought a large pig from one of them. P.m. stood out of the bay. At sunset shortened sail.

Saturday 22 November Throughout this day very unsettled weather. Sometimes hard breezes, variable and then calms for the same space of time. The wind from all points of the compass.

Sunday 23 November Weather more settled. Latter part fine. Cruising about the bay. At sunset, shortened sail for the night. Portland Island bore E. by N.

Monday 24 November First part of the day fine. Latter part, fresh breezes with light showers of rain. Carpenter making a topsail yard. Cruising about the bay.

Tuesday 25 November Light breezes and fine weather throughout the 24 hours. Hands variously employed. The carpenter finished the topsail yard and gave it a coat of tar.

Wednesday 26 November Sent a boat on shore for some sand. They brought two goats off with them from Portland Island. At sunset, shorten sail for the night. Portland Island E. by S. about 3 miles.

Thursday 27 November Fresh breezes with light showers of rain at times. Standing off and on the Mahia Land.

Friday 28 November Moderate breezes and fine weather. Sent the main topmast stay down and repaired it and got it up again. P.m. saw spouts, lowered the boats and pulled up to them. Proved to be finbacks.

Saturday 29 November Fresh breezes throughout the 24 hours. Cruising about the bay. At sunset, shortened sail for the night. Portland Island E.S.E. 6 or 7 miles.

Sunday 30 November Throughout this day fine weather. Stood up the bay. One of the shore boats came off. At sunset, stood further out in the bay.

Monday 1 December First part of this day fine. Middle and latter parts, hard breezes from N.E. with light mizzling rain. Standing off and on the Mahia in smooth water.

Tuesday 2 December Throughout this 24, hard gale with light mizzling rain. At 4.00 p.m. came to an anchor in the N.E. corner of the bay in 10 fathoms. Coarse sand and shells. At 8.00 set anchor watch.

Wednesday 3 December Hard gale throughout the 24, with sunlight, mizzling rain.

Thursday 4 December First part of this day hard breezes. Middle and latter part, more moderate. p.m. got underway and stood out in the bay.

Friday 5 December First part of this day fresh breezes. Middle and latter part fine. Cruising about the bay. Employed repairing a topsail.

Saturday 6 December This day begins with light breezes and cloudy. Middle and latter part of the day, blowing hard from S.S.W. with rains. Working out of the bay with single reef topsails. At sunset, Portland Island bore E.N.E. Distant about 2 miles.

Sunday 7 December This day begins with strong breezes. Middle and latter part fine. At sunset, Portland Island bore E. by S. 6 or 7 miles.

Monday 8 December Light breezes and fine weather. P.m. the mate went on shore at Portland Island. At sunset the boat came on board and brought three pigs.

Tuesday 9 December Throughout this day, light breezes and fine weather. Cruising about the Bay. Employed repairing a topsail.

Wednesday 10 December This day commenced with light breezes and dark gloomy weather. Middle and latter part strong breezes with rain.

Thursday 11 December Strong breezes with dark gloomy weather with thunder and lightning with some light drops of rain. Working out of the Bay with single reef topsails. At sunset, shortened sail for the night. Portland Island bore E. by S. 6 or 7 miles.

Friday 12 December First part of this day strong breezes and cloudy. Middle and latter part fine. Cruising about the bay. At sunset, Portland Island E.N.E. about 8 miles.

Saturday 13 December First part of the day, light airs and variable. At noon, the breeze settled at N.E. and blowed fresh. At 5.00 p.m. saw sperm whales. Lowered the boats and got two of them and got them secured alongside by dark. Midnight, the breeze hauled to the West. Lost about 30 fathoms of whale line.

Sunday 14 December Fine weather throughout the 24 hours. Employed cutting-in at sunset. Lit the work for the first time.

Monday 15 December Fine weather throughout the 24 hours. Employed cutting-in and trying-out.

Tuesday 16 December Weather same as yesterday. Finished cutting-in the whales. Still trying-out last one of the carcases with about 20 fathoms of line.

Wednesday 17 December Weather still fine. Employed trying-out and stowing down.

Thursday 18 December Fine weather. Employed as yesterday.

Friday 19 December Light breezes and fine weather throughout the 24 hours. Employed trying-out and stowing down the oil.

Saturday 20 December Weather the same as yesterday. Finished trying-out and stowed the oil down. The whales have made 130 barrels of oil. A very good day's work.

After nearly three weeks of totally unproductive searching for whales, the captain's relief at his eventual success is evident. For the crewmen, time spent cruising about with no particular destination in mind, and only the captain's hunch to guide them towards whales, would have tried the patience of all on board. Throughout this time, lookouts would have been stationed at the mastheads, their eyes straining to diligently scan the horizon; and on deck, work would have had to be found to occupy the attention of idle hands.

Sperm whales, one of the largest creatures on the planet, can yield a great quantity of valuable oil and are also a principal source of the even more valuable spermaceti. To have succeeded in catching two of these rich prizes should have done a lot to restore the spirits of the ship's company.

Sunday 21 December First part of the day, light breezes and cloudy. Employed boiling out the fat, bone and other fragments of the whale in water.

Monday 22 December Fresh breezes and cloudy. Employed as yesterday.

Tuesday 23 December Strong breezes from the west and southwest. Could not keep the work alight. Employed working under the weather shore.

Wednesday 24 December Hard breezes throughout. At 4.00 p.m. came to anchor in Low Ridge Bay. I went on shore to try to get something for Christmas dinner. Lit the works and finished boiling out the fragments.

Thursday 25 December Fine weather throughout the 24 hours. Done no duty this day.

Friday 26 December Employed this day cleaning the ship and getting casks ready for filling water. At 6.00 p.m. gave the mate and four hands liberty to go on shore for the evening. The men would not come on board when the mate wanted them. He stopped till daylight and then came on board with two men. John Roach and John Brown would not come on board.

Saturday 27 December Fine weather throughout the 24 hours. Took the casks on shore for water, taking one of the natives to show the way. Found the place about four mile from the ship and very difficult get down, the river being very shallow to float the full casks and very bad quality of water. Brought two tun such as it was.

Sunday 28 December At daylight hove short and set the sails, but could not start for the want of a breeze. Being a dead calm which continued for the remainder of the day, I went on shore and sent the boatsteerer to the two men to ask them if they would come on board, but they refused.

Despite the recent success and 130 barrels of sperm whale oil in the hold, it does not sound as if the captain had a happy Christmas. His attempt to celebrate by going ashore to find something for Christmas dinner does not perhaps tell us the whole story. Was he trying to reward his crew, or to persuade them of his good nature by seeking to provide a treat and a welcome relief from the ship's rations – or were the ship's rations beginning to run out? His success or failure in his hunting, foraging or bartering mission is not recorded. His generosity in declaring Christmas Day a holiday and in allowing several men shore leave the next day went unappreciated, as another two men refused to return to the ship the following day.

Monday 29 December At daylight, got underway and sailed out of the bay with a light breeze from the S.W., which died away about noon. The vessel then was about 8 miles from the anchorage.

Tuesday 30 December The first part of this day, light airs. At 10.00 a.m. I went on shore on the west side of the bay to try to get some potatoes and a watering place. I had not been long on shore when a strong breeze set in from E., which caused a heavy surf on the beach. I did not wait to get any potatoes, but put off from the beach. The boat got upset in the surf and stoved her and lost the trade but saved everything belonging to the boat. By the help of some tools and nails we got from a man on shore, was able to repair the boat so as to take us on board by sunset, the wind and sea going down fast by that time.

Wednesday 31 December First part of this day, light breezes with light mizzling rain. Latter part, blowing hard from the east. Was obliged carry on hard to get off the lee shore. At daylight, Cape Kidnapper bore south 9 miles.

Thursday 1 January 1852 Strong breezes with dark gloomy weather. Working the ship to the eastward.

Friday 2 January Moderate breezes and fine. Working to the eastward. At sunset took one reef in the topsails.

Saturday 3 January Weather the same as yesterday. At sunset Portland Island bore E. about 15 miles.

Sunday 4 January Throughout this day, light breezes and fine weather. At noon I went on shore at Portland Island to look for a watering place. Found several very small springs out of the foot of the island.

Monday 5 January First part of the day, light breezes and fine weather. At 11.00 a.m. came to anchor opposite a run of fresh water on the west side of the Mahia. At the same time saw a small vessel coming down the bay with colours at the masthead. I went on board of her. The captain informed me the shore party had got a great number of whales on Friday last and that there was some dead whales floating about the bay. I immediately got under way and commenced cruising, but saw nothing. Latter part strong breezes.

On 14 April 1852, the *Hobart Town Courier* reported that in January 1852, the *Prince of Denmark* was spoken to by the *Venice*, three months out from Hobart Town. She was carrying 13 tuns of sperm whale oil.

Tuesday 6 January Moderate breezes and fine weather. Cruising about the bay but saw nothing.

Wednesday 7 January This day begins with light airs and fine weather. At 3.00 a.m. the mate gave notice of a reef being close to the ship and she would not stay. I ran on deck and found the vessel within 20 fathoms of a reef of rock on the lee beam. I ordered the anchor to be let go, which was done as soon as it was possible to get it ready, and laid out about 17 fathoms of chain. The lead and line being over the side at the same time in my one hand, there was three fathoms as I supposed by the marks on the line, I found the vessel to strike the ground aft. I then hove in 3 or 4 fathoms of chain. —— more after heaving in the chain. I then run a kedge out with 200 fathoms of line and hauled her off in deep water, and run out the kedge a second time and made sail. When the vessel struck the ground, the rudder rose as far as the wood stock would allow. I afterwards found the lead line was marked wrong by a fathom ——.

Prompt action by the captain had saved his ship from an extremely perilous situation. The light wind had meant that when the mate sighted a reef in the early hours of the morning, the vessel did not have sufficient way for the helmsman to put her about and steer her away from danger. The lack of either accurate detailed charts of the area or any means of establishing an exact position make it difficult to be critical of the fact that the *Prince of Denmark* nearly ended up grounded on a reef. It is a little surprising, therefore, that the captain mentions finding that the lead line was wrongly marked. If he was trying to exonerate himself from responsibility for the incident when the owner came to study the log, he was likely to be unsuccessful, as one of the many stressful features of being a ship's captain is that one is responsible for all that occurs on board. If the lead line was wrongly marked, the captain should have known about it long before this incident.

Thursday 8 January Light breezes and fine weather throughout the 24 hours. The vessel making no more water than usual. At sunset, Portland Isle bore E.S.E. 5 or 6 miles.

Friday 9 January This day begins with light breezes. At 4.00 a.m. sent the two boats on shore for fresh water and got one raft off by 8.00 a.m. Got breakfast and took the cask on shore again. At 11.00 a.m. the mate came on board with some of the natives and said the natives had seized the casks and the other boat till they were paid for the pigs and goats and likewise the wood and water, which request I was obliged to comply with.

Saturday 10 January At daylight got under way and sailed out of the bay with the intention of going further to the south. At sunset Cape Kidnapper bore W. by N. 15 to 20 miles.

Sunday 11 January First part of this day, light breezes and cloudy. Middle and latter part, fresh gales with light showers of rain.

Monday 12 January First part of this day, hard breezes. Middle and latter part, fine. At sunset, Cape Paller [Palliser] bore W. by S. 20 to 25 miles. Latitude at noon 41.50.

Tuesday 13 January This day begins with light breezes and cloudy weather. Middle and latter part, hard gale from S.S.W. with showers of rain. Standing off and on Cape Palliser.

Wednesday 14 January Weather the same as yesterday. Standing off and on Cape Palliser. Close reefed main topsail and foresail.

Thursday 15 January This day commences with strong breezes. Middle and latter part of the day, fine. Unbent the fore-topsail and bent on another. At sunset, Cape Palliser bore N.N.W. 20 to 25 miles.

Friday 16 January Throughout this day —— breezes and fine weather. Standing off and on the ——.

Saturday 17 January First part of this day, fine. Middle and latter part, strong breezes with a high sea. No men at the masthead. Latitude at noon 42.06. Longitude by Chr. 175.15.

Sunday 18 January Hard breezes throughout the 24 hours. Latitude 42.15 Longitude 175.07.

Monday 19 January This day begins with hard breezes, which died away as the day broke and continued fine till after noon. The breeze then began to freshen and by 6.00 p.m. it blowed a hard gale from the north. We ran to the south till midnight then hove to under the close-reefed main topsail.

Tuesday 20 January First part of this day, hard breezes. Middle and latter, parts fine. A.m. saw Banks Peninsula to the W.S.W. P.m. got a porpoise. Latitude 43.14 Longitude 174.05.

Wednesday 21 January Light breezes and fine weather throughout the whole of this day. Two sail I sight to the westward. People variously employed. At sunset, the peninsula bore S.W. by W. 15 to 20 miles.

Thursday 22 January Weather the same as yesterday. Got two porpoises.

Friday 23 January This day begins with light breezes and fine weather. At sunset, the S.E. point of the peninsula bore W.S.W. 12 to 15 miles. Latter part of the day fresh breezes with rain.

Saturday 24 January Fresh breezes and thick foggy weather with light mizzling rain at times. [No name given] refused duty for which I put him in the ship's press.

Sunday 25 January This day begins with light airs and cloudy. At 6.00 a.m. a violent gale came on from the south. At 8.00 squared the yards and run for the peninsula. At 11.00 a sea struck the starboard boat and knocked her into small pieces. Saved all the gear but two oars. At 2.00 p.m. anchored in Akaroa.

Monday 26 January Hard breezes and passing clouds. Unbent the main topsail to repair it. A shore boat came off and offered firewood for sale which I bought as I could not trust any of the men on shore.

Tuesday 27 January First part of this day fine. Several of the natives came on board, and while I was getting breakfast, three of the men got on shore in one of the canoes, taking one oar, leaving me in distress for men and oars. I immediately went on shore and gave notes to the district constable and offered a reward for the men. I stopped on shore till evening in hopes of getting the men, but did not succeed. A sudden gale came on that prevented me from getting on board.

Wednesday 28 January Still blowing a hard gale throughout the day. The men been not apprehended, I thought it best to get more in their place. Accordingly I shipped two men. One of them ran away as soon as he got his advance. Latter part moderate.

Thursday 29 January Moderate breezes. Could not get any more men with out giving advance money. This I would not do as they were likely to run away as soon as they got it. At noon, came on board and got under way and sailed out of the harbour.

Another unhappy and uncomfortable few days for the captain, with a mutinous crewman under lock and key, a smashed boat and the loss of not only more men but also the cash that had been advanced to them. The decision to sail regardless presumably meant that the crew was again short-handed.

Friday 30 January Light breezes and dark gloomy weather throughout the 24 hours.

Saturday 31 January Throughout the whole of this day, light winds and thick foggy weather.

Sunday 1 February Light breezes and thick foggy weather and light mizzling rain.

Monday 2 February Weather the same as yesterday.

Tuesday 3 February Light breezes and fine clear weather throughout the day. Saw finbacks. Latitude 44.42. Longitude 173.00.

Wednesday 4 February Light airs and variable and a heavy swell from the south. Three sail in sight. Latitude 44.38. Longitude 173.00.

Thursday 5 February Fine weather throughout the 24 hours. Carpenter getting stuff ready to build a boat. P.m. saw a small vessel standing to the north. Latitude 44.18. Longitude 172.44.

Friday 6 February First part of this day fine. Middle, hard breezes, which died away towards sunset. Saw finbacks. Latitude 44.45 Longitude 172.30.

Saturday 7 February Throughout this day, moderate breezes and thick hazy weather with light mizzling rain at times.

Sunday 8 February First part of this day, thick hazy weather. Middle and later part, fine. A sail in sight to the N.E. Latitude 44.22 Longitude 172.49.

Monday 9 February This day begins with light breezes and fine weather. Middle and latter part, blowing hard from the N.E. Latitude 44.27. Longitude 172.10.

Tuesday 10 February First part of this day, strong breezes. Middle and latter part, fine. Unbent the fore-topsail to repair it. Carpenter getting a boat's keel ready.

Wednesday 11 February Fine weather the whole of the day. Finished the repairs of the fore-topsail and bent it. Saw finbacks. Latitude 45.02. Longitude 172.26.

Thursday 12 February Light airs and calms at times. Saw a great number of finbacks. Carpenter commenced to build a small boat. Latitude 45.04. Longitude 172.39.

Friday 13 February Light breezes and fine weather throughout the whole of this day. Latitude 44.31 Longitude 172.07.

Saturday 14 February Weather the same as yesterday. Saw finback all day. Latitude 44. 54. Longitude 172.36.

Sunday 15 February Light breezes and dark gloomy weather with light mizzling rain.

Monday 16 February This day begins with light breezes and dark gloomy weather. At daylight, a strong breeze from S.S.W. and by a.m. it blowed a hard gale. Took in the main topsail and set the fore trysail. About noon, while I was taking the sun, a very heavy sea struck the vessel and hove her on her beam-ends. I was forward at this time with the quadrant in my hand. The sea rushed over me as I lay hold of the windlass bitts and was soon sent completely under water. When I got above water, I saw nothing of the starboard boat but the stem and sternposts hanging to the davit. At this time the whole of the vessel's rail was below the water. I ordered the helm to be put hard up which was done and the lee gangway giving way, the vessel righted and run before the gale. On examination I found several articles washed overboard and the larboard boat badly stoved and the try-work greatly shook. Lost the following articles: one boat, four oars and two tubs of line. Two lance warps, three lances, three irons, one spade, boat hook, boat keg, —— mast and sail, two mincing tubs, three cutting-in falls, 8 fathom of 4-in rope and quadrant. We are now completely disabled from prosecuting any further on the voyage in our disabled state. Towards evening the gale moderated. At 10.00 p.m. passed Banks Peninsula, steering N.N.E. for Cook Straits.

Tuesday 17 February Fine weather throughout the 24 hours. Saw finbacks. At sunset, the east end of the peninsula bore S.S.W. by compass, 15 to 20 miles.

Wednesday 18 February Moderate breeze from the N.E. At sunset, a sudden shift of wind to the N.W. and blowed hard. Close reefed the topsails and stowed the jib and mainsail. The east end of the peninsula S.W. by W. the west end [*sic*]. Latter part of the day light breeze.

Thursday 19 February Light wind and variable. Saw finbacks. At sunset, abreast of the Key ——.

Friday 20 February Weather the same as yesterday. At sunset Cape Campbell N.W. by compass about 20 miles.

Saturday 21 February Light breezes and fine weather. At sunset, Cape —— bore E. and Point Sinclair S. At sunset, stowed the main topgallant sail.

Sunday 22 February Light breezes from the N.E. with fine weather. At sunset, Cape Stephens bore W.S.W. about 15 miles.

Monday 23 February Weather still fine. At sunset, Stephen Island bore S.W. by W. Cape Farewell S.W. by S. Got the boat inboard for repairs. Two sail in sight.

Tuesday 24 February First part of this day, light airs and cloudy weather. Middle and latter parts, strong breezes from W.N.W. A sail in sight.

Wednesday 25 February Throughout the whole of this 24 hours, strong breezes and then calms and very unsettled weather. At sunset, the east end of the sand spit of Cape Farewell bore south about 6 miles.

Thursday 26 February Light airs and strong breezes and unsettled weather. At 6.00 p.m. Cape Farewell bore S.E. by E., from which I take my departure.

Friday 27 February Very unsettled weather throughout the 24 hours. Finished the repairs of the boat and got her out on the cranes. Latitude by ac. 39.32. Longitude by ac 171.38.

Saturday 28 February Light breezes and variable. Carpenter building a small boat. Latitude by ac. 39.02. Longitude 171.24.

Sunday 29 February First part of this day, light wind and cloudy. Middle and latter part, strong breeze. At 2.00 p.m. the wind shifted from W.N.W. to W.S.W. Latitude by ac. 39.43. Longitude by ac. 170.34.

Monday 1 March Strong breezes with squalls of wind and rain. Steering to the N.W. under reef sails. Latitude by ac. 39.09. Longitude by ac. 169.16.

Tuesday 2 March Throughout the whole of this day, hard gale from W.S.W. with showers of rain. Heading N.W. Latitude by ac. 38.34. Longitude by ac. 168.46.

Wednesday 3 March First part of this day, hard gale. Middle and latter part, more moderate. Made sail accordingly. Latitude by ac. 37.14 Longitude by ac. 167.40.

Thursday 4 March Light breezes from the south. Carpenter building a small boat. At 8.00 p.m. lowered after black fish but could not get fast. Latitude by ac. 37.14. Longitude by ac. 166.41.

Friday 5 March First part of this day light winds and fine weather. Middle and latter part, fresh breezes from S.E. Latitude by ac. 37.38. Longitude by ac. 164.57.

Saturday 6 March Moderate breezes and cloudy weather. All sail set. Steering W.S.W. Latitude by ac. 38.03 Longitude by ac. 162.13.

Sunday 7 March First part of this day, moderate breezes and dark gloomy weather. Middle and latter part, light breezes. Latitude by ac. 38.25. Longitude by ac. 159.07.

Monday 8 March This day begins with moderate breezes from the S.E. At 6.00 a.m. a sudden shift of wind from S.E. to W. with rain that lasted about half an hour, and then the wind hauled to the N.E. Latter part of the day, light breezes and fine weather. Latitude by ac. 39.00 Longitude by ac. 157.35.

Tuesday 9 March Moderate breezes and fine weather throughout the whole of the day. Latitude by ac. 39.25. Longitude by ac. 155.53.

Wednesday 10 March Light airs and calms throughout the 24 hours. Latitude by ac. 39.32. Longitude by ac. 155.32.

Thursday 11 March Weather the same as yesterday. Latitude by ac. 39.52 Longitude by ac. 154.32.

Friday 12 March Light airs and calms at times with thick foggy weather. Latitude by ac. 40.21. Longitude by ac. 154.04.

Saturday 13 March First part of this day, light airs. Middle and latter part, moderate breeze from N.W. to S.W. with some rain. Latitude by ac. 40.26. Longitude by ac. 153.32.

Sunday 14 March This day begins with light breezes. At 4.00 a.m. a moderate breeze sprung up from the north which continued the remainder of the day. All sail set. Standing to the west. Latitude by ac. 40.36. Longitude by ac. 152.20.

Monday 15 March The first part of this day, moderate breezes. Middle and latter, part light air. Sighted St. Patrick's Head bearing west by compass.

Tuesday 16 March Light airs and calms throughout the day. The land in sight to the west.

Wednesday 17 March Light breezes and fine weather. Spoke the *Flying Fish* and sent a letter to town by her.

Thursday 18 March Weather the same as yesterday. Spoke the *Yarro* bound to Hobart Town. At 8.00 p.m. passed Cape Pillar and steered S.W. by W.

Friday 19 March 1852 Light airs and calms off the ——.

The last few entries in the log are missing, but within a few days of 19 March 1852, the *Prince of Denmark* was safely back at Hobart Town to be unloaded, repaired and equipped for her next voyage. Robert Heays had been the longest serving captain of the *Prince of Denmark* and probably knew the vessel better than anyone else, but his voyage to New Zealand seemed to indicate that he was perhaps losing authority and may have been ready for a well-earned rest.

Sketch map of New Zealand

13   Planks, Palings and Petty Crime

At an unknown date between 1851 and 1855, George Watson became involved in the management of the *Prince of Denmark*. He is thought to be the same George Watson who had previously owned her in 1843, but no details have been found to clarify how that came about. It has been assumed that George Watson, who was a former whaler and ship-owner, and George Watson, who was a timber merchant, are the same person, but proof of this has not been found. Contemporary newspapers describe George Watson as the owner of the *Prince of Denmark*, but the surviving registration documents do not seem to bear this out and it is possible that Mr. Watson may have simply chartered her from Richard Cleburne.

Following the *Prince of Denmark*'s return from whaling, she commenced a lengthy period of trading in timber. It was common for the same people who were involved in whaling to have extensive interests in both agriculture and the timber trade, and George Watson seems to have fitted in to that pattern.

Whilst the *Prince of Denmark* was engaged in trade between Hobart Town, Launceston and a variety of South Australian ports, her captain and crew could perhaps have encountered the 296-ton barque *Rory O'More*, which called at Launceston on 25 June 1852 and left for Sydney a few days later on 29 June. On 14 December the same year, *Rory O'More* called at Port Phillip, leaving a week later for Sydney, and in February of 1853, she sailed from Sydney bound for Calcutta. If the two vessels did ever meet, their respective masters and crews would probably be unaware that their ships were built within a hundred yards of each other in Kirkcudbright. *Rory O'More* was built in 1842 and made a few voyages to Montreal and Quebec between 1846 and 1850, while under the ownership of Charles Moore and Co. of Liverpool.

My interest in the schooner *Prince of Denmark* began when I realised that there was a possibility that either a painting or a photograph of her might be found in Australia. Sadly, apart from finding Thomas Gay's little sketch, my quest was unsuccessful. My secondary research into the history of the barque *Rory O'More* has, however, produced a magnificent painting of her by an unknown artist (*see* opposite). This painting is the

130

Barque Rory O'More (*Courtesy of the National Maritime Museum, London UK*)

only known detailed illustration of any ship built in Kirkcudbright, and does much to confirm the excellent reputation of Kirkcudbright's shipbuilders.

On 22 December 1854, the *Hobart Courier* carried an advertisement for the sale of the cargo of the *Prince of Denmark*, to take place on 27 December. A total of 22,000ft of joists, quartering boards and beams were offered with 25,000 palings, in 5ft or 6ft lengths. Having successfully weathered storms and overcome adversity of astounding variety for 66 years, the *Prince of Denmark* came close to catastrophe on 23 March 1855, as a result of nothing other than petty crime. The incident was described in the following account from the *Hobarton Mercury*:

> **A Cool Deed** – On Wednesday week, as a small craft was making for her mooring place at the wharf, her anchor got foul of the warp of the *Prince of Denmark* belonging to Mr. George Watson. The man in the craft very coolly took out a knife and cut the warp away from his anchor, setting the *Prince of Denmark* adrift, and leaving her anchor at the bottom of the harbour. Mr. Watson happened to be close by, and was an eyewitness to the transaction; and the man having been taken into custody on suspicion of being an absconder, Mr. Watson came to the police officer on Wednesday, to lay a charge against the man. Mr. Wilmot told him he could only proceed by information for wilfully damaging his property to the amount of £5. Mr. Watson thought this rather hard, as the damage amounted

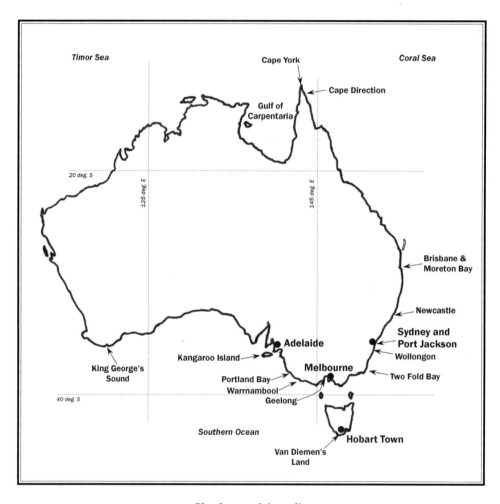

Sketch map of Australia

to nearly £14. He thought a man would be in a better position if met by a robber on the highway, than to have his property destroyed in this cool and wanton manner. He would however lay his information.

Mr. Watson had further need for recourse to law after a pair of revolvers belonging to him was stolen from the *Prince of Denmark* in August of 1855. The *Hobarton Mercury* reported, on 3 October 1855, that Mr. John Hunter had been charged with stealing the pistols. He and a Mr. Henry Newman had been hired by Mr. Watson to work aboard the *Prince of Denmark* and the pistols were noticed to be missing thereafter. John Hunter was found guilty and sentenced to hard labour for six months. The captain at the time was Mr. R. W. Johns, the cook was John Harding, and both gave evidence at John Hunter's trial.

On Monday 6 August 1855, the *Hobart Town Courier* carried the following advertisement:

> Tuesday 7th August 1855, at half past ten for 11 o'clock
> 40,000 prime 5ft paling by Mr. W. A. Guesdon
> On Tuesday 7th August, the time as above,
> at the Constitution Dock, N.E. side, alongside the *Prince of Denmark*
> 40,000 prime paling, 5ft, in lots to suit purchasers.
> Terms – cash.

The general decline in the fortunes of the whaling industry continued to have devastating effects for the many people involved. In November of 1855, George Watson's house at Barton Vale was advertised for sale and in January of 1856, his brother John Watson was forced to advertise the sale of his shipyard and several of his vessels. George Watson, timber merchant, was declared insolvent on 28 May 1856 and on 12 November 1856, 1,577 acres of land belonging to him were advertised for sale. On 2 June 1856, the *Hobarton Mercury* published an advertisement for the *Prince of Denmark*'s sale by auction at Constitution Dock on 9 June. She was described as having new yards, masts and sails. The cost of these items and the associated costs of removing the old masts and spars and re-rigging the entire vessel would have been considerable.

On 17 December 1856, Hubert Beard Evans was recorded as master of the *Prince of Denmark* at Hobart Town in place of Robert Heays. Under the command of her new master, the *Prince of Denmark* was engaged in extremely brisk trade between Sydney, Newcastle, Hobart Town, Melbourne, Geelong, Hobson's Bay, and a variety of other ports in South Australia and Tasmania. Although she was a small and now elderly vessel, her reputation for speed and her familiarity in so many ports must have been of great assistance to her owners and to her captain in securing cargoes. The growth of communities, both large and small, around the coast created a demand for building materials and manufactured goods, and the rapidly expanding cities needed agricultural produce. This resulted in the *Prince of Denmark* rarely having to sail in ballast or without a cargo, and frequently carrying mixed cargoes of great variety.

On the day after the appointment of Captain Evans, the *Hobart Courier* reported that she left Hobart Town, bound for Sydney, carrying 50 tons of potatoes, 15,000ft of battens and 5,000 palings, arriving on 30 December 1856.

> Crew: John Lewis, Mate, 28, England: Edward John McFie, O.S., 18, Tasmania: N. G. Clarke, O.S., 21, Norfolk: John Bell, A.S., 22, Edinburgh: Franklin Allen, Cook, 28, London:
> Left Hobart Town, 18th December. Arrived Sydney, 6th January 1857.[*]

The *Colonial Times* of 5 February 1857 recorded her return to Hobart Town on 3 February 1857, carrying 100 tons of coal and one cabin passenger: Mr. G. Hill.

---

[*] *(Transcribed from an original document in the* State Records of New South Wales*)*

Little information has so far been given about the men who formed the various crews of the *Prince of Denmark* and the conditions under which they served. The ship's log only mentions them when they have deserted, fallen ill, died, caught a whale, or been disciplined. The owners and captains were generally men of substance whose names are known in other areas, both professionally and socially. In contrast, the background of the crewmen is largely unknown unless in the event of them having a criminal record. By the mid-19th century, however, legislation was making increasing demands on masters and owners to treat their employees more equitably and to keep better records. An assortment of papers has survived relating to the *Prince of Denmark*'s crews, and they, or facts gleaned from them, are reproduced in this chapter in chronological order.

Although no logs for any of these voyages are known to have survived, crew lists, and the crew's terms of engagements have been found and provide some valuable insight to where these men came from, how they lived and how they were rewarded for their labours.

16th February 1857:

Agreement for foreign-going ships

Name of Ship – *Prince of Denmark*, official number – 32050. Port of Registry – Hobart Town. Port No. and date of registry – 52/1857. Registered tonnage – 70. Name of Master – Hubert Beard Evans. Date and place of first signature – 16th February 1857, Hobart Town. Signed Jas. Hawthorn.

The Several Persons whose Names are hereto subscribed, and whose Descriptions are contained below, and of whom three are engaged as Sailors, hereby agree to serve on board the said Ship, in the several capacities expressed against their respective Names, on a voyage from Hobart Town to Sydney and/or any other Port or Ports in the Australasian Colonies and back to Hobart Town, there to be discharged. Full period of service not to exceed three Calendar Months from the date of the agreement.

And the Said Crew agree to conduct themselves in an orderly, faithful, honest, and sober manner, and to be at all times diligent in their respective duties, and to be obedient to the lawful commands of the said Master, or of any Person who shall lawfully succeed him, and of their Superior Officers, in everything relating to the said Ship, and the Stores and Cargo thereof, whether on board, in boats, or on shore, in consideration of which services, to be duly performed, the said Master hereby agrees to pay to the said Crew as Wages the said Sums against their names respectively expressed, and to supply them with Provisions according to the annexed scale. And it is hereby agreed that any Embezzlement, or Wilful or Negligent Destruction of any part of the Ship's Cargo or Stores, shall be made good to the Owner out of the Wages of the Person guilty of the same. And if any Person enters himself as qualified for a duty which he proves incompetent to perform, his Wages shall be reduced in proportion to his incompetency. And it is hereby also agreed that if any member of the Crew considers himself to be aggrieved by any Breach of the Agreement or otherwise, he shall represent the same to the Master or Officer in charge of the Ship in a quiet and orderly manner, who shall thereupon take such steps as the case may require. And it is also agreed that the crew shall consist of six hands all told.

The scale of provisions to be allowed and served out to the crew during the voyage was as follows:*

1 lbs. of bread each day of the week.
1.5 lbs. of beef on Sundays, Tuesdays, Thursdays and Saturdays.
1.25 lbs. of pork on Mondays, Wednesdays and Fridays.
0.5 lbs. of flour on Sundays and Wednesdays.
1/3 of a pint of peas on Mondays, Wednesdays and Fridays.
¼ of an ounce of tea per day.
½ of an ounce of coffee per day.
Two ounces of sugar per day.
Three quarts of water per day.
No spirits allowed.

In witness whereof the said Parties have subscribed their Names hereto, on the days against their respective Signatures mentioned. Signed by Hubert Beard Evans, Master, on the 16th day of February 1857.

Christopher Harrison, 40, British, ship in which he last served – *Iris* of Hobart Town. Date and place of discharge – 1st February 1857, Hobart Town. Place and date of entry in this ship 17th February 1857, Hobart Town. In what capacity engaged – Mate. Amount of wages per calendar month £10.00. Wages from the morning of 17th February 1857.

David Williams, 20, Wales, *Sir William Wallace* of Hobart Town, 8th February 1857. February 16th Hobart Town. Cook / Steward. £5.00 Wages from the morning of 11th February up to 1st May 1857.

Timothy Hallahan, 34, London, *Sir William Wallace* of Hobart Town 8th February 1857.16th February 1857, Hobart Town. Able Seaman, £5.00. Wages from the morning of 11th February.

Henry Lewis, 20, England, *Creole* of Hobart Town. 3rd February, Hobart Town. 16th February 1857, Hobart Town. Ordinary seaman £4.5s. Wages from the morning of the 16th February up to 27th April 1857. Two months and 18 days, discharged at Sydney.

William Brown, 28, London. First voyage. 16th February 1857, Hobart Town. Able seaman, £5. Wages from the morning of 16th February 1857.

The *Prince of Denmark* sailed for Sydney on 6 March 1857, the *Hobart Courier* of 4 March having described her cargo as consisting of 24,000ft of timber, 8,000ft of battens and 16,000 palings.*

Crew: C. Harrison, Mate, 40, England; Timothy Hallahan, A.B., 30, England; William Gleeson, A.B., 30, England; Henry Lewis, O.S., 18, England; David Lewis, Cook, 25, England.

Left Hobart Town, 6th March 1857. Arrived Sydney, 14th March 1857.

---

*(*Transcribed from an original document in the* Archives Office of Tasmania)

She was reported to be off Wollongong (a little to the south of Sydney) on 21 April 1857; on 27 April 1857, the *Hobart Courier* reported her return to Hobart Town from Newcastle (to the north of Sydney) with coals. In May of 1857, the same newspaper reported that:

> We regret to announce the death, under the most painful circumstances, of Mr. George Watson, an old colonist of many years standing, well known as having been connected with the shipping interests of this port.

No details of the circumstances of Mr. Watson's death have been traced, but it would not be surprising if the financial stress he had undergone was either a direct or an indirect cause. The *Prince of Denmark* was reported to be at Two Fold Bay in early July, at Melbourne in late July, and on 12 August 1857, the *Hobart Town Mercury* reported that she had sailed from Hobart Town for Geelong, with 10,000ft timber and 50,000 palings.

> 2nd September 1857:
>
> Port of Geelong, Victoria, Outward manifest of the brig *Prince of Denmark* of about 70 tons, British built with 6 men besides H. B. Evans a British Master for this present voyage to Hobart Town, in ballast. 2nd September 1857, Custom House, Geelong.
>
> Crew: R. Turner; L. Davis; R. Duff; D. Evans; R. Proudfoot; J. Smith.
>
> Stores: 18 lbs. tea; 5 lbs. coffee; 30 lbs. sugar.
>
> Left Geelong, 2nd September 1857.

> 18th September 1857:
>
> *Prince of Denmark*, British built, about 70 tons, with 5 men besides Master H. B. Evans, a British Master for this present voyage from Geelong, in ballast. Arrived at Hobart Town, 18th September 1857.
>
> Crew: R. Turner; R. Proudfoot; John Thomas; R. Duff; Thomas Mullens.
>
> Arrived Hobart Town, 18th September 1857.[*]

On 25 September 1857, the *Hobart Town Mercury* reported that the *Prince of Denmark* had sailed from Hobart Town for Warrnambool (between Portland Bay and Geelong) carrying 33,000ft of timber, and 23,000 palings. She returned to Hobart Town from Geelong on 25 October 1857, with 490 firkins of butter. A few days later, on 5 November 1857, she sailed from Hobart Town bound for Sydney, carrying 20,000ft boards, 10,000ft timber, 15,000ft battens, 10,000 palings, 40,000 shingles and 20,000 laths. Both cargoes were listed in the *Hobart Courier*:

> Crew: E. J. Ledwell, Mate, 40, England; William Ward, A.B., 40, England; Robert Duff, Ordinary, 20, Scotland; Thomas Mullens, A.B., 23, England; R. Proudfoot,

---

[*]*(Transcribed from original documents in the* Archives Office of Tasmania)

Cook / Steward, 39, Scotland; Robert Gordon, Ordinary, 37, England; Thomas Smith, Ordinary, 20, England.

Left Hobart Town, 5th November 1857. Arrived Sydney, 16th November 1857.*

Her cargo was later advertised in the *Sydney Empire* of 24 November, to be sold at auction by Bowan and Threlkeld, at Messrs. Macnamara and Son's wharf. The advertisement gives much more detail than the lineal footage of timber previously mentioned, and describes joists, floorboards, battens, laths, palings, shingles, Oregon red pine deals, Bangor duchess slates, cement, six-panelled doors and cockle shell lime.

The *Hobart Town Mercury* of 9 December 1857 reported the *Prince of Denmark*'s return to Hobart Town from Newcastle (to the north of Sydney) on 8 December 1857, with 110 tons of coal and one cabin passenger: Mr. W. Clarke. On 23 December 1857, the *Hobart Courier* recorded her departure from Hobart Town, bound for Sydney with 30,000ft of timber, 20,000 palings, 70,000 shingles and 20,000 laths. She arrived at Sydney on 31 December 1857.

> Crew: Elb Elphedes, Mate, 40, England; Thomas Mullens, A.B., 23, England; Samuel Menz, Cook, 30, England; Henry Grish, Ordinary, 18, Germany; Charles Dawson, Ordinary, 18, England.*

On 27 January 1858, she returned to Hobart Town from Sydney, having left Newcastle on 20 January after loading 100 tons coal. Less than a month later, on 14 February 1858, she sailed from Hobart Town for Sydney with sundries, arriving there on 28 February 1858. After a further voyage to Hobart Town, the *Prince of Denmark* returned to Sydney on 2 March 1858.

> Crew: Thomas Mullens, Mate, 30, Great Britain; R. Proudfoot, Cook, 25, Great Britain; John Thomas, A.B. 22, Great Britain; John Smith, Ordinary, 20, Great Britain; H. Tinsley, A.B. 24, Great Britain; William Jones, Ordinary, Great Britain; Henry Shaw, Passenger.*

Despite an extremely busy schedule, in the course of which a small crew seem to have handled a substantial amount of cargo, profits must have been low. The *Sydney Morning Herald* carried the following report on 5 April 1858:

> Hubert Beard Evans, Master of the ship *Prince of Denmark* was sued by 5 seamen belonging to that ship, and they recovered the amounts claimed, *viz*: Thomas Mullins, £15.14s.; Richard Jones, £6.15s.; James Holland, £2.6s.8d.; Robert Proudfoot, £11.4s.; and Levi Davis, £2.6s.8d.

A few days later, Willis and Lucas were given authority to sell the *Prince of Denmark* for £50 within six months. Joseph Scaife Willis had arrived in Australia in 1840 from

---

(Transcribed from an original document in the State Records of New South Wales)

Kirkoswald in Ayrshire and set up in business with William Lucas Merry as Willis, Merry and Co. Merchants and Shipping Agents. The following notice appeared in the *Sydney Morning Herald* on Saturday 10 April 1858:

> The British Built Schooner *Prince of Denmark*
>
> 69 tons register
>
> In the Water Police Court, Sydney, Thomas Mullens and four others v. Hubert Beard Evans.
>
> Messrs. W. Dean and Co. have received instructions to sell by auction, at their warehouse, Pitt and O'Connell Streets, on Monday 12th April at 12 o'clock, in pursuance of warrants of distress issued by the Bench and Magistrates, at the Water Police Office, Sydney, in the case of Thomas Mullens and four others, v. Hubert Beard Evans, The British Built schooner *Prince of Denmark*, 69 tons register, as she now lies off the Corporation wharf, near King Street, where she may be inspected.
>
> She was built on the Clyde for the Revenue Department, is exceedingly well-found in sails, stores, *etc. etc.* and is well and favourably known in the Hobart Town Trade.
>
> Terms at Sale.

The *Prince of Denmark* was not, of course, built on the Clyde, but it is interesting that her supposed history as a revenue cutter is again mentioned. She became the property of Charles McKellar on 14 April 1858, and he registered her in Sydney (Registration No. 4) on 11 May 1858.

It seems that, yet again, an owner of the *Prince of Denmark* was struggling financially. The brisk trade in timber and coals, the hard work of the crew in loading and unloading quickly, and good fortune with fair winds allowing a minimum time spent in port, had not been enough to ensure a profit. The fact that she had been offered for sale for only £50 is ample indication that she was no longer generally seen as a good investment. Charles McKellar, however, must have been both an enthusiast and an optimist.

14 A Chinese Banquet

On 30 September 1858, the emigrant ship *St Paul* was wrecked on a reef close to Rossel Island in the Louisiade Archipelago, to the southeast of New Guinea. She had been chartered to sail from Hong Kong, bound for Sydney, and was carrying 327 Chinese passengers, who had been intending to seek their fortunes in the gold fields of Australia. In 1854, 4,341 Chinese people had left Hong Kong for the same purpose. The photograph overleaf, dating from the 1880s, is of a procession in the town of Cooktown on the north-east coast of Australia, and illustrates the considerable extent of the Chinese population at that time, many of whom were engaged in gold digging.

Despite the loss of their ship, the captain, his crew of nine, and all of the passengers safely boarded the ship's boats and landed successfully on a small and uninhabited island. The rather unfortunate decision was then taken that the captain and all of the European crew would sail in one of the boats to seek help, leaving the passengers to fend for themselves. After a voyage of some 600 miles, they landed on a beach near Cape Direction, close to the northeastern tip of Australia, and went ashore in search of assistance, food and water. Finding no signs of habitation, they went back aboard their boat and sailed southwards, apparently leaving behind one of their number, a 12-year-old cabin-boy, named Narcisse Pelletier, who had become separated from his colleagues and was considered to be in too feeble a state to have survived.

Fifteen days after the loss of the *St Paul*, the captain and his eight crewmen were picked up off the islands of the Sir Everard Home's Group by the schooner *Prince of Denmark*. Unfortunately, it seems that the rescued men had to spend two months on board the *Prince of Denmark* before Captain McKellar put them ashore at New Caledonia. The French steamer *Styx* was then immediately sent to Rossel Island to rescue the Chinese passengers, though none of the various accounts that are made of this incident mention any attempt to investigate the fate of the missing cabin boy. The *Hobart Town Daily Mercury* of 8 February 1859 reported that:

> Captain Pennard of the *St. Paul*, came up in the *Styx*; he states that he was 62 or 63 days on board the *Prince of Denmark*, before being landed at New Caledonia;

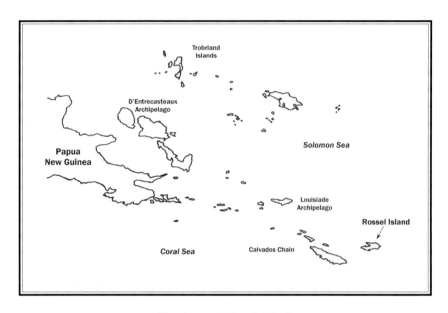

Sketch map of Rossel Island

A Chinese funeral in Cooktown, Australia (Courtesy of the Royal Geographical Society and the Institute of British Geographers, London, UK)

that he begged of Captain McKellar to take him to some place at once to obtain assistance, but he refused to do so, giving as a reason that he had a party at an island gathering *bêche-de-mer*, who would be out of provisions, did he not attend to them first.

When the *Styx* eventually arrived at Rossel Island and went to the scene of the abandonment of the passengers, only one small Chinese boy was there, and despite searches of the area, no trace of the other 326 passengers was found. When the surviving boy was taken to Sydney, he gave, through an interpreter (Mr. H. Leru Appa), the following lurid account of his experiences, which was published in the *Sydney Herald* in 1859:

The ship went on shore during the night, and when she struck the passengers all rushed on deck, making a great outcry, upon which the captain drove them all below again. When daylight broke, we landed by means of the boats on an island, where we remained two days without any water, when some of us went on board the ship again to get some, as also provisions. The captain left in his boat with some of the crew, and we were not disturbed by the natives for a month after he was gone; they then came over from the mainland, distant about three quarters of a mile, and made an attack on us. Some of us had double-barrelled carbines, but we got frightened, and threw them away. The only white man left with us, after the departure of Captain Pennard, was a Greek, who, having armed himself with a cutlass, fought desperately, and killed a great many of the natives before he was overpowered. They then took all our clothing, *etc.*, which they partly destroyed. Any valuables that they found, such as sovereigns, rings, *etc.*, they placed in a net bag, which each man carried round his neck. A watch particularly excited their attention, as they were continually opening it to observe the reflection of their faces in the glass. At night we were placed in the centre of a clear piece of ground, and fires lit in several places, the natives keeping a regular watch over us, and during the day they would select four or five Chinese, and after killing them, roast the flesh, and eat it, what was not consumed being deposited in their nets.

Their mode of proceeding was as follows: the victims being decided on, they were taken out and beaten all over (excepting the head) with a kind of club, and then despatched by ripping the stomach open. The body was then cut up in small pieces and divided, the fingers, toes, and brains being eagerly sought after. The bones were then collected, and either burnt or thrown away. I saw ten of my fellow passengers killed in this way. On one occasion some of the Chinese took a boat, which belonged to the ship, and went over to the mainland at night to get some water, but never returned, so we thought they had been killed. Every day they brought us cocoa-nuts, or some wild roots to eat, and appeared to be quite friendly with us. This state of things continued until I was taken off the island. When I left there were only four Chinese and the Greek alive, all the rest having been killed. I saw these five the day the steamer came in sight, but when the natives saw the boats coming on shore, they took them up the mountains. I was sick and lame, and they would not carry me, so that I watched my opportunity and contrived to conceal myself among the rocks until the boat came on shore. They are very numerous, but do not appear to have any chiefs among them.

> They live on cocoa-nuts, of which there are large quantities, and a kind of yam, which they roast before eating; but beyond a few dogs I saw neither animals nor fowls of any kind.

The foregoing account was generally accepted as true, and was given further credibility by its inclusion as a cautionary tale in the British Admiralty Sailing Directions for the area. The story of cannibalism went unchallenged for at least 30 years after the incident.

When investigations were eventually made by Sir William MacGregor, the first Australian administrator of New Guinea, reports were received of Chinese people still living in the vicinity of Rossel Island, though nobody was found. Today, it is generally believed that the passengers, thinking themselves abandoned, soon found that food was surprisingly plentiful, particularly the much valued seafood, *bêche-de-mer*. After some time, it is thought that the survivors either decided to make for New Guinea in the ship's remaining boats, or that they were picked up by another passing trader. Perhaps they had come to realise that if they ever did reach the goldfields of Australia, they would face a lifetime of toil in order to repay the loans they must have received to cover the cost of their passages. In New Guinea, they could be free, debt-free, and could fend for themselves.

The first census ever taken of the population of New Guinea is reported to have revealed a considerable number of people of Chinese origin, but of course, no explanation of how they came to be there was given. The Chinese people in general were not well treated by Europeans, and it was common for passenger lists of ships in the mid-19th century to give the full names and origins of all European passengers, and to merely add: 'and 47 Chinese'. The following extract from a letter written by James Stobie in Adelaide to his aunt in Fife, Scotland, on 27 August 1857 displays a lamentable disregard for Chinese immigrants that was probably widespread at the time:

> May I tell you that we are having shiploads of Chinese every month landing in the colony to go to Melbourne overland to the diggings; a distance of 400 miles. They land here to save 10 pounds sterling which they have to pay at Melbourne before they can enter into the interior or even the city. A filthy, deceitful and unnatural lot they are and ought to be prevented from intermingling with a class of men who have some regard for decency, honesty and straightforward conduct. I would not trust a Chinaman, however honest he might appear to be.[*]

However, the strange story of the survivors of the *St Paul* does not end on an entirely inconclusive note. On 11 April 1875, 17 years after the loss of the *St Paul*, Captain Fraser of the brig *John Bell* found a European man living near Cape York with a group of aboriginal people of the Uutaainganu Tribe. He was described as having bronze skin, a pierced nose, an elongated ear lobe and decorative scarring on his upper body.

---

[*]*(Quoted from an original letter in the author's collection)*

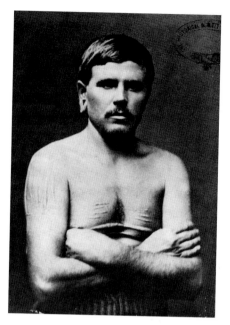

Mr. Narcisse Pelletier (Courtesy of the Royal Historical Society of Queensland, Australia)

After some initial difficulty, due to the fact that virtually all memory of his native language had gone, it was established that he was Narcisse Pelletier. He was apparently taken by force and against his will from his adoptive family and was eventually placed in the care of the French Consul. If rumours that he had to leave behind two or three children are true, this would clearly have added to the trauma of his enforced departure from a people who had shown him great kindness. Narcisse Pelletier was returned to his birthplace in France – Saint-Gilles-Croix-de-Vie – on 2 January 1876. He wisely declined offers of employment in a circus, eventually securing a job as a lighthouse keeper near St. Nazaire. He later married a seamstress and settled at Port Charlotte. He died on 26 September 1894 at St. Nazaire.

15 *From Sea Slugs to Sperm Whales*

The *Prince of Denmark*'s first voyage under the ownership and command of Captain Charles McKellar was to the northeast of Australia and to New Caledonia, commencing at some time after May 1858. The purpose is not clear, but it was probably to investigate markets such as the trade in sea slugs, sea cucumbers or *bêche-de-mer*. Captain McKellar did not engage a large crew, so cannot have had whaling in mind. Labour and expertise for the gathering of *bêche-de-mer* would have been provided by local Pacific Islanders, some of whom subsequently returned with the *Prince of Denmark* to Sydney.

Bêche-de-mer can be gathered all the year round from the reefs off Australia and the Pacific Islands generally. Most are consumed in China, and their high protein levels make them valued as an aphrodisiac throughout Asia. Their processing involves boiling, cutting open, boiling again, gutting and drying or smoking. The resulting dried product is then used in soups and stir-fries. Depending on their size and on the quality of the drying process, *bêche-de-mer* are of medium or high value.

A letter to the *Perth Gazette and Western Australian Journal* in November 1836 referred to the potential market for *bêche-de-mer* as follows:

> The Gulf of Carpentaria (according to the information I have received) abounds with a species of sea slug called by the Malays 'Trepang', or *bêche-de-mer*, and an immense quantity brought from that place annually by the Macassar proas, yields an extraordinary revenue to the Dutch when taken to China.

Bêche-de-mer were certainly being exported from Western Australia in 1859, and the following article, under the heading *Uncommon Good Eating*, appeared in the *South Australian Advertiser* on 13 June 1859:

> The Chinese gloat over sea slug, or *bêche-de-mer*, and a dish of a certain sea worm is one of the events of life to the dwellers in the islands of the South Pacific.

In the crew list for this first voyage under the new owner, the tradition of all crewmen being of British origin is maintained. Charles McKellar (the spelling of his surname varies from 'McKellar' to 'Mackellar' throughout the records) was both master and owner and is presumed to have been British. All crew lists quoted in this chapter have been based on original documents held by the State Records Authority of New South Wales. The original documents are, in some cases, very difficult to read and the spellings, particularly of unfamiliar names, are often bizarre. In cases where the real name can be reasonably deduced, the spelling has been altered accordingly, and in all other cases, it has been quoted in as near to the original form as can be discerned.

> Crew: J. C. Bennett, Mate, 33, British; Alfred Vaughan, A.B., 25, British; James Leggatt, A.B., 27, British; William Cochrane, A.B. 27, British; Dominick Kelly, O.S., 20, British.
>
> Passengers: 6 native South Sea islanders.
>
> Left Sydney, date unknown. Returned to Sydney, 16th January 1859.*

The voyage does not seem to have gone entirely smoothly, as immediately after the *Prince of Denmark*'s return to Sydney, the following report appeared in the *Sydney Morning Herald* of 25 January 1859:

> Alfred Vaughan, a seaman belonging to the schooner *Prince of Denmark* was convicted of continued disobedience of lawful commands while at sea, having refused to do duty for about six weeks. Sentenced to four weeks imprisonment, with hard labour, to forfeit two days pay and ordered to pay costs of court and prosecution. Mr. Brenan for complainant, Mr. Moffat for the defence.

The *Prince of Denmark* left Sydney for the South Seas on 7 May 1859 and John Charles Bennett, originally from Plymouth in England, who had been mate on the previous voyage, sailed for the first time as captain. The voyage may well have been a trying one for him, as the crew list includes only one seaman and nine passengers. Of the nine passengers, seven were South Sea Islanders, one was the owner, and the other the owner's friend, Mr. G. H. Chalk. Captain Chalk had been master of the schooner *Deborah* of London, in which Charles McKellar was a passenger when she arrived in Port Jackson from San Francisco on 21 September 1851. Prior to that, Captain Chalk had been master of the *Lady Howden*, which was lost on a reef in Fijian waters on 28 May 1850. After sailing to the South Seas in the *Deborah* in 1850, Captain Chalk commanded the *Gipsy* and the *Ellen*, carrying passengers between Maitland and Two Fold Bay. On 13 October 1852, the brig *Wanderer* sailed from Maitland to Melbourne, and her passengers included both Captain G. H. Chalk and Charles McKellar.

The South Sea Islanders were doubtless working their passages and perfectly capable of carrying out any reasonable task they were given, but Captain Bennett must have

---

(Transcribed from an original document in the State Archives of New South Wales)

been at all times conscious of the scrutiny of his superiors. Keeping the lone Scots crewman happy and attentive to his duty in such circumstances might also have been a challenging task.

> Crew: William Brunson, seaman, 36, Scotland.
>
> Passengers: Charles McKellar esquire, gentleman; Mr. G. H. Chalk, gentleman; 7 South Sea Islanders.
>
> Left Sydney 7th May 1859 bound for South Seas. Returned to Port Jackson, Sydney 21st September 1859.*

The *Maitland Mercury and Hunter River General Advertiser* gave the following account of the voyage on 24 September 1859:

> The *Prince of Denmark* has been cruising in the equator and has obtained 100 barrels of oil. Captain Bennett has also on board 20 large turtles which he captured on one of the islands.

Lessons must have been learned on these first two voyages under the ownership of Captain McKellar, for as soon as the *Prince of Denmark* returned to Sydney, the following advertisement appeared in the *Sydney Morning Herald*:

> Wanted, a headsman and boatsteerer. Apply on board the Schooner *Prince of Denmark* at Smith's Wharf.

In October 1859, on the first voyage with John Charles Bennett as captain, free from the influence of Charles McKellar as an owner / passenger, there was an immediate change in the composition of the crew, which became much more representative of the new Australia and incorporated men of a great many different nationalities. The purpose of this voyage was whaling, which would require men with high degrees of specialist skills. Some of these men would have been Australian-born, and others recruited from American and British whaling vessels that were active in the area. A few may have been ex-convicts and many more were Pacific Islanders who started off as deck passengers, but soon made themselves sufficiently useful to earn places as crewmen.

> Crew: W. H. Pasfield, Chief Officer, 31, Sydney; W. Bryant, 2nd Officer, 38, Sydney; J. R. Thomson, 3rd Officer, 30, England; B. Thresher, Boatsteerer, 35, United States; John Wilson, Boatsteerer, 44, England; F. Ives, A.B., 30, England; E. Allan, A.B., 21, England; A. Simmons, Cook / Steward, 38, Barbados; J. Hazzo, Cooper / Carpenter, 33, Bristol; W. Pincott, Cook / Steward, 38, United States.
>
> Passengers: 9 South Sea Islanders.
>
> Left Sydney, 15th October 1859, bound for the South Seas. Returned to Sydney, 17th April 1860.*

---

*(*Transcribed from an original document in the* State Archives of New South Wales)

No details have been found to illustrate where these voyages were destined, or how successful they were. Subsequent events, however, will show that Captain Bennett had detailed knowledge of the whaling grounds in the vicinity of the Chesterfield Islands, to the west of New Caledonia, and it is likely that he had been working in this area. The *Prince of Denmark* set off on a further whaling voyage at some time after April of 1860.

> Crew: William Bryant, Chief Mate, 39, Sydney; John Francis, 2nd Mate, 37, Marseilles; George Price, 3rd Mate, 23, Cork; Benjamin Pease, 4th Mate, 26, Massachusetts; Henry Vassal, 28, Boatsteerer, London; William Day, Boatsteerer, 34, Norfolk; Richard McCain, A.B., 29, Liverpool; John Williams, Cook / Steward, 48, London; Manual Mustag, A.B., 30, Portugal; Antonio Silva, Boatsteerer, 24, Flores; Edwin Oram, Seaman, 27, Penzance; George T. Walker, Seaman, 28, London; Manuel Pris, Boatsteerer, 29, Brava; Charles Bettink, A.B., 35, Graciosa; Peter Gray, A.B., 23, Glasgow; George Reynolds, Carpenter, 19, London; Antonio Pereira, A.B., 23, Fagal; Joseph Robinson, A.B., 30, Lisbon; Conens, Cook / Steward, 35, China.
>
> Passengers: 9 South Sea Islanders – Bob, Cooley, Gachi, Cooma, Ganna, Harry, Soup, Munsa and Jerry.
>
> Left Sydney, date unknown. Returned to Port Jackson, Sydney, 23rd October 1860.*

The foregoing list includes names for the nine South Sea Islander passengers, but it is obvious that the names given are either nicknames or wildly inaccurate spellings of the true names of the individuals concerned. The same names (or similar ones) occur in several subsequent lists of passengers and crew, and have been quoted as accurately as possible in the manner in which they appear in each original list.

The purpose of the next voyage is not known, but it involved only a small crew, and once more included the owner, Mr. Charles McKellar, as a passenger.

> Crew: Joseph Robinson, A.B., 35, [sic] Lisbon; Edward Coburn, A.B., 46, England; C. Oroney, Cook / Steward, 34, China.
>
> Passengers: Charles McKellar, and 5 South Sea Islanders – Bob, Cooley, Cooma, Ganny and Harry.
>
> Left Sydney, date unknown. Returned to Sydney, 28th December 1860.*

On 15 January 1861, the *Sydney Morning Herald* reported that Captain Bennett had appeared in the Water Police Court, charged with illegally detaining certain wearing apparel *etc.* (value £6.15s.), the property of Bob, a South Sea Islander. Captain Bennett was ordered to make reparation of the goods.

When the *Prince of Denmark* sailed again for the whaling grounds at an early date in 1861, Bob was not among the crew. During 1861, Charles McKellar died, and his widow, Isabella McKellar of Sydney, inherited the vessel. Captain Bennett, unaware of these

---

(Transcribed from an original document in the State Archives of New South Wales)

events, remained in command and continued with his whaling voyage, sailing to Bampton Shoal in the Chesterfield Islands, not returning to Sydney until November of 1861.

> Crew: Alexander Ducker, Mate, 41, Berwick; Simon Bachelor, 2nd Mate, 40, N. Hampshire; Frank Fratis, 3rd Mate, 22, Flores; Joseph Smith, Cooper / Carpenter, 32; William Thomas, Cook / Steward, 48, London; John Topson, Boatsteerer, 25, Nantucket; James Ring, Boatsteerer, 24, Ireland; Peter Brown, Boatsteerer, 26, Pecopecon; William Ferrier, A.B., 45, Milford Haven; William Marshall, A.B., 19, Altringham; John Hogen, O.S., 19, Windsor N.S.W.; Francesco Rodriguie, O.S., Pecopecon.
>
> Passengers: Charles Hogan; 8 South Sea Islanders – Jack Tieka, Harry Tieka, Billy Bush, Harry Sandwich, Farampton Sandwich, Sawwood Sandwich, Tommy Sandwich, Bingmoss Sandwich.
>
> Left Sydney, date unknown. Returned to Sydney, 2nd November 1861.*

In the foregoing list of names, the words 'Sandwich' and 'Tieka' probably refer to the islands to which the people concerned belonged. The best-known Sandwich Islands were of course Hawaii, but it is possible that the island referred to here is Efate, one of the main islands of Vanuatu, formerly the New Hebrides, which was once named Sandwich by Captain Cook. In the eastern part of the New Caledonia group lies an island called Tika, which being in the same general area could be the source of the name 'Tieka'. An alternative might be Tikei in the Tuamotu Archipelago.

In October 1861, the *Prince of Denmark* was reported to have been at Brampton Shoal in the Chesterfield Group, with 600 barrels of humpback whale oil on board. In early November, she was back in Sydney, and her captain was advertising for a new chief officer and a steward. One crewman – Billy Bush – died on board her at Sydney on 8 December 1861, aged only 20 years. The circumstances of his death are unknown and he is buried in Camperdown Cemetery at Sydney. Although he is referred to in the list of crew and passengers as a South Sea Islander, other sources refer to him as being an Aborigine.

On his return to Sydney, Captain Bennett wasted no time in finding a partner with whose help he could afford to buy the *Prince of Denmark*. In 1862, Captain John Charles Bennett and J. C. McDougall – a Sydney chandler – became joint owners of the vessel, and registered her in Sydney (Registration No. 31). A further voyage was embarked on, the purpose of which was stated to be whaling, but the crew seemed to lack the necessary numbers and specialist skills (such as officers and boatsteerers). One South Sea Islander, Jackey Ticka, aged only 20, had been promoted to ordinary seaman.

> Crew: R. McDonald, Cook / Steward, 29, Greenock; John Hamilton, Cooper / Carpenter, 53, Falkirk; William Ferrier, A.B., 40, Milford Haven; Jackey Ticka, O.S., 20, Toka Little Island.

---

*(*Transcribed from an original document in the* State Archives of New South Wales)

Passengers: Mrs. Chalk; 8 South Sea Islanders – Harry Sandwich, Bingmoss, Lukeboy, Lawncloths, Tabanglow, Brughow [?], Showman, Jannett.

Left Sydney, date unknown. Returned to Port Jackson, Sydney, 17th February 1862.*

In the above list, Jackey Ticka's home is given as 'Toka Little Island'. No island of exactly that name has been located, but a small island called Toka lies adjacent to Puka Puka in Rarotonga.

The appearance of Mrs. Chalk – presumed to be the wife of Mr. G. H. Chalk – as a passenger on the return voyage suggests that whaling was not taking place. Perhaps Captain Bennett and his new partner Mr. McDougall were merely exploring new markets while keeping their options open. The Chesterfield Group had almost certainly been visited during this voyage, as the list of donations to the Australian Museum during March 1862 includes coral from the Chesterfield Bank, donated by Captain Bennett of the Schooner *Prince of Denmark*. Captain Bennett would seem to have had a lively interest in the diversity of marine life, as the following extract from the *Maitland Mercury and Hunter River General Advertiser* of 20 February 1862 illustrates:

> The *Prince of Denmark* from the South Seas has not sighted any vessels since leaving this port, but Captain Bennett has on board no less than 300 live turtle, of only three inches in length, which he collected on the coral reefs and has kept in a large cask. Such a sight has never been witnessed in the colonies. He has also some 200 more preserved in spirits, together with several soldier crabs, a peculiar kind of fish found only on the reefs, and to the curious in such matters, really well worth seeing.

A further clue to the diversity of the activities undertaken by the crew of the *Prince of Denmark* – and the difficulties they sometimes faced – is given in the following extract from an article entitled *Wanderings in Tropical Australia No VIII, Torres Straits Cruise*, published in the *Sydney Morning Herald* on 21 February 1862:

> The Darnley Islanders informed me that although it was peace between white men and themselves, at Mater, the largest Murray Island, it was war. This I was not surprised at, having known that some people of the *Prince of Denmark*, schooner, when trading there for tortoiseshell in the previous year, had killed a native during a quarrel in which the islanders were the aggressors, having tried by force to repossess themselves of the tortoiseshell which they had sold and had been paid for.

Captain Bennett made another appearance at Sydney's Water Police Court in early May of 1862, but on this occasion it was as a witness. He told the court that while he had been preparing the *Prince of Denmark* for departure from Smith's Wharf, he had

---

(Transcribed from an original document in the State Archives of New South Wales)

gone ashore with one of his seamen, a South Sea Islander named Jerry, to procure supplies. At a butcher's shop, Captain Bennett had given Jerry a package of meat and groceries to take back to the ship, and had followed him a short time later. Jerry, in the meantime, had been robbed by four men, of tea and sugar to the value of 14 shillings. With the assistance of Constable McHale, a labourer named Patrick Murphy and a tinsmith named John Carroll were arrested after a chase and accompanied to the lock-up. Patrick Murphy was later acquitted, but John Carroll was found guilty and was sentenced to labour on the roads and other public works for three years.

It was not long before the *Prince of Denmark* was again ready and fully crewed for a whaling voyage to the South Seas. She sailed in the early part of 1862, with a crew of 16 men and nine passengers. Pacific Islanders Harry Sandwich and Wainboa had joined Jackey Tieka as ordinary seamen.

> Crew: William Bryant, 1st Mate, 38, Sydney; Alexander Ducker, 2nd Mate, 42, Berwick; William Ring, 3rd Mate, 29, Sydney; Henry James, Boatsteerer, 22, Barbados; Joseph Alvey, Boatsteerer, 23, Foreign [*sic*]; John Hazzel, Cooper / Carpenter, 42, Bristol; Thomas Henry, Cook / Steward, 28, Gambia; Antonio Nunis, O.S., 30, Singapore; Nicholas Bertram, A.B., 22, St. Domingo; J. N. O. Dennis, A.B., 38, Prussia; Jackey Tieka, O.S., 20, Tieka; Harry Sandwich, O.S., 28, New Hebrides; William Alworth, Boatsteerer, 40, Limbeck; Wainboa, O.S., 25, Caledonia; Thomas Thompson, A. B., 27, Northumberland; S. M. Wood, O.S., 20, England.
>
> Passengers: 9 South Sea Islanders.
>
> Left Sydney, after May 1862. Returned Sydney, 8th December 1862.*

The fact that Harry Sandwich's place or country of origin is given as 'New Hebrides' gives some credibility to the theory that the name 'Sandwich' refers to an island in the New Hebrides – or Vanuatu, as it is now known – rather than Hawaii.

The *Sydney Morning Herald* of 16 February 1863 published the following letter from Captain Bennett:

> Sir,
>
> Seeing a paragraph in this morning's issue relative to the schooner *Prince of Denmark* getting on shore yesterday at Bradley's, and which, in the manner in which it is worded, would lead many astray as to the nature of it, and would no doubt, most materially affect the value of the vessel if I wished at any time to dispose of her, I beg you will insert the following *viz*:
>
> The schooner, in working down the harbour yesterday, and when off Bradley's with a light wind, was caught by the eddy tide there, and in spite of all due precautions being taken in hauling head sails down *etc.*, payed off to the point, and touched with her forefoot, but so slightly that it was not felt on board. Mr. Gibson with his boat's crew were getting a tow down by me, and kindly rendered

---

*(*Transcribed from an original document in the* State Archives of New South Wales)

all assistance in getting an anchor and warp astern and heaving it out. The *City of Newcastle*, fortunately for me, came by; the swell she made took the vessel cleverly off without receiving any damage whatever, as I have ascertained by my divers on board.

By inserting this, you will extremely oblige.

Charles Bennett,

Master, schooner *Prince of Denmark*.

P.S. Your reporter must have been misinformed. I had no intention of staying the vessel, fully expecting to clear; consequently she could not have misstayed.

Captain Bennett had an obvious pride in his seamanship and a shrewd grasp of the adverse effect of bad publicity. Despite this minor setback, he was applying himself to the whaling industry in a professional and purposeful manner. His combination of personal skill, the hiring of multiracial crews who were evidently experienced whalers, and an ongoing relationship with indigenous people of the Pacific Islands was perhaps beginning to pay dividends. Sadly however, everything was about to change.

16 *A New Caledonian Ending*

In early February of 1863, the *Prince of Denmark* set sail from Sydney for the whaling grounds in the vicinity of the Chesterfield Islands, to the west of New Caledonia. She was again under the command of Captain John Charles Bennett, who had bought out the half-share owned by his former partner, John Graham McDougall (a Sydney ship chandler).

The *Prince of Denmark* was then in her 74th year, much of her working life having been spent in the particularly arduous trade of whaling. Whalers were normally built to high specifications and were of unusually heavy construction to help them withstand the extreme conditions in which they would be operating. In the case of the *Prince of Denmark*, however, it is most unlikely that this was so, as neither the town in which she was built, nor the men who built her had any known connection with the whaling trade. If she was originally commissioned as a revenue cutter, she would have been designed and built to high standards, but the aim of those setting the standards would have been to procure a vessel that was outstandingly fast. This would probably have been achieved by combining a very large sail area, a lofty rig and a low displacement. One way of keeping displacement low was to ensure that construction was as light as possible, which in the 18th century was not normally compatible with longevity.

It is sometimes said that whaling vessels which were fortunate enough to escape such events as collision, fire or shipwreck, could have an unusually long working life, due in part to the fact that their timbers, from the deck to the bottom of the hold had been perpetually steeped in whale fat and oil. Whilst there is probably some truth in this theory, in the case of the *Prince of Denmark*, the effect would, to a great extent, have been offset by the ravages of the climate in which she had been operating. Weeks of exposure to the heat of the tropical sunshine in the waters around Samoa and New Caledonia, followed by weeks of sleet and snow in the roaring forties and to the south of Tasmania, would have caused expansion and contraction of her planking, opening and closing caulked seams and making maintenance of her deck and superstructure a demanding and expensive task.

Charts of the Pacific Ocean in the early 19th century were neither as comprehensive nor as accurate as those of modern times; thus in addition to the known hazards to navigation, there were a great many reefs and shallows which were unknown and uncharted. Voyaging in these waters is still difficult and dangerous and the huge Pacific Ocean swells can break heavily over such shallow areas. Nowadays, virtually all vessels from ocean liners to tiny yachts are equipped with satellite navigation systems that allow their masters to know their exact positions at all times. Prior to their invention, the master of a sailing ship making a lengthy passage would be fortunate if he was always entirely certain of his position. Either the lack of opportunity to take a noonday sight of the sun due to adverse weather, or an inaccuracy in the ship's chronometer, could easily cause doubt. In such circumstances, fate frequently dictated that landfall would be made, not in clear weather and bright daylight, but at night, during mist and rain. The master of a sailing vessel could then easily find that the first warning he received of a hazardous situation was the awful sound of breaking surf. In many cases, wind conditions would then leave him with neither the power nor the sea room to avoid disaster.

Coral reefs, which are the normal accompaniment to any landmass in the Pacific, however small, can extend over several square miles of the seabed. They are normally submerged, extremely hard, sharp-edged and destructive, both to timber vessels and to any human beings unfortunate enough to be swept against them. Timber and flesh are almost equally prone to laceration, and flesh wounds caused by coral have the additional complication that they invariably turn septic. The coral reefs of the Pacific are the natural habitat of several different species of shark. Fortunately, the reefs are so densely populated with fish that sharks do not normally need to attack human beings. Nevertheless, hungry sharks that are trapped within a reef system on a falling tide can easily succumb to the temptation provided by a distressed human being thrashing around in the water and bleeding from a coral wound.

The *Prince of Denmark*'s underside had been sheathed in copper, but there had been many incidents in her lengthy past that would have damaged her hull and sheathing, providing opportunities for marine borers to invade her structure, imperceptibly weakening her planking and timbers. A weakened hull coming into contact with a coral reef in a heavy swell could be completely shattered in a matter of a few terrifying minutes.

The Chesterfield Group is an archipelago in the Coral Sea, roughly half way between Australia and New Caledonia, and is now part of the territory of New Caledonia. The land consists largely of reefs and sandbanks, some of which are at times covered by the sea and are prone to shifting their position due to the effects of wind and tide. The larger islands have been stabilised by the growth of grass, scrub and low trees, but none is inhabited. The islands surround a deep lagoon, which covers an area of 1,350 square miles.

The largest island in the group is Isle Longue, which is approximately one mile in length, but only a little over 100 yards in width and 30ft in height. A few miles to its

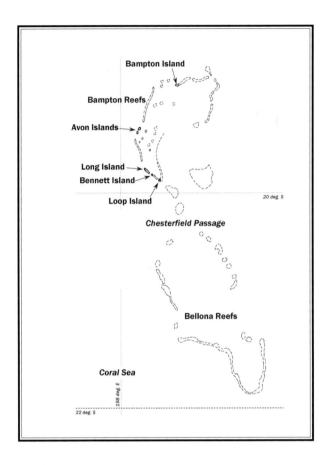

Sketch map of Chesterfield Islands

southeast lies Passage (or Bennett Island), on which Captain Bennett had established a whaling station in 1862. The Chesterfield Group was known to be an area where whales gathered to spend the winter months and Captain Bennett must have considered it worthwhile to establish a base there, which would enable him to tow whales ashore, fire up his try-works on land and boil down the blubber into oil in the safety and relative comfort of the shore.

Despite the many hazards described previously, Captain Bennett brought the *Prince of Denmark* safely to anchor off his whaling station on 20 February 1863. She carried a quantity of timber planks with which to complete construction of the station, and also a large amount of equipment. The further the ship was anchored offshore, the more difficult the task of unloading would have been, and it is likely therefore that Captain Bennett would have chosen a temporary anchorage very close to the shore. On 19 March 1863, when the task of unloading was all but completed, a sudden and violent squall caused the anchor cable to break and the *Prince of Denmark* was quickly swept onto the reef. The breakers and the coral soon caused her to disintegrate, and her captain and crew, who came ashore clinging to pieces of wreckage, were fortunate to escape with their lives. Captain Bennett later gave the position of his whaling station as being latitude 19.58 south, longitude 158.23 east, and the Australian National Shipwreck Database gives a position for the shipwreck of latitude 19.983317 south, longitude 158.55 east. The *Queensland Guardian* published the following account of her loss:

> **Wreck of the Schooner *Prince of Denmark*** – From the information we were able to gather yesterday respecting the wreck of this vessel, it appears that she left Sydney about the beginning of February last, for one of the islands of the Chesterfield Group, on which is situated a whaling station. She was loaded with stores for this station, where she arrived about the 20th February. She had landed successfully nearly the whole of her cargo when on the 19th March, during a heavy gale, she parted her cables and went ashore. In about half an hour scarcely a vestige of the vessel was to be seen. The whole of the crew with great difficulty succeeded in saving their lives by either swimming or floating on the debris of the wreck to the shore. On the second day after the wreck, the weather became calm, and some of the island blacks, by diving, succeeded in bringing up from the wreck sundry small articles, among which were several of the carpenter's tools and a spy-glass and one or two chests belonging to the seamen.

When he had recovered from the initial shock of his experience, Captain Bennett's first tasks were to determine what was salvageable from the wreck, estimate how long he and his crew could survive on the available water and provisions, and assess the time that might elapse before a passing ship might find them. Captain Bennett would be as able as anyone to work out that equation, and must have made an early and wise decision to depend only on what was under his own control. Early investigation of the wreck probably enabled him to recover the ship's boats (either intact or damaged), the cargo of timber planks, and much of the provisions. The ship's complement consisted of around 21 men, who would have provided him with a skilled and able workforce, but also required a large amount of food and water. Eleven of these men are believed to have been Pacific Islanders, and would have been adept at identifying, catching and gathering food from the reef system – but for how long could 21 men hope to survive on such a tiny island?

17 *A Ghostly Rising*

After a very short period of time spent appraising his situation and that of his crew as castaways, Captain Bennett took the almost unbelievably bold decision to build a vessel using whatever materials he could muster, capable of carrying all (or a large part) of his crew to safety. The audacity of that decision defies description and leaves one wondering whether or not it was merely a ploy to exercise the minds and maintain the spirits of his crew while he secretly hoped for rescue; or a carefully considered plan, following detailed analysis of the available resources. To run out of materials such as timber, bolts, nails and caulking material would mean the end of the venture. To complete construction and to then find the vessel too heavy to move to the sea would have been cruel beyond words. There are no big tidal ranges in this part of the Pacific Ocean to assist in launching, so levers, ropes and the brute force that could be exerted by a limited number of exhausted and perhaps undernourished men, was all that was available.

The *Prince of Denmark*'s planking would almost certainly have been unusable, but her timbers (the adze-hewn oak frames that gave her hull its shape), were more likely to have survived in a usable form. These timbers, combined with the planks Captain Bennett had brought to extend his whaling station, were almost certainly the basis of the new vessel.

Given the skills of the ship's carpenter on a typical whaler, repair of the ship's boats would have been a fairly straightforward matter. These boats, however, are unlikely to have been larger than 25ft in length, narrow in beam, and very lightly constructed. Captain Bennett may have decided that they were too small to safely make the long passage through open water to Australia. A vessel of between 30 and 40ft in length would have been roughly half the length of the *Prince of Denmark*, but would have afforded a much better chance of carrying the necessary provisions and reaching safety. Contemplating construction of a vessel of such size would have raised the possibility of using only every second frame of the original vessel. Damaged frames could then be repaired by splicing in pieces of the neighbouring frames, and those too badly damaged to repair could have been fabricated by adapting sections of the adjacent frames which most closely resembled their shape. By this means, a shorter vessel could have been devised, minimising the difficulty in achieving a reasonably well-shaped hull. The resulting beam could have been disproportionately large and the freeboard too high, but some reshaping of the timbers – both at their junction with the keel and at their junction with the deck beams – could have made this manageable. The masts, spars, sails, deck fittings, cordage and anchors were presumably salvaged from the wreck.

On 17 June 1863 – only a little under three months after the shipwreck – the new vessel was complete and ready for sea. Displaying both a sense of humour and a degree of literary knowledge, Captain Bennett named his new command *Hamlet's Ghost*. She set sail for Brisbane, 600 miles away, manned by the pick of the *Prince of Denmark*'s crew but leaving 11 Pacific Islanders behind to await rescue. On 27 June 1863, *Hamlet's Ghost* arrived safely (though only just) at Moreton Bay, Brisbane. The editor of the *Brisbane Courier* wisely chose to use Captain Bennett's own words to tell the astonishing story in the paper's issue of 2 July 1863:

> The subjoined report of the passage of the *Hamlet's Ghost*, schooner, from Bennett's Whaling Station, on the Chesterfield Islands, in latitude 19 deg. 58 mins. S., and longitude 158 deg. 23 mins. E., was furnished to us by her Captain and owner, Mr. J. C. Bennett:
>
> **Wednesday 17 June** At noon we left the station, in company with the barque *Offley*, (Robinson, Master) of Hobart Town, six weeks out, all well. He desired me to report him, and I received every kindness that the case demanded, he giving me charts, clothes, a compass, preserved meats *etc.*, I having lost everything in the schooner except two chronometers and a quadrant. From Captain Wybrow of the *Bonnie Doon*, I received yams and preserved meats, and was also heartily cheered by both crews, and which was as heartily answered by the crew of the *Hamlet's Ghost*. The assistance rendered to me by the two vessels I am truly thankful for, and shall often think of it with pleasure. We had steady breezes from E.S.E., and S.E., and fine weather.
>
> **Thursday 18 June** Steady breezes from S.E., and fine weather. Steering to the S. and W. for Wreck Reef in company with the barque *Offley*, she having kindly offered her company and assistance as far as Wreck Reef, which was eagerly accepted, as the boat was making a little water. Latitude at noon, 21 deg. 22 mins. S., longitude 157 deg. 5 min. E.
>
> **Friday 19 June** At 4.00 p.m. Wreck Reef bore S.W. true 70 mins; steady breeze and fine weather; 9.00 p.m. light N.E. winds; midnight ditto. At 4.00 a.m. light N.E. and showers. At 6.00 a.m. Wreck Reef bore W.S.W. 35 mins. At 8.00 a.m. light N.N.E. wind; parted company with *Offley*. At noon, latitude by observation 22 deg. 7 mins. S., longitude 156 deg. 5 mins. 5 sec. E.
>
> **Saturday 20 June** Light winds and variable, principally S.S.W. At 6.00 p.m. spoke the brig *Victoria*, Hentestalk Master, 6 weeks out, clean. Had tea on board of her and obtained a few candles and two tins of preserved meat. He told me that the brig *Amherst* and barque *Caernarvon*, and several American vessels were to the Southward. We parted company from him and stood to S.W. Winds light and veering to the S.E. Midnight puffy and heavy rain. Lightning S.E. shortened sail. At 4.00 p.m. fresh breezes from S.E. and showers with heavy sea. At noon Lat. observed 22 deg. 26 min. S. long. 155 deg. 54 min. 30 sec. E. Squally S.S.W. winds and heavy sea.
>
> **Sunday 21 June** Light variable winds. Schooner working to the S.S.W. Lat. Obs. 22 deg. 40 min. S. long. 156 deg. 17 min. 15 sec. E.

Monday 22 June Fresh breezes S.S.W. and fine. Noon to 4.00 p.m. steady and fine; midnight puffy and lightning from S.E. and S. Nasty cross sea on; tacked to W. Winds light and variable; at 8.00 a.m. barque *Eliza* of New Bedford, (Devoule, Master) in sight; exchanged colours. Was boarded by him and supplied with water, pork, and some oil. Desired me to report him 32 months out with 1,000 barrels of sperm, and last from Monganui, N.Z. At noon latitude by observation 23 deg. 30 min. S. long. 156 deg. 30 min. E.

Tuesday 23 June Found a strong set to the N.E. Winds light and variable; latter part fresh breezes S.E. and S.S.E. Heavy sea. Schooner standing to S. and W. The latter part of the day puffy and variable; lightning to the S. and S.E. lat. 24 deg. 16 min. S. long. 155 deg. 33 min. 45 sec. E.

Wednesday 24 June Puffy and variable; nasty sea on; Schooner standing to the S. and W. Latter part squally and heavy rain. At noon, squalls, very sudden calms and heavy rain; no sights; no meridian altitude. Course and distance from yesterday at noon, 116 miles S., 31 W.

Thursday 25 June Light and variable, principally N. and N.N.E. At 4.00 p.m. backed to N.N.E.; heavy rain, everything and everybody wet and miserable, cold, and very dirty looking weather; at 6.00 p.m. puffy from N.E. and clear. Midnight fine breezes but variable; At 4.00 a.m. strong breeze N.E., and fine; at 5.00 a.m. sighted Moreton Light, bearing —— at 8—[?] Moreton Light bore W. ½ N. 15 miles; at noon steady breeze and fine. Lat. by obs. 27deg. 26 min. S. Stradbroke N.E. point bore W.S.W.

Friday 26 June Light winds and fine. At 5.00 a.m. Point Danger bore W. by N ½ N. Mount Warning bore S.S.W. ½ W. Winds light and variable; At 8.00 a.m. puffy from S.S.W. and heavy sea. Shortened sail and stood to the S. and E. At 4.00 a.m. same weather and every appearance of a dirty S.W. wind. Rain all night; at 8.00 a.m. a grey dingy appearance to the S.S.W. Schooner standing in for the land: at noon close in with the land. Mount Warning, S.W., Point Danger W. by S.; bore up for Moreton Light; blowing strong from S.S.W.

Saturday 27 June Blowing heavy from S.S.W. 6.00 p.m. more moderate; at 9.30 p.m. anchored under Moreton Light in 5 fathoms. Light bearing E. At 1.00 a.m. heavy squalls; rain from S.W. Let go the second anchor. At 4.00 a.m. same weather; at 8.00 a.m. weather squally and showers. At 11.00 a.m. got under way and worked into the bay and came to in 8 Fathoms close to W. bank. Red light pilot station bore xxx 1 mile; at 7.00 p.m. moderate and clear, wind W.S.W. Sun and clear hard-looking horizon.

Note: In working into the bay, the pilot boat was running and she crossed my stern and asked if I wanted a pilot; I told him no, but that I had a shipwrecked crew and wanted assistance. He very likely did not understand me as he waved me to tack and go towards the pilot station. I did so. After standing to the westward a little longer, the pilot boat went towards Moreton Light; a ship followed her out. A little while after dark, the pilot boat got back to her moorings before she came round the beacon point I had a large —— —— at the mainmast head to attract attention, thinking of course that he would send a boat off, but no boat came. At 1.00 a.m. the boat parted her chain, it blowing strong at the time from S.W. and a strong ebb setting out. Made sail on the boat and stood to the W. under —— reefed mainsail and reefed staysail; hoisted a light and kept it burning, thinking again a boat would come off. The light at the pilot station was out but no boat came out. At 2.00 a.m. bore round and stood for what I supposed to be the pilot boat's light, intending to let go the anchor close to her and run a line to her to hold on to her until morning. Ran the boat with all confidence, but was terribly disappointed to find myself close in with the beacon light on the point. Rounded the boat to and let go the anchor, and found the anchor would not hold, being too much tide. Managed to save her from going on shore by getting her head to the westward again running the sails up and cutting the anchor adrift. Kept under way, tacking to and fro. At daylight made sail; at 8.00 a.m. hoisted the ensign upside down. The pilot boat came out some time after and lowered his boat and came alongside with Mr. How. I told him I had lost both my anchors and wanted the loan of one, some firewood, a little tea and sugar and some beef. I told him I expected someone last night, that I had a —— up before he came round the point, also a light after I broke adrift. His answer to me was that he did not see it, but that they intended and were preparing to come this morning. He said he would go up with me to Brisbane and also get an anchor for me. He went back to the boat and obtained the articles, all but the anchor, and came on board. We kept under way all night and in the morning, 29th June, were tacking to and fro under Mud Island; at high tide crossed the bar and at 10.00 p.m. made fast alongside Mr. Campbell's wharf, and was very thankful for it. Had the light on the pilot schooner been burning, or had a boat come out to me after the pilot boat got to her moorings, I should most likely have saved my anchors. The words 'a shipwrecked crew' in answer to the pilot boat's question, was quite enough, I should think, to induce any man with a grain of humanity to have sent a boat to me, after bringing the pilot boat to her moorings. Who is to blame is not for me to say. I leave that for abler hands than mine.

Captain Bennett, having already endured a mariner's worst nightmare with the loss of the *Prince of Denmark*, had made a prodigious personal effort in inspiring his crew to build *Hamlet's Ghost*. Despite probable exhaustion and the stress that must have resulted from handling a new and untested vessel in bad weather, he had then brought his ship and his crew successfully to within a very short distance from his destination, only to be faced with the awful prospect of losing her, and perhaps the lives of himself and his crew, on the rocks of his home shore.

His relief at finally tying up alongside Mr. Campbell's wharf is palpable, and his hurt and anger at the pilot who let him down at the time of his greatest need is understandable. It is perhaps better, however, to recall the kindness of the captains of the various ships that seemingly appeared from nowhere, and escorted *Hamlet's Ghost* safely through the crucial early stages of her maiden voyage.

After a brief period of celebrity status, *Hamlet's Ghost* became merely one of many small vessels carrying cargo in and around the port of Brisbane. For some of this time, her captain was George Elliot, and the *Brisbane Courier* of Wednesday 15 June 1864 records that he was fined £2.10s. and 3s. costs for failing to show a light on board his vessel during the night. The *Brisbane Courier* of Thursday 6 October 1864 records that on Tuesday 5 October, *Hamlet's Ghost* left town with a cargo of hides, bound for the *Young Australia*, which had commenced loading for her outward voyage. A further cargo of cotton was then carried to the *Young Australia* on Thursday 20 October.

At an unknown date, *Hamlet's Ghost* (Ship no 52224) was sold for £100 to George Harris – sometimes referred to as the Merchant Prince of Brisbane. He was a member of the upper house of the first parliament of Queensland, and had a reputation for entertaining on a lavish scale, with a budget of over $20,000 per year. He used *Hamlet's Ghost* as a yacht, sporting six small bronze swivel guns (three per side), and in December 1864, he entered her for Cleveland's second annual regatta, which was to be held on

Monday 2 January 1865. The *Brisbane Courier* for Tuesday 3 January 1865 reported that *Hamlet's Ghost* finished in third place in the third race, but was second on corrected time, despite having carried away her topmast and split her mainsail during the race.

From the following advertisements, published in the *Brisbane Courier* in July 1865, it would appear that Mr. Harris had tried, without success, to dispose of *Hamlet's Ghost*. Perhaps he was unable to realise the price he had anticipated and decided instead to keep her, or perhaps she changed hands within the Harris family. Precise details are unknown.

> To lightermen and others employed in the bay and river trade, Arthur Martin has received instructions from Messrs. J. and G. Harris to sell by auction at their wharf on Saturday 22nd July, at 11 o'clock, that first class, faithfully built and well found ketch known as *Hamlet's Ghost*, at present in thorough order, with all her rigging and fittings quite new and in working order, completely fitted out with all necessary masts, sails, ropes, chains, anchors, booms, gaffs, sweeps, galley with American stove, winch, water casks *etc*. Her tonnage is about 25 tons burthen, 44ft in length, 12ft 6in in beam and good depth of hold. As this vessel is quite new, and admirably adapted for the river and bay trade, the auctioneer invites intending purchasers to inspect her, and learn all particulars previous to the day of the sale, which will be on Saturday 22nd inst. at 11 o'clock on Messrs. Harris's wharf
>
> Mr. A. Martin at 11 o'clock at the City Auction Mart: the ketch *Hamlet's Ghost*, kerosene oil and lampware, horse pump, coffee-mill, stove, cigars, furniture, tobacco, boots, groceries, and oilmen's stores, sugar, maize, and hay, bottled beer, whisky, brandy, wooden wares.

The *Brisbane Courier* of Friday 16 February 1866 reported that *Hamlet's Ghost* had been re-launched as a schooner after a refit and extensive alterations had been carried out. Her new rig included two flying gaff topsails, a cock-billed yard to carry a square sail, but no main topmast staysail. She had not been successful in the lightering trade as she had insufficient space for cargo, and she had been laid up for some time by her owner. Elijah Monk, a shipwright and boat builder of South Brisbane, had carried out her conversion to a yacht, adding an elliptical stern, altering her stem from being straight to overhanging, sheathing her hull in cedar planking and coppering her bottom. He had also added a cabin, lined internally with diagonal pine boarding, with accommodation for 12 people, and had re-laid her decks in colonial beech. The finishing touches were two neatly designed headboards with her name in gold letters on a ribbon. It later transpired that the cost of this conversion far exceeded the probable cost of commissioning a new vessel and Mr. Monk and Mr. Harris ended up in court in May of 1866 in a bitter dispute over payment.

Mr. Harris's irritation and frustration would not have been eased by an incident that occurred during St Patrick's Day celebrations in March of 1866, only a month after his vessel had been re-launched. Mr. Harris was entertaining some distinguished friends, including the colonial secretary, Sir Robert George Wyndham Herbert, and Captain Henry Dowdeswell Pitt R.A., aboard *Hamlet's Ghost*, and was awaiting favourable winds in Moreton Bay. Mr. Harris accepted a tow from the passing excursion steamer *Settler*, which was laden with passengers enjoying a St. Patrick's Day outing. The barque *Yaletta* was at anchor close by, and the helmsman of the *Settler* badly misjudged the situation, allowing *Hamlet's Ghost* to collide with one of the projecting yards of the *Yaletta*. The result was the complete destruction of the masts and spars of *Hamlet's Ghost*, which came crashing to the deck. It was fortunate that there were no injuries other than to the pride and the pocket of Mr. Harris.

Repairs must have been quickly carried out, as George Harris, vice commodore of Brisbane Yacht Club, sailed *Hamlet's Ghost* in the first races held in Moreton Bay on 14 July 1866, under his black, yellow and red flag. The extra weight of his lavish conversion seemed to have been a handicap however, as he finished in last place. When His Royal Highness Prince Alfred Ernest Albert, Duke of Edinburgh, visited the area in February 1868, Mr. Harris anchored *Hamlet's Ghost* near to where the government steamer *Kate*, bearing the prince, was expected to pass. *Hamlet's Ghost* was bedecked with flags and bore a banner which read 'Welcome to the Sailor Prince'. The press reported that Mr. Harris had done further honour to the prince by dipping his ensign and firing a salute, which was returned by the dipping of the *Kate*'s ensign.

Mr. Harris eventually tired of his expensive plaything, and on 29 June 1868, *Hamlet's Ghost* was sold for £500 to a gentleman described in the bill of sale as 'Graf von Athems, a native of the empire of Austria'. This mysterious nobleman had arrived in Sydney on the *Northampton* of London, on 20 April 1868, and sailed from Brisbane in his new vessel on 7 July. The *Cleveland Bay Express* recorded his arrival thus:

Mr. George Harris (Courtesy of the John Oxley Library, State Library of Queensland, Australia)

> Among the new arrivals this week, we have the pleasure of Count Von Attems. This nobleman is taking a tour for pleasure, and arrived here on Thursday last, in his splendid yacht, *Hamlet's Ghost*. This beautiful little vessel is, without exception, the prettiest model we remember to have seen on our waters. The Count, last evening, entertained several of our leading townsmen with a supper at Will's Hotel.

The dashing Count and his much-admired yacht had clearly made a good initial impression. The cabin of *Hamlet's Ghost* was reportedly lined with grained maple panelling and gold mountings, and her company consisted of the count, a captain, a first officer, three seamen, a cook, a steward and a servant. They headed northwards, calling at Maryborough and arrived off Keppel Bay on 14 July 1868. *Hamlet's Ghost* then sailed on up the coast to Mackay and Port Denison (Bowen), leaving there on 31 July. The unsuspecting people of these ports were not to know that their visitor had made a career out of the creation of favourable first impressions, but the penny quickly dropped – as the following account from The *Otago Witness* of 5 September 1868 illustrates:

> A few months ago a gentleman, newly arrived in Sydney, introduced himself to one of the foreign Consuls here as the distinguished Austrian Count Von Attems. He had with him such books, private papers, and photographs of members of his illustrious family, as perfectly to satisfy the Consul in question as to his identity. The result was that he soon became known to all the 'best people' in Sydney. He was received in society, installed at the Union Club, hunted at the Opera, caressed at Government House; and yet the impostor – for such he was – carried about with him evidence of his rascality sufficient to excite suspicion. His manners and appearance were those of an ostler. There was not a vestige of high birth or polished manners about him. Your correspondent met him at the Flore Australienne in George Street a few days after his arrival, and remarked at the time that the 'Prince' was a very strange specimen of royalty; a doubt which was considerably strengthened in your correspondent's mind when he heard that the prince had no money with him, but was borrowing it on the strength of his representations, and of certain non-negotiable bills on the 'Anglo-Austrian Bank'. After spending a pleasant month or two here, our illustrious visitor resumed his tour, and was last heard of as having touched at Bowen, in Northern Queensland, in command of his yacht *Hamlet's Ghost*. Intelligence received by the last mail has inflicted a heavy blow upon the insinuating foreigner's confiding friends. It is found that he is not the Count Von Attems at all (a punster might say there was not von atom of truth in his story). The real Count, it is said, died at Sierra Leone a short time ago, and the gentleman who has honoured us with his acquaintance is, or was, his valet, who had managed to possess himself of the defunct nobleman's travelling effects. This laughable little affair reminds us of Gentleman Chucks, who excused himself for a similar "mistake" by saying the "only thing of my poor master's I took was his name, which he had no further occasion for, poor fellow!" Our late visitor can lay no such salve to his conscience, if he had one.

Gentleman Chucks – 'a boatswain who appeared to have received half an education' – was one of the most famous characters created by Captain Frederick Marryat, and appeared in his popular novel, *Peter Simple*. Journalists of the day were as able as their modern counterparts to recognise a good story when they found it: more and more details emerged of the fraudster's activities, and increasingly colourful accounts like that in the following extract from the *Gladstone Observer* were published:

> The *Hamlet's Ghost*, with the spurious Count on board, put into Somerset (Cape York) on or about the 15th August. On being boarded by the police boat, he made enquiries as to whether a frigate had arrived there, and on being answered in the affirmative became agitated and eagerly inquired about her movements, but appeared relieved when told that the vessel was HMS *Virago*, and that she had left the settlement in January. He remained eight days, and during the whole time kept a bright lookout for vessels in the offing. The captain and crew were discharged in consequence of a row between the 'Count' and the captain, in which revolvers were drawn. The crew refused to put the captain in irons. It appears that the Count had kept them in awe by threatening to give them twenty-five lashes apiece when he fell in with the Austrian frigate he was always expecting. The acting police magistrate induced the crew to re-ship under a fresh agreement, all but the captain and steward, who remained behind. While in port, the Count was always dressed in the uniform of an Austrian captain of cavalry, and wore a sword when on shore. He made a great display of the money he had with him, and purposely left bills of exchange lying about his cabin for visitors to see, many of which were filled in for large amounts, and only wanted his signature. He succeeded, in imposing upon the authorities, taking supplies for his vessel and paying for them in bills, which the holders will doubtless discover are about as valuable as drafts upon Aldgate pump. Among those who were swindled are two naturalists – one named Thorpe. The Count bought stuffed birds, *etc.*, from them to the amount of about £30; but some slight compunction must have touched him, for, contrary to custom, he paid them half cash and half by a bill. He sailed for Batavia on the eighth day, leaving letters for the captain of the Austrian frigate and his bankers in Sydney. The frigate was ordered to follow him to Timor. The captain he has with him is one Austin, late master of the brig *Reliance*, which was wrecked on the Solomon group. He was picked up and brought into Bowen, whence he shipped as mate on board *Hamlet's Ghost*. Two days after she left Somerset, the schooner *Captain Cook* arrived from Bowen, with a warrant for the arrest of the Count.

Mr. Thorpe, one of the two men who sold stuffed birds to the bogus count is likely to have been J. A. Thorpe, a naturalist and taxidermist of some distinction. Between 1863 and 1879, a government settlement was in existence at Somerset, close to Cape York, at the northern tip of Australia. The ships that brought supplies to the settlement also brought naturalists, and J. A. Thorpe had spent many months collecting in the vicinity. In 1867, he was taxidermist to the Australian Museum.

Hamlet's Ghost eventually appeared in Surabaya in late 1868, where the Count Von Attems was arrested, charged with fraud and false pretences under his real name of Kurt Schwartz (sometimes reported as Curt Oswald Shmalz), and imprisoned. Aged only 22 years and a former apprentice cobbler, he had confessed to six years of criminal activity, having been responsible for fraud and deception in Holland, Spain and other

European countries, as well as in Turkey and Egypt. He then went to North America and enlisted in the 2nd Massachusetts Cavalry, in which he was promoted to captain. After the American Civil War was over, he travelled to Rio de Janeiro, Montevideo, Buenos Aires, Lima and Havana, and later used fraudulently obtained cash to buy a passage from New York to Sierra Leone. He was then employed by the real Count Von Attems as a valet for six months prior to that gentleman's death in Sierra Leone.

The photograph below is from the Walter B. Woodbury Photographic Collection, and is entitled '*Hamlet's Ghost*, Sourabaya [*sic*], Java, (Boat with Passengers and Crew) *c*.1865'. Walter Woodbury was a pioneering English photographer who travelled to Java in 1857 and set up a photographic business there, in partnership with James Page. Walter Woodbury left Indonesia in 1863, but the firm he founded continued in business there until 1908. This photograph cannot have been taken before late 1868, and should therefore probably be attributed to the firm of Wooodbury and Page, rather than to Walter B. Woodbury. The discovery of the existence of this picture at the very end of the research process was astonishing, and must bring to a satisfying end the speculation that anyone reading this account might reasonably have about the nature and quality of a vessel of such improbable origins.

The schooner Hamlet's Ghost *(Courtesy of the W.E.B. Du Bois Library, University of Massachusets, Amherst, USA)*

Woodbury and Page's excellent picture shows a surprisingly yacht-like vessel with a rakish sheerline, narrow on the waterline at both bow and stern, and carrying a generous sail area, but with unusually light-looking masts and spars. The scrollwork at the bows, the altered stern, and the cabin structure added by Elijah Monk, can all be clearly seen, and the rig, altered by him for Mr. Harris, is indisputably that of a schooner. *Hamlet's Ghost* appears to be in tidy condition with rigging properly set up, jib and fore-topmast staysail in stops, mainsail and foresail neatly stowed, and tropical awnings rigged over the booms. It seems probable that the picture was taken not long after her arrival in late 1868, perhaps even in that period when her captain and crew had time to pose for a picture while their employer awaited trial, and they anticipated the sale of the vessel and the making of arrangements for their passage home.

Captain Hamlin, the first commander appointed by the spurious 'Count Von Attems' had been dismissed at Maryborough within a few weeks of his engagement, and John McQuade, who had originally been mate, was appointed captain in his place. James Blair was appointed as A.B., and an experienced seaman named William Williamson also joined the crew, together with a French cook / steward and a valet. John McQuade and William Williamson wisely resigned before they even left Maryborough, which led to the appointment of William Howes as captain, Edmonds Brown as mate and William Henry as an additional seaman. Edmonds Brown resigned at Thursday Island and Captain Howes resigned at Somerset on 29 September 1868. The position of captain was then filled by John Austen. Of the crew members who found themselves marooned in Surabaya, James Blair shipped in a vessel bound for London, and did eventually find his way back to Brisbane. William Henry stowed away on a brig bound for Hobart by clinging to the bobstay for three hours, and also returned safely to Brisbane. Nothing is known of the fate of the others.

The *Surabaya Haudelsblad* of 2 August 1869 gave a lengthy report of an escape attempt by the so-called count, who had succeeded in forcing his way through two bars at the window opening of the prison hospital. After an unsuccessful attempt to board the steamer to Malacca, he departed on horseback, purporting to be Captain Stone of the American man-of-war *Hartford*, involved in the laying of a telegraphic cable. News of the escape preceded the so-called Captain Stone's arrival at Pamakassan, and suspicions were soon aroused about him, resulting in his arrest and return to jail. Kurt Schwartz was held in prison without trial, in squalid conditions, clad in rags, until he was sentenced (in 1870) to a fine and six years in the house of correction, followed by an additional six years in prison. It was later determined that his sentence was over-lenient, and his term in the house of correction was increased to ten years.

Hamlet's Ghost was sold in Surabaya on 4 December 1868 for the sum of £200. She was reported to have become an inter-island trader and was later lost in a cyclone.

Epilogue

Mariners have consistently shown affection for the better ships in which they have served, and the longer a ship's life, the greater (generally) was the mariners' affection and the more fanciful their claims with regard to her qualities. Some ships had almost supernatural powers attributed to them, their crews naively believing that vessels so favoured were able to anticipate trouble and forewarn of dangers such as rocks, shoal waters or lee shores. Ships which were well designed and well built would perform well, and given able captains and crews, could fight clear of hazards to which lesser vessels might have succumbed. Some fast and handsome ships were admittedly unfortunate enough to be lost on their maiden voyages, but there are very few examples of ungainly and poorly performing vessels having long lives. A fast ship was generally a good ship if properly handled and the *Prince of Denmark* was clearly such a vessel.

However, her qualities as a fast and handsome vessel were not enough to save her from the onset of obsolescence. By the last 30 years of the 19th century, steam ships had revolutionised both coastal and international trade and the advent of efficient railways had dealt a mortal blow to coastal trade under sail. Although the more modern sailing vessels survived for a few more decades, elderly sailing vessels were particularly costly to maintain and could rarely carry large enough cargoes to be viable.

The various owners and masters of the *Prince of Denmark* seem to have had more than their fair share of misfortune: William Stewart was imprisoned for debt and later died in poverty in 1851; Henry Wishart was killed by sharks; John Wallace Murdoch was made bankrupt in 1839, and again in 1850; Michael Connors II became an alcoholic and died in 1853 after falling out of bed while drunk; James Kelly had made and lost a fortune by 1842 and died in 1859; Thomas Raine was practically bankrupt in 1829 and died in 1860; George Watson was bankrupt in 1851 and in 1856; and Hubert Beard Evans was declared bankrupt in 1857 and again in 1876 (he was an Alderman of Hobart 1875–1876 and died in 1886).

The Chesterfield Islands seem to have held a fatal attraction for Captain Bennett, for on 15 November 1863, he was again wrecked at Bampton Shoal while in command of the whaling brig *Sporting Life*. He and his crew subsequently met up with the crew of the *Hope*, which had also been wrecked, and both crews sailed together for the mainland in a flotilla of nine whaleboats. All reached Brisbane successfully.

Richard Cleburne and Captain Peter Williams outlived their vessel, dying in 1864 and 1868 respectively. Richard Cleburne, like Hubert Beard Evans, was an Alderman of Hobart in 1846–1847. Even George Harris, the wealthy merchant who bought *Hamlet's Ghost* and converted her to a yacht, was not immune to financial misfortune. In 1876 he was declared insolvent and he died in1891.

Two of the more colourful characters associated with the *Prince of Denmark* were Baron De Thierry, and Kurt Schwartz – the bogus Count Von Attems. The amazing career of the flamboyant, visionary and intrepid Baron De Thierry continued to fall short of his lofty aspirations until he died in Auckland in 1864. In 1872, a distinguished member of the Australian Club of Melbourne is reported to have received two pairs of boots from a Mr. Schwartz, who was then incarcerated in prison in Batavia. Kurt Schwartz subsequently vanished into the prison system.

The timbers fashioned by Kirkcudbright's craftsmen into the *Prince of Denmark*, re-fashioned by Captain Bennet's crew into *Hamlet's Ghost*, and repaired by Elijah Monk of Brisbane, were strewn across Indonesian beaches by a typhoon. They could then have simply rotted away or been used as firewood, but there is also just a chance that these fine old timbers, steeped in whale oil, were salvaged by beachcombers and utilised in construction or repair of the fine sailing vessels that still grace these islands.

Appendix 1
Fitting out at Hobart Town
April to July 1836

Please note that the logs in these appendices have been edited to remove entries that record no activity or nothing of significant interest

List of articles received on board the *Prince of Denmark* between 25 April and 30 May 1836.

25 April 1 bag of sugar 117 lbs. from house. 1 ditto biscuits 60 lbs. ditto.

10 May 1 cask pork 284 lbs. from house. 28 lbs. biscuits from house.

18 May 1 coil spun yarn from house 56 lbs. ditto. 1 coil 3 yds. spun yarn. 2 —— from Haig. 2 bolts repaired by Morill.

19 May 1 bag biscuits 56 lbs. from house.

20 May 4 iron bolts repaired by Morill.

21 May 1 gallon Stockholm tar – house. 2 battens for the yard.

22 May 40 lbs. flour from the house. 15 lbs. beef from Bayntous.

24 May 36 lbs. leather ditto.

26 May 5 no. 20ft deals from the house. 36 trunnels Grays. 2 —— house. 11 bolts weighing 21¾ lbs. from Morrill.

27 May 10 lbs. five-inch nails from the house. 1 piece 4in rope 97 lbs.

28 May 8 lbs. ditto. 5 deals 20ft long, 10in by 2in 2 coils 6 thread rattling.

29 May 15 lbs. fresh beef.

30 May 1 bag potatoes 100 lbs. 2 gum planks, 16ft.

Tuesday 26 April First part light winds and cloudy weather. At 8.00 a.m. sent two hands to scrub the ship —— and the rest of the crew clearing away the hold. Opened one cask of pork then headed it up again, the pork being cured. Six hogs, two sows and nine pigs belonging to the sows. Middle and latter part ditto wind and weather from the S.W. Covered up the hogs with staysail and square sail.

Wednesday 27 April First part light winds and heavy weather. The hogs tore the sails very much. At 6.00 a.m. commenced to discharge. Discharged five hides and six tierces of pork. Discharged 40 hogs and 320 coconuts and 240 ditto. Employed one man from the shore James Muligan —— and John Forman. Middle and latter parts light winds and cloudy weather. Wind from S. to S.W.

Thursday 28 April First part fresh breezes and showers of rain. At 6.00 a.m. commenced discharging. Discharged 22 tierces, 14 hides, two half pipes, two quarter ditto. Hoisted the spare sails up to get the air. Middle and latter parts fresh breezes and clear weather. Wind at W.S.W.

Friday 29 April First part fresh breezes and clear weather. At 6.00 a.m. commenced to discharge. Discharged six hides and three half pipes, and two tierces of pork, one tierce of lard and nine small kegs of ditto and 400 coconuts. Middle and latter part ditto wind and weather. The boat got adrift from alongside and was picked up at the other side, the ship brought from the S.W. anchor. Winds from W. to N.W.

Saturday 30 April First part fresh breezes and clear weather. At 6.00 a.m. sent the boat to Cox Bay for the tow the other. At 10.00 a.m. the boat came back. Then began to unbend the sails then stowed them down in the hold. At 2.00 p.m. the Harbour Master came on board and hauled the ship further in shore and moored her with both anchors. Middle and latter parts strong gales and clear weather.

Sunday 1 May First part light wind and pleasant weather. At 7.00 a.m. hoisted the colours. People all paid off from the ship. Middle and latter parts light winds and variable from S.W. to N.W.

Monday 2 May First part light winds and clear weather. At 8.00 a.m. gave the hogs some meat. Discharged 11 kegs of powder to the magazine. Sent the remainder of the trade to Mr. Kelly, being 11 pieces of calico, 11 remnants of ditto, two-dozen of comforters, 131 collars and — —, 56 pieces of prints, 18 pieces of handkerchiefs and three single ditto, 11 runs of coloured calico, 31 shirts. Middle and latter part light wind and clear weather.

Wednesday 4 May First part light winds and variable. Middle part strong breezes from the S.E. Sent one hog on shore to Mr. Kelly's own house. One strange man on board getting his tickets. Latter part light wind and thick cloudy weather inclining to rain.

Thursday 5 May First part fresh breezes and clear weather. Middle part light winds and heavy rain. Took the longboat to her moorings and left her. Got one bundle of straw for the hogs from Mr. Kelly. Latter part light winds and clear weather. Wind at N.W.

10 May Shipped Henry Douglas, John Snedmore, John Forman.

14 May Shipped Joseph Davis.

16 May Shipped Edward Stevens.

17 May Mr. Dawson commenced work aboard the schooner.

20 May Mr. Gray commenced work.

Thursday 26 May The first part of this 24 hours moderate breezes and fine pleasant weather. The people employed rigging sheaves and lifting the foremast for shortening. Two carpenters employed. The latter part ditto weather.

Friday 27 May A.m. light winds and fine weather. People employed tanning in the fore-rigging with sundry other jobs. Two carpenters employed. The middle and latter part ended with light winds and clear.

Saturday 28 May The first part of this 24 hours commenced with fine pleasant weather. People employed variously about the rigging. Two carpenters employed. People signed articles. The latter part ditto weather.

Sunday 29 May The first part calm and fine pleasant weather. An East India Company brig arrived and the *Menafee* from Two Fold Bay with cattle.

Monday 30 May The first part of this 24 hours commenced with fine pleasant weather. The captain joined us this day. People employed lifting the mainmast and shortening 3ft and variously about the rigging. One carpenter employed. The latter part calm and clear.

Wednesday 1 June The first part of this 24 hours commences with light winds and fine weather. People employed variously about the rigging. Four carpenters employed. The middle and latter part ends with light winds and clear.

Thursday 2 June The first part of this 24 hours commenced with moderate breezes and fine weather. Carpenters employed fishing the foremast. Four employed people employed variously about the rigging. The latter part end with light wind and cloudy.

Friday 3 June The first part of this 24 hours commences with light winds and cloudy. People employed variously about the rigging. Four carpenters employed. The middle and latter part ends with light winds and clear.

Saturday 4 June The first part of this 24 hours commences with moderate breezes and fine pleasant weather. People employed about the rigging with sundry other jobs. Four carpenters employed. The middle and latter part ends with light winds.

Wednesday 8 June The first part of this 24 hours commence with strong winds and squalls snow and sleet. People employed variously. No carpenters employed. The latter part ends with cloudy squally weather attended with snow showers.

Thursday 9 June The first part of this 24 hours commences with strong winds and squalls snow and sleet. People employed variously. No carpenters employed. The latter part ends with cloudy squally weather attended with snow showers.

Saturday 11 June The first part of this 24 hours commence with moderate breezes and fine weather. People employed variously about the rigging. Two carpenters employed. The middle and latter part ends with light winds and cloudy.

Monday 13 June The first part of this 24 hours commence with light winds and fine weather. People employed rattling the —— rigging with necessary work. One carpenter employed caulking the ship's side. The latter part ends with light winds and cloudy.

Tuesday 14 June The first part of this 24 hours commence with moderate breezes and hazy weather. People employed rattling the rigging down with sundry other jobs. One carpenter employed. The latter part ends with thick hazy weather.

Wednesday 15 June The first part of this 24 hours commenced with moderate breezes and fine weather. People employed painting and rattling the rigging down. One carpenter employed on board. Shipped two seamen, John Dawson and Robert Eliott. The middle and latter part ends with light winds and clear.

Friday 17 June The first part of this 24 hours commences with moderate breezes and fine weather. People employed as necessary about the rigging. One carpenter employed. The latter part ends with light winds and clear. One ship arrived from England.

Sunday 19 June The first part of this 24 hours commences with light winds and cloudy. People employed unmooring ship and hauled alongside the new wharf, then heaved down. The latter part ditto weather.

Monday 20 June First part of this 24 hours commence with light winds and fine weather. People employed getting all clear for heaving down. One carpenter and labourer employed. The middle and latter part ends with light winds.

Tuesday 21 June The first part of this 24 hours commenced with fresh breezes and fine weather. People employed heaving down. Two carpenters employed repairing the copper. At 5.00 p.m. eased up for the night. The latter part ditto weather.

Wednesday 22 June The first part of this 24 hours commence with moderate breezes and fine weather. People employed heaving down and two carpenters employed repairing the copper. At 5.00 p.m. eased her up for the night. Latter part ditto weather.

Thursday 23 June The first part of this 24 hours commence with light winds and fine weather. People employed heaving down and two carpenters employed and one labourer. The latter part ditto weather.

Friday 24 June The first part of this 24 hours commence with light winds and fine weather. Two carpenters and one labourer employed heaving down and repairing the copper. At 5.00 p.m. eased her up for the night. The latter part fresh breezes and cloudy. John Dawson absent on shore, sick.

Saturday 25 June The first part of this 24 hours commences with moderate breezes and fine weather. People employed heaving down and repairing the copper. Two carpenters. At 4.00 p.m. hauled away from the wharf and made fast to the hulk. The latter part ends with light winds and cloudy.

Tuesday 28 June The first part of this 24 hours commences with light wind and rain. One carpenter employed half a day. People employed mooring ship and getting fore and topsail yard up with sundry other jobs. The latter part ends with light winds and clear.

Wednesday 29 June The first part of this 24 hours commence with fresh breezes and cloudy weather. People employed rattling the topmast rigging down and scraping the ship sides, with sundry other jobs. One carpenter employed. The latter part cloudy squally weather.

Thursday 30 June The first part of this 24 hours commences with moderate breeze and hazy. People employed scraping and painting with sundry other jobs. One carpenter employed. The latter part ends with light winds and hazy weather.

Friday 1 July The first part of this 24 hours commence with fresh breezes and fine weather. People employed scraping and painting with sundry other jobs. One carpenter employed. The latter part ends with light winds and cloudy.

Monday 4 July The first part of this 24 hours commence with light winds and fine weather. People employed painting and blacking the beams with sundry other jobs. One carpenter employed. The latter part ends with light winds and clear.

Tuesday 5 July The first part of this 24 hours commences with moderate breezes and fine weather. People employed getting the sails on board and bending them, with sundry other jobs. The latter part ends with light winds and cloudy. One carpenter employed.

Wednesday 6 July The first part of this 24 hours commences with moderate breezes and fine weather. People employed setting the lower rigging up and bending sails, with other necessary work. The latter part ditto weather.

Saturday 9 July The first part of this 24 hours commence with light winds and fine weather. People employed variously about the ship. Received on board one anchor. The latter part ditto weather.

Monday 11 July The first part of this 24 hours commences with moderate breezes and fine weather. People employed getting three casks of water from the shore and one boatload of ballast with sundry other jobs. Shipped steward / carpenter. The latter part ditto weather.

Tuesday 12 July The first part of this 24 hours people employed variously. Received on board nine casks of water. The ship *Eagerly* arrived from England this day. The latter part ends with light wind and clear.

Wednesday 13 July The first part of this 24 hours commences with moderate breezes and fine weather. People employed taking in 19 empty oil casks and three casks of beef and two ditto of pork with sundry other jobs. The latter part ditto weather.

Thursday 14 July The first part of this 24 hours commences with light winds and mostly fine weather. Employed taking in 21 empty oil casks with sundry other jobs. The latter part ends with light winds and cloudy.

Friday 15 July The first part of this 24 hours commences with light winds and fine weather. People employed taking in one boatload of ballast and stowing the hold. At 3.00 p.m. unmoored ship and came to in the stream ready for sailing. The latter part ditto weather.

Saturday 16 July The first part of this 24 hours commences with light winds and fine weather. People employed taking in ten empty oil casks with sundry other jobs. Douglas absent from duty. The latter part ends with light winds.

Tuesday 19 July The first part of this 24 hours commenced with cloudy squally weather with snow and sleet. People employed variously. One seaman shipped, Edward Dunn[?]. The latter part ditto weather.

Wednesday 20 July The first part of this 24 hours commences with moderate breeze and fine. People employed getting stores on board and making all clear for sailing. Shipped steward / carpenter. The latter part ends with light winds and cloudy.

Thursday 21 July A.m. moderate breezes and fine weather. At 10.00 weighed anchor and made sail from Sullivan's Cove, the wind from the N.N.W. Captain Kelly on board. Sent Robert Eliott on shore at his own request in consequence of his being badly of the —— and unable to work and fill his duty, which state he has been in for the last ten days. At 6.30 p.m. came to off Captain Kelly's farm in 9 fathoms of water with 80 fathoms of chain. Iron Pot Light bearing E.N.E. The latter part light wind with mizley rain.

Friday 22 July The first part of this 24 hours commenced with moderate breezes and cloudy. People employed getting on board from the farm 21 bags of potatoes, one bag of turnips and three live sheep, two pigs and 12 fowls. The latter part light winds and cloudy.

June 22 1836 Stores received on board: 20 sheets copper and 40 lbs. nails, one iron plate and nails, 8 lbs. of nails.

25 June One cask of pork, 6 lbs. of copper nails, 30 lbs. potatoes, 17 lbs. of fresh meat.

27 June 28 lbs. of flour, 8 lbs. of sugar.

29 June 46 lbs. of bread, 5 lbs. of tea, 2 gall. paint oil, 5½ lbs. of mutton.

30 June 30 lbs. of potatoes, 5 lbs. of nails.

1 July 1 bottle of spirits turpentine, 6 lbs. mutton.

5 July 1no. 13-inch double block

6 July 2no. 12-inch single blocks, 2no. 10-inch double, 3no. 9-inch double, 7no. 9-inch single, one coil 1½-inch rope, one ditto 2¾-inch, one ditto 2¾-inch, one ditto 2-inch, 14 lbs. meat.

7 July 44 lbs. of spun yarn, 4 lbs. of seaming twine, 2 ditto of roping twine.

8 July One chest of tea.

9 July One bag of sugar 161 lbs., one bag bread 60 lbs., 30 lbs. of flour, 16 lbs. of beef.

11 July Six tumblers, six wine glasses, three tin dishes, six table spoons, six tea spoons, 30 lbs. of potatoes, 3no. 15ft oars, 6no. 16ft oars, 3no. 17ft oars, 2no. 22ft oars, 1no. 21ft oar, one coil rope 2½-inch, two boat's masts, three-dozen ale, four tin pots and four pannikins, one tureen and ladle, one glass lamp, five bags of flour 660 lbs., 12 bags bread 919 lbs., one-dozen of brandy, four bottles of mustard, fouir knives and forks, four bars of soap, two bottles of pickles, one bottle of vinegar, one case wine, three bolts of canvas, two gimlets and nails, four muskets and ——, one bag of flints, 5 lbs. of candles, scrubbing brush, two —— paper, two balls of lamp cotton.

3 June 1836 Stores received on board: 3no. planks 20ft long, 36 lbs. of oakum, 14 bolts 13 lbs.,

¾, 6 lbs. of 7-inch nails from Mr. Stockels, 7 lbs. of 5-inch ditto from the house, one coil of 2½-inch rope, 42 lbs. of pitch, 10½ lbs. of meat for ship use.

5 June 18½ lbs. of meat for ditto, one bolt of no. 3 canvas, one chain plate, 14 bolts, 14¾ lbs., 14 rings.

6 June 44 lbs. of pork, one-dozen trunnels, Grays.

8 June 24 lbs. of spun yarn from Haigs, 28 lbs. of rope, 2¾-inch from Mr. Clark, 12 lbs. of lead from Mr. Haigs, 2 lbs. of copper nails from the house, 7½ lbs. of fresh meat for ship's use.

11 June ¼ cwt. of spun yarn from Haigs, 17 lbs. of meat for ship's use, 56 lbs. of pork, 48 ditto of flour, 4 ditto of tea, one bottle of mustard.

14 June 2 gallons of paint oil, ½ ditto of turpine, 6no. 7-inch blocks, 36 lbs. of rattling from the house, 43 lbs. of pitch, two dead eyes and bands from Mossels[?].

15 June 7¾ lbs. of mutton, 24 lbs. of pork.

16 June One coil of whale line, one piece of wood for the rail.

17 June Received on board one —— of rum, 66 lbs. of biscuits, 40 lbs. of potatoes.

18 June 45 lbs. of pork, 18 lbs. of fresh meat from Mossels[?]

Appendix 2
A Voyage from Hobart Town to Two Fold Bay
July and August 1836

Saturday 23 July The first part of this 24 hours commenced with moderate breezes and dark cloudy weather. At 3.00 a.m. weigh and made sail with the wind from the N.N.E. At noon, abreast of Cape Raoul, off shore 3 or 4 miles. This log contains 12 hours in order to commence the sea log.

Sunday 24 July p.m. calms and fine weather. Abreast of Cape Raoul, offshore 4 or 5 miles. At 6.00 Tasman Island N.E. by N. 4 or 5 miles. At 8.00 ditto strong winds from the N.W. In topgallant sail and first reef the topsail and mainsail and stowed the jib. Cape Pillar N. 5 or 6 miles. At midnight cloudy squally weather. Tacked to the N.N.W. At 4.00 a.m. Tasman island W. by S. Tacked to the E.N.E. At 11.00 ditto strong winds from the N. Running to Fortesque Bay in consequence we could not get to windward. At noon came to on the east of the bay in 7 fathoms of water with 30 fathoms of chain.

Monday 25 July The first part of this 24 hours commences with strong winds with squalls. The sea watch kept with muskets loaded for fear of the prisoners. Employed variously about the ship. The latter part ends with strong winds and cloudy. This log contains 36 hours in order to commence the civil day.

Tuesday 26 July The first part of this 24 hours commences with light and variable winds and fine weather. People employed variously about the ship. At 3.00 p.m. weighed and made sail from Fortesque Bay with the wind from the west. At 8.00 p.m. light winds and hazy weather with rain. The south end of Frederick Hendrick bore W.N.W. 6 or 8 miles. Midnight moderate breezes with rain. Took in fore-topgallant sail.

Wednesday 27 July At 2.00 a.m. Maria Island W.N.W. 10 or 12 miles. Set topgallant sail. At 8.00 a.m. ditto moderate breezes and fine weather. Schouten Island west 5 or 6 leagues. At noon ditto breezes and hazy. Southernmost Schouten island S.W. by S. St. Patrick's Head N.W. by N. distance off shore 18 miles. All possible sail set. Lat obs. 41.57 south.

Thursday 28 July a.m. moderate breezes and hazy. All sail set. At 8.00 a.m. ditto weather. At midnight fresh breezes and cloudy. At 3.00 a.m. a shift of wind from the northward with thunder lightning and heavy rains. In 2nd reef the topsail and double reef the mainsail and stow the jib. At 8.00 a.m. more moderate. Made more sail. At noon cloudy squally weather with a high sea and heavy rains. Latitude obs. 39.45 south.

Friday 29 July p.m. cloudy squally weather with flying showers of rain. In 2nd reef the topsail and reef the foresail and sent the fore-topgallant yard down. At 6.00 p.m. strong gales with a high sea going. Took in the fore-topsail. Midnight cloudy squally weather with heavy rains and a high sea. At 4.00 a.m. ditto weather. Set the topsail. At 9.00 a.m. wore ship to the S.E. At noon dark cloudy weather with constant rain.

Sunday 31 July p.m. cloudy squally weather. Made the Sisters bearing S.W. by W. 12 miles. At 3.00 ditto all hove to the wind on the starboard tack at 4.00 ditto the Northern Sisters S.S.E. 4 miles. At 5.00 ditto the island bearing S. by E. 6 miles. Strong squalls with rain. Took in the fore-topsail and mainsail and laid her to under the gaff foresail. At midnight ditto. At 6.00 a.m. more moderate. Made sail, the Sisters bearing S.E. by S. 4 or 5 leagues. Bore away for Kent groups. At 11.00 a.m. came to in Kents Groups in 6½ fathoms with the two bow anchors with 30 fathoms of chain each way to the S.E. and S.W. John Steward, carpenter down below absent from duty, likewise the two last days. The latter part ends with cloudy squally weather with constant rain. This log contains 36 hours in order to commence the civil day.

Monday 1st August The first part of this 24 hours commences with strong winds and rain. People employed unmooring and mooring ship with sundry other jobs. Carpenter absent from duty. The latter part ends with moderate breezes and rain.

Wednesday 3 August The first part of this 24 hours commences with moderate breezes and fine weather. People employed getting one boatload of ballast from the shore with sundry other jobs. At 4.00 p.m. weigh and made sail from Kents group with the wind from the N.N.E. At 6.00 the island bearing west 5 miles. At 8.00 ditto fresh breezes and cloudy. Tack to the N.W. At 10.30 ditto strong winds with heavy squalls and rain. Close reefed the topsail and single reefed the main and foresails and took in the jib. At midnight ditto.

Thursday 4 August At 4.00 a.m. more moderate. Made more sail. At 8.00 a.m. Kents group S.W. by W. to 5 or 6 leagues. At noon steady breezes with mizzling rain. Set fore-topmast studding sail. The island bearing S.W. 10 leagues. This log contains 12 hours to commence the sea log. Latitude obs. 39.07 south.

Friday 5 August p.m. cloudy squally weather with rain. At 8.00 ditto strong winds with squalls and rain. In main topmast staysail and flying jib. At midnight strong gales with heavy squalls and rain. Took in the fore-topsail and hove to with her head to the S.W. with the single reef foresail. At 6.00 a.m. made Cape Howe bearing S. by E.½E. distance 4 or 5 leagues. Bore away and made sail. At 10 ditto came to 7 or 8 miles to the S.W. of Cape Howe, 1 mile off shore in 7 fathoms of water and Captain Kelly went on shore to look at river and found it to be a very extensive one. At 11.30 a.m. weigh and made sail and steered along the land. At noon steady breezes and fine weather. Green Cape bearing N.N.E. 7 leagues. At 4.00 p.m. gentle breezes running along the land. At 6.00 ditto abreast of Cape Haydock Point. At 10.00 ditto light winds and clear. Came to in Two Fold Bay in 12 fathoms of water. At midnight ditto weather. This log contains 36 hours to commence the civil time.

Saturday 6 August a.m. commences with light winds and fine weather. At 10.00 a.m. ditto weigh and made sail to go in to the cove. At noon came to in 5 fathoms of water with 30 fathoms of chain. The *Lindsay*, the *Merope*, and the *Brougham*, barques laying in the cove and the barque *Thomas Lowery* arrived, whaler. The latter part light winds and clear.

Sunday 7 August The first part of this 24 hours commence with moderate breezes and fine weather. At 10.00 p.m. weigh and made sail from the cove and run over to the south of the bay and brought up in three and a half fathoms water with 30 fathoms of chain. Latter part ends with moderate breeze and rain.

Monday 8 August The first part of this 24 hours commences with light winds and rain. People employed landing 50 oil casks at Mr. S—— and brought three casks of water off from the shore with sundry other jobs. The latter part ends with light winds and cloudy.

Tuesday 9 August The first part of this 24 hours commences with light winds and fine weather. People employed getting two boatloads of ballast and eight —— of beef from Mr. Ranns. At

10.00 weigh and made sail from the south side of the bay and came to in the north side. The latter part ends with light winds and cloudy.

Wednesday 10 August The first part of this 24 hours commence with moderate breeze and fine weather. People employed getting beef and repairing sails and sundry other jobs. The *Brougham* barque sails this day and the *Lindsay* for Hobart Town. The latter part ends with light winds and clear.

Thursday 11 August a.m. moderate breezes and cloudy weather. At 6.30 ditto weigh and made sail from Two Fold Bay with the wind from the south. At 8.00 ditto hove to and lowered the boat down and Captain Kelly went on board the *Thomas Lowery*. At 10.00 a.m. Captain Kelly came on board. At 11.00 abreast of Haydock Point. At noon ditto breezes and fine weather. The barque *Brougham* in sight. This log contains 12 hours in order to commence the sea log.

Friday 12 August p.m. moderate breezes turning to windward the barque *Brougham* in company. At 5.00 ditto Reid Point[?] west 5 leagues. Cape Howe S.S.W.½S. Midnight steady breezes and fine weather. Set fore-topmast studding sail. At 8.00 a.m. ditto breeze and fine weather. Set the square sail. The *Brougham* in sight running. At noon ditto breezes and pleasant weather. All sail set to advantage. Latitude Obs. 38.44 south.

Saturday 13 August Towards Hobart Town. P.m. steady breezes and fine weather. The barque *Brougham* in sight astern. At 8.00 ditto breezes and clear. Midnight dark cloudy weather. At 6.00 a.m. saw the land bearing west. At 8.00 ditto Cape Barren bore W. by N. 6 or 7 leagues. At noon light winds and fine weather. Cape ——land[?] west 5 or 6 leagues. The *Brougham* on the larboard quarter. Latitude obs. 40.56 south.

Sunday 14 August p.m. light winds and fine weather. All sail set to advantage. At 6.00 ditto, St. Patrick's Head S.W.½W., St Helen's W. Midnight moderate breezes and cloudy. Set topmast studding sail starboard side. At 8.00 a.m. gentle breezes and fine pleasant weather. Abreast of the Schoutens, Maria Island S.W. by S.½S. At noon ditto weather. Latitude obs. 42.34 south.

Monday 15 August p.m. fine steady breezes and pleasant weather. The barque *Brougham* —— her courses in the water. Cape Pillar S. by W.½W. 4 leagues. At 8.00 ditto Cape Pillar N. by W. 3 or 4 miles. At midnight abreast of Cape Raoul off shore 6 or 7 miles. At 8.00 a.m. steady breezes turning up Chase[?] Bay in company with the *Brougham*. At noon light airs and calms. Come to in Storm Bay till a breezes spring up. At 2.00 p.m. weigh and made sail. His Majesty's ship and the government schooner passed us. At 8.00 ditto light airs and variable from the S.E. and N. At midnight ditto weather. This log contains 36 hours in order to commence the harbour day.

Tuesday 16 August a.m. commences with moderate breezes and clear. At 3 ditto. Came to in Sullivan's Cove with 25 fathoms of chain. People employed variously about the ship. The latter part ditto.

Monday 22 July 1836 Received from Captain Kelly's Farm: 15cwt. of potatoes, three sheep, one bag of turnips and two boat-loads of firewood and a quantity of hay.

Sent on shore at McRann Stations, 8 August: 40 lbs. sugar, 6 ditto of tea, 4 ditto of tobacco, four bags of flour, 8 lbs. of biscuits, three bags of flour, 399 lbs., 4 cwt. of potatoes, 86 lbs. of biscuits, eight quarters of beef of 942 lbs. received.

Appendix 3

Whaling in Recherche Bay

August to November 1836

Thursday 18 August 1836 The first part of this 24 hours commences with steady breezes and fine weather. People employed in repairs to sails with sundry other jobs. Two ships arrived from England. The latter part ends with light winds and clear.

Monday 22nd August Light breezes and fine weather throughout. People employed getting on board empty casks. Received on board two bags of sugar and a half chest of tea.

Wednesday 24 August At 6.00 a.m. got under weigh and made sail down the river for Recherche Bay. At 2.00 p.m. came to off the farm. Sent two boats to Bull Bay for potatoes. 6.00 p.m. calm. The boats returned.

Thursday 25 August At 4.00 a.m. weigh anchor and drop down the river with the tide. At 4.00 p.m. no wind and flood tide. Came to anchor off Simpson's Point. Midnight calm.

Friday 26 August At 2.00 a.m. light airs from N.N.W. Got under weigh. 4.00 Calm. 8.00 light airs from the westward. Noon abreast Southport. Lowered after a whale. No one got her. Up boats and proceeded on. 5.00 p.m. came to and moored ship in the bay.

Friday 2 September Strong gales and squally throughout. Variously employed on shore. John Mansfield got a whale.

Friday 16 September Lying in Recherche Bay. Light breezes and fine weather. All boats out. Spare hands variously employed. Loose sails.

Sunday 18 September Hard gales for the most part. All boats out and nothing got. Spare hands employed on sundry jobs on shore.

Monday 19 September Hard gales throughout. All boats out. A.m. Chase killed a whale. Sunk outside the reef. Loosed sails to dry.

Tuesday 20 September Moderate breezes and fine weather. P.m. John Smedmore got half a whale with one of Lindsay's boats. Sunk outside the Black Reef.

Wednesday 21 September Moderate breezes and fine. P.m. Chase brought home his whale. Nothing seen today.

Friday 23 September Light winds and fine pleasant weather. Three boats out, one boat cutting-in the half whale and trying-out on shore.

Monday 26 September Commences strong gales and squally with showers of rain. 11.00 a.m. weighed and sailed for town. Noon abreast Southport. At 11.00 p.m. came to with the small bower in Sullivan's Cove. Midnight calm.

Tuesday 27 September a.m. commences light airs and fine weather. People employed loading the vessel with empty casks.

lying in Recherche Bay Wednesday 28 September a.m. strong gales and squally. Finished loading. Received on board from the *Marianne* two boat anchors from Mr. Hewitt, two bundles of coopers flags, 4 lbs. of rivets, one side of beef 269 lbs. from Mr. Hewitt, one coil of line and a quantity of hooping. From the house a bag of sugar 140 lbs. 5.00 p.m. sailed. 11.00 calm. Came to off Brown's River.

Thursday 29 September a.m. commences calm fine weather. 5.00 got under weigh with a light air from S.W. Noon abreast Green Island. P.m. hard gales throughout. Beating down under single reef sails. At 7.30 came to under Partridge Island in 20 fathoms. Midnight moderate and cloudy.

Friday 30 September a.m. light airs from N.E. 5.00 a.m. weighed and made sail. At 11.00 came to in Recherche Bay and moored ship with the —— bowers. P.m. loaded all the casks with other articles from the shore.

Sunday 2 October Moderate breezes and fine weather. Received on board 12 casks of oil. John Mansfield and Chase got a whale each. P.m. all hands towing brought both whales home to the schooner.

Monday 3 October Hard gales throughout with constant rain. No boats out today. Employed cutting-in two whales and boiling-up blubber.

Thursday 6 October Moderate breezes and fine. Three boats out. Finished trying-out. Took in all the oil from the shore.

Saturday 8 October Commences hard gale attended with heavy squalls and hail showers. At daylight unmoored ship. At 8.00 got underway. At 8.30 run aground in a hailstorm on the Denmark Rock. Remained about 10 minutes. Started two tuns of oil. Noon abreast Partridge Island. Blowing excessive hard. P.m. abreast the farm. Hard gales from the northward. Came to off the retreat. Midnight ditto weather.

Sunday 9 October Commences hard gales attended with heavy squalls. Daylight, got underway. Noon, came to off the Battery Point. P.m. hard gales and squally throughout. Lying at single anchor. [Sketch in margin implies one whale got by Roger].

Monday 10 October Hard gales and squally throughout with constant rain. A.m. hauled in alongside the wharf and moored ship. P.m. commenced discharging the oil. George the cook returned to duty.

Tuesday 11 October Strong gales throughout. Employed discharging oil. [Sketch in margin implies 1.5 whales caught by Mansfield and Smedmore].

Wednesday 12 October a.m. finished unloading the oil and hauled off from the wharf. Received on board 15 lbs. fresh beef, 10 lbs. of rivets and bundle of flags. P.m. sailed for Recherche. 7.00 p.m. came to anchor at the back of Southport[?] Latter part strong gales and dark rainy weather.

Sunday 16 October Commences hard gales. 5.00 a.m. more moderate. Got the anchors and made sail. Hard gales. Close reefed the sails. Attended with very heavy squalls. Bore up again seeing no chance of getting down. Noon came to again under Southport[?] with both anchors. P.m. blowing a perfect storm.

Monday 17 October Lying in Recherche Bay. A.m. stormy weather throughout. Sent the boat on shore for water. P.m. more moderate. Hove up the best bower.

Tuesday 18 October a.m. commences calm cloudy weather. 8.00 a.m. a light air from the N.W. Noon abreast the Aileens[?] Wind N.E. 3.00 p.m. came to in Recherche and moored ship with the two bowers. Latter part hard gales from the W.N.W.

Wednesday 19 October Hard gales throughout attended with heavy squalls. Three boats out. One crew getting out bone.

Monday 24 October Fresh breezes and cloudy with passing showers of rain. Unbent the topsail to repair. Three boats out, one crew and spare hands employed cleaning bone.

Tuesday 25 October Moderate breezes and cloudy. All boats out. Myself repairing the topsail.

Wednesday 26 October Moderate breezes and cloudy. A.m. Mr. Chase got a whale. P.m. Mansfield a whale. Got them both home. Myself repairing the topsail and on sundry jobs about the rigging. Received from Petchy vessel, one cask of pork and one bag of sugar. [A note in the margin says: 'Nine whales got today, 15 to 20 seen'].

Thursday 27 October Moderate and fine. Three boats out. Cut-in two whales. Took the blubber on shore and lighted the works. [A note in the margin says: 'Four whales got, 11 seen'].

Friday 28 October Moderate breezes and fine weather. John Mansfield got a whale and half. Remainder of the hands employed trying-out on shore.

Sunday 30 October Moderate breezes and fine weather. People employed as yesterday throughout. Myself on sundry jobs on board.

Wednesday 2 November Light breezes and fine weather. All hands employed in loading the vessel.

Thursday 3 November a.m. moderate breezes and fine. Sent two boats and crews to town. Got all the stores from the fishery. 11.00 sailed for town. Noon abreast of Southport. 8.00 p.m. come to in Sullivan's Cove. Moored ship with warp.

Appendix 4

A Voyage to Portland Bay
November 1836 to March1837

Friday 4 November 1836 a.m. employed getting the vessel alongside the wharf and mooring. P.m. commenced discharging the oil.

Saturday 5 November a.m. finished unloading the vessel. P.m. hauled off from the wharf and moored ship with small bower and hawsers. Six men employed for those away.

Monday 7 November a.m. hard gales and squally weather. P.m. more moderate. Unmoored and sailed for Recherche Bay. At 11.00 p.m. came to in the mouth of the passage. Midnight ditto weather.

Tuesday 8 November Commences with light airs. Inclined to calms. 6.00 a.m. got underway. Noon hard gales. Abreast P—— Island. 2.00 p.m. squally. Came to off ——. *Count Tamar* and *John Pirie* at anchor.

Tuesday 31 January Commences with light winds and fine weather. People employed getting the ballast out. Middle and latter, ditto weather. Received from the store one-quarter cwt. bread.

Wednesday 1 February Throughout all these 24 hours light wind and fine weather. People employed as yesterday. Received from the house 10 lbs. beef.

Thursday 2 February First part of these 24 hours fresh breezes and clear weather. Shipped two men Israel Mazey and Haycorn. At 6.00 p.m. got all the ballast out. Middle and latter part ditto weather. Received from the house 10 lbs. beef.

Friday 3 February Throughout all these 24 hours moderate breeze and clear weather. People employed getting all ready for heaving down. William Fling, absent for two days came to work this morning.

Saturday 4 February First part of these 24 hours fresh breezes and cloudy. Winds variable. Received from the house 30 lbs. sugar, 14 lbs. ——, 54 lbs. bread. People variously employed.

Sunday 5 February Throughout all these 24 hours fresh breezes. Received on Saturday for today 14 lbs. beef.

Monday 6 February First part of these 24 hours fresh breezes and cloudy. People employed variously getting all ready for heaving down. Middle and latter part ditto weather. Winds variable. Received from the house 14 lbs. beef.

Tuesday 7 February Throughout all these 24 hours light winds and moderate weather. Winds from S. to S.E. Received from the house 14 lbs. beef and 117 lbs. potatoes. People employed as yesterday.

Wednesday 8 February Commences with light winds and pleasant weather. Winds variable. Middle and latter part ditto weather. Received from house 14 lbs. beef and 35 lbs. salt ditto.

Thursday 9 February First part of these 24 hours moderate and clear weather. At 6.30 a.m. hove the schooner down and found the false keel hurt a good deal. At 8.00 a.m. eased her up again. People employed getting the fore-topmast down and sundry other jobs. Middle and latter ditto weather. Winds S.E. Shipped John Rowo this morning.

Friday 10 February Throughout all these 24 hours moderate and clear weather. Winds S.E. People employed about the rigging. Discharged Israel Mazey for refusing to do what he was told to do. Received from the house 60 lbs. bread, 32 lbs. salt beef.

Saturday 11 February Throughout all these 24 hours light winds and fine weather. People employed tarring the rigging fore and aft. Received from the shore 3½ gallons tar, 14 lbs. b——.

Sunday 12 February Commences with light winds and variable weather. Winds from S.W. to S.E. Middle and latter ditto weather. An order came from Mr. Kelly to send the Blue Peter and the purchase fall on board the *Eliz. Ann*, which accordingly I did.

Monday 13 February Throughout all these 24 hours light winds and variable. People employed scraping the masts and sundry other jobs. Received from the shore 56 lbs. sacking and 31 lbs. pitch. Two carpenters employed caulking her upper-works. Two-dozen spoke nails.

Tuesday 14 February Throughout these 24 hours light winds and variable. People employed variously. Two carpenters employed caulking the deck and other jobs. Received 35 lbs. salt beef 3 lbs. of tea. Mr. McDougal, the mate, left the ship.

Wednesday 15 February First part these 24 hours strong breezes from the S.W. People employed at sundry jobs. Unshipped the windlass to repair the bitts. Two carpenters employed at sundry jobs. Received on board 3½ lbs. of nails from stock. One bolt 3½ lbs. from Morral.

Thursday 16 February Commences with light airs from the S.E. Two carpenters employed about the windlass and the false keel. Two men absent, John Haycorn and [blank]. Received on board 12 lbs. of fresh beef. Went with three hands to the carpenters yard and towed a stage round to the schooner.

Friday 17 February Commences with fresh breezes from the S.E. At 6.00 a.m. commenced heaving down. Two carpenters at work put a ——- on and caulked the garboard strake. The hands employed pumping. Shipped Thomas Burges as chief mate, John Wilkins, seaman. Received 30 lbs. of bread. At 6.00 p.m. eased the ship up again. Latter part ditto wind and weather. Discharged John Welsh.

Saturday 18 February Commences with light airs and clear weather. At 6.00 a.m. commenced heaving down. Two carpenters employed coppering the keel. Received 15 lbs. of fresh beef, 30 lbs. of sugar. At 5.00 p.m. eased the ship up and unrove one of the falls. Latter part ditto wind and weather.

Monday 20 February Commenced with calms and clear weather. At 7.00 a.m. hove the schooner down. Two carpenters employed in caulking the topsides. Received 35 lbs. salt beef. At 11.00 a.m. eased the ship up. Thomas Burgess, John Wilkin, Thomas Charlton signed articles this day. The latter parts light winds from the E.S.E.

Tuesday 21 February Commenced with light breezes. Two carpenters employed in caulking the decks. People employed in shifting the sheers. Shipped James Harvey. The latter parts small rain and light winds.

Wednesday 22 February First part of these 24 hours light winds and fine weather. At 9.00 a.m. canted the ship round for heaving down. Received 14 lbs. fresh beef. Two carpenters employed in caulking the decks. At 5.00 p.m. set up the main rigging. Latter part of this 24 hours strong winds from the S.E.

Thursday 23 February Commenced with light air and clear weather. At 6.00 a.m. hove the ship down. Two carpenters employed coppering the keel. People employed pumping ship. Received 30 lbs. bread, 30 lbs. salt beef, 6 lbs. tea, 25 lbs. potatoes. At 3.00 p.m. eased the ship up. Latter parts strong breezes from N.N.W. and clear weather.

Friday 24 February Commenced with strong breezes and variable. At 6.00 a.m. hove the ship down. Two carpenters employed about various jobs. At 9.00 a.m. eased the ship up. People employed unrigging the sheers and getting up the fore-topmast and fore-topsail yard. Shipped Stilman White. The latter part of this 24 hours light winds and fine weather.

Saturday 25 February Throughout all these 24 hours strong winds from W.N.W. and cloudy weather. Two carpenters employed in coppering the rudder and repairing the windlass. People employed in getting the ballast on board. Shipped James Chumpy. Received on board two knives, two pine planks 17ft, ten bolts for windlass 30 lbs, 6 lbs. copper nails, 1,000 bricks and 16 lbs. fresh beef. Casks one 300, two 260, one 210.

Sunday 26 February Commences with strong breezes from W.S.W. At 8.00 a.m. hoist the ensign. Middle and latter parts ditto weather. Received 75 lbs. bread, one bag potatoes.

Monday 27 February Commence with light winds. Two carpenters employed in caulking the decks. People employed in getting on board the ballast. Shipped Phillip Haines, Thomas Blake, James Vallaley. Received 68 lbs. salt beef, a fresh cask and 24 lbs. fresh beef. 3.00 p.m. got up the fore-topgallant mast and topgallant yard. Latter parts ditto weather.

Tuesday 28 February Commence with light winds and fine weather. Two carpenters employed in caulking the decks and lining the windlass. People employed in getting on board the cargo. Stilman White absent without leave half a day. Latter part winds from E.S.E.

Wednesday 1 March Commence with light winds from west and clear weather. Middle part strong winds from S.W. and small rain. Two carpenters employed in caulking the decks and repairing the windlass. People employed as yesterday. Discharged Stilman White for being absent without leave. Received 20 lbs. sugar. Latter parts ditto weather.

Thursday 2 March Commenced with light winds from W.N.W. and clear weather. Two carpenters employed in caulking the decks and other jobs. People employed in bending the sails and stowing the cargo. Discharged Phillip Haines for being absent without leave. Received 30 lbs. salt beef. Latter parts ditto weather.

Friday 3 March Commence with light air of winds from N.W. and clear weather. Two carpenters employed in repairing the boat and other jobs. People employed in stowing the cargo. Shipped Stilman White again this morning. Latter parts strong breezes from E.S.E. and fine weather.

Saturday 4 March Commence with light winds and variable. Two carpenters employed in repairing the boat and other jobs. At 4.00 p.m. haul the ship from the wharf to her anchor. Latter parts ditto weather.

Tuesday 7 March Commence with light winds and clear weather. At 7.00 a.m. loose sails to dry. People employed at sundry jobs. At 10.00 a.m. furled the topsail and topgallant sail. At 4.00 p.m. got under way and stood off and on. At 6.30 p.m. came to anchor and furled sails. Latter parts of the 24 hours clear weather.

Wednesday 8 March Commenced with light airs of winds from the N.W. and clear weather. At 9.00 a.m. got under way. Took the pilot on board. At 2.00 p.m. sent the boat on shore to Mr. Kelly's farm and received five bags of potatoes and six sheep. At 7.00 p.m. came to anchor. Latter part calms and clear weather. Killed one sheep 36 lbs.

Thursday 9 March A light rain. Winds from N. Shortened in cable and loosed sails. At 6.00 a.m. weighed anchor. Passed Partridge Island at 12 ——.

Friday 10 March Fine breezes and clear weather. At 5.00 p.m. passed Recherche Bay. At 7.00 p.m. the South Cape bore north distance 4 miles. The Mewstone bore S.W. by W. At 9.30

p.m. the Mewstone bore N.N.W. distance 3 miles. At midnight light airs and clear weather. 2.00 a.m. took the square sail in and set the foresail. At 7.00 a.m. the South Cape bore E. by N. distance 6 leagues. At 9.00 a.m. South Cape bore E. distance 8 leagues. Light winds and clear weather. At —— a.m. course N.W. by N. Latitude obs. 43.16 south.

Saturday 11 March Commence with light wind and —— weather. At 2.00 p.m. the wind shifted round to the N.W. At 8.00 p.m. tacked the ship. Took in the fore-topgallant sail. At midnight the wind shifted to the west and cloudy. At 12.00 a.m. pumped ship. At 4.00 a.m. light winds and dark cloudy weather inclining to rain. At 6.30 a.m. took in the foresail. At 8.30 tacked ship and set the fore-topgallant sail. At —— a.m. tacked the ship and stood off. At 11.00 a.m. Rocky Point bore N.E. by N. distance 10 miles. At noon light and hazy weather with —— at times. Killed one sheep 30 lbs. Latitude ob. 43.10 south.

Sunday 12 March Commence with light winds and clear weather. At 4.00 p.m. pump ship. At 6.00 p.m. tacked ship, fresh breezes. At midnight tacked ship, fresh breezes. At 4.00 a.m. tacked ship. At 7.00 a.m. freed[?] ship. Looking wild like. Point Hibbs bore N.E. by E. distance 4 leagues. At 9.00 a.m. took a reef in the topsail and mainsail and stowed the flying jib. At 10.00 a.m. Point Hibbs bore E.N.E. Strong breezes from N.N.W. and cloudy weather. Killed one sheep 34 lbs. Latitude ob. 42.50.

Monday 13 March First part strong gales and ——. At 3.00 p.m. the wind shifted round to the west with heavy rain. Tacked ship at 5.30 p.m. Let one reef out of the topsail and set the topgallant sail. At 8.00 p.m. light winds and heavy rains. At 11.30 a.m. took a reef in the topsail and stowed the flying jib. Rain and squally weather. At 4.00 p.m. strong breezes and squally attended with rain. At 8.00 a.m. pumped ship. At 10.00 a.m. set the square sail. Strong breezes with a heavy cross-sea running. Killed one sheep 30 lbs. Latitude obs. 41.29.

Tuesday 14 March Commence with strong breezes and a heavy sea. At 3.30 p.m. set a reef topsail and set the topgallant sail. Took in the square sail and pump ship. At 6.00 p.m. heavy squalls. At 8.00 p.m. fresh breezes and squally. Pump ship. At 10.00 p.m. set the square sail. At 4.00 a.m. fine breezes and clear weather. At 12.00 took the reef out of the mainsail. Killed one sheep 30 lbs. Lat. obs. 39.7 south.

Wednesday 15 March Commence with fresh breezes and squally weather. At 6.00 p.m. pump ship. At midnight light winds and clear weather. At 5.00 a.m. let a reef out of the topsail and set the topgallant sail and flying jib and kept ——west. At noon fresh breezes and cloudy weather. At 8.00 a.m. found we had overrun our distance. Lat obs. 38.27. Hauled the ship in by the wind. It being so hazy could not see the land. Thought it was the Barwons. By standing inshore found it to be Cape Bridgewater. Strong breezes and thick showers of rain. Could only see the land at times.

Thursday 16 March Commence with fresh breezes. At 1.30 p.m. tacked ship and stood off. At 4.00 p.m. tacked ship. At 7.00 p.m. Cape Bridgewater bearing east, distance 7 miles. At 8.00 p.m. pump ship. Fresh breezes inclining to rain. At 2.00 p.m. tacked ship. At 9.00 p.m. tacked ship. Light winds and small rain. Killed one sheep 30 lbs. This log contains 36 hours to commence the harbour log. At 4.00 p.m. came to anchor in Portland Bay. Hoisted out three boats and sent them on shore.

Friday 17 March Commenced with fresh breezes and thick weather. People employed in discharging the cargo. Latter parts ditto weather. This log contains 12 hours.

Monday 20 March Commence with strong breezes and thick weather. People employed in getting on board the ballast and setting up the rigging. Latter parts ditto weather.

Wednesday 22 March Commence with strong breezes. At 2.00 p.m. hoist the boat in and hove up one anchor. At 6.00 p.m. got underway. Lances Point bearing N.N.W. distance 4 miles. Midnight moderate breezes and clear weather. At 8.00 a.m. strong breezes and cloudy. At 10.00 set the square sail. Fresh breezes and squally with rain. At 11.00 strong gales and heavy squalls. Took in the mainsail. At noon fresh breezes and clear weather. Latitude obs. 40.31.

Thursday 23 March Commence with strong breezes and squally. At 1.00 p.m. took in the square sail and one reef in the mainsail and set it, the wind inclining to draw forward. At 8.00 p.m. pumped ship. At midnight strong breezes and cloudy inclining to showers at times. At 4.00 clear weather. At 8.00 pleasant breezes. Set the square sail. At noon light breezes and hazy, inclining to rain. Latitude obs. 40.00 south.

Friday 24 March Commence with fresh breezes. Rainy weather. 6.00 p.m. squally with rain. At 8.00 p.m. light winds and clear weather. Midnight light winds and squally with rain. At 6.00 a.m. set the square sail and made the land bearing N.E. At 8.00 a.m. set the topmast studding sail and pumped ship. At 9.30 the Mewstone bore north distance 4 miles. At 1.30 p.m. took the pilot on board. At 2.00 p.m. the pilot went on shore. At 8.00 p.m. came to anchor. This log contains 36 hours to commence the harbour log. Expended 2½ yds. canvas for draw bucket.

Saturday 25 March Commence with strong gales and heavy squalls with rain. At 4.00 a.m. tried to get the anchor and could not. At 8.00 a.m. hove up the anchor and got under way. At 12.30 took the pilot on board. At 1.00 p.m. came to anchor in Hobart Town. The latter part of this 24 hours ditto weather with heavy rain.

Sunday 26 March Commence with strong breezes and easy weather. At 6.00 a.m. washed the deck and pumped ship. At 8.00 a.m. hoisted the ensign and burgee. Latter parts strong breezes inclining to rain. Log Stilman White for being absent without leave 36 hours.

Monday 27 March The first of this 24 hours strong breezes from N.E. and moderate weather. At 6.00 a.m. washed the deck and pumped ship. At 7.00 a.m. loosed the sails to dry. People employed about sundry jobs. At 10.00 stowed the sails. Received 10 lbs. fresh beef. Expended 17 yds. canvas for repairing the mainsail. Latter part light winds and fine weather.

Thursday 30 March Commence with light breezes and clear weather. At 10.00 a.m. loosed the sails to dry. Received 15 lbs. fresh beef. Expended 5 yds. of canvas and one skein of twine repairing topgallant sail. At 3.00 p.m. stowed the sails. Latter parts ditto weather.

Friday 31 March Commence with calms and fine weather. People employed in repairing the topgallant sail and rigging. Received two boats on board and hoist them up. Middle and latter parts light winds from E.S.E. and clear weather.

24 February Received on board 20 sheets of copper, two pump boxes and one repaired, one sheave, four dogs, six bolts from the blacksmith.

25 February Received two knives, two pine planks 17ft, ten bolts 30 lbs. for the windlass, 6 lbs. copper nails, 1,000 bricks ——.

28 February Received one pine plank 25ft for lining the windlass

1 March Received 14 bundles of iron hooping

2 March Two Wilton planks and 100 spike nails. Two try-pots, 6 lbs. 3-inch nails, ½ lb. copper ditto, one coil of —— rope, 56 lbs. of oakum.

4 March Received 12 skeins twine, one bolt of no. 5 canvas, four bags sugar 522 lbs., six bags bread 30 lbs. each, three bags flour 150 lbs. each, two chests tea, one coil whale line[?], one cask beef, one ditto pork, one coil ratline line, six bolts for the clamps of the windlass.

6 March 20 lbs. fresh beef, 13 ——, one boat hook, two boat sails, one coil lance line, five bundles iron hooping, one grinding stone, 12 lances, two boat's anchors, three iron pots, two drawing knives, two saws, two ——, one bag nails, two knee bolts, five boards.

List of articles received on board the *Prince of Denmark*

1 February ¼ cwt. of bread.

2 February 10 lbs. fresh beef.

3 February 10 lbs. ditto.

5 February 14 lbs. ditto, 30 lbs. sugar, 54 lbs. bread.

6 February 14 lbs. ditto.

7 February 14 lbs. ditto.

8 February 14 lbs. ditto, 115 lbs. potatoes.

9 February 14 lbs. ditto, 35 lbs. salt beef.

10 February 32 lbs. salt beef and 60 lbs. bread.

11 February 14 lbs. of fresh beef.

14 February 35 lbs. of salt beef and 3 lbs. of tea.

17 February 30 lbs. of bread.

18 February 15 lbs. of fresh beef and 30 lbs. of sugar.

20 February 35 lbs. of salt beef.

22 February 14 lbs. of fresh beef.

23 February 30 lbs. of bread, 30 lbs. salt beef, 6 lbs. tea, 25 lbs. potatoes.

25 February 16 lbs. fresh beef.

26 February 75 lbs. bread, one bag potatoes.

27 February 68 lbs. salt beef, a fresh cask and 24 fresh ——.

1 March 20 lbs. sugar.

2 March 30 lbs. salt beef.

4 March one bag potatoes, 20 lbs. fresh beef.

List of stores received on board

March 1 Six casks of beef, four casks of pork, flour no. 5 – 532 lbs., flour no. 4 – 500 lbs., flour no. 6 – 476 lbs., bread no. 2 – 507 lbs., bread no. 1 – 400 lbs., bread no. 7 – 519 lbs., bread no. 3 – 412 lbs.

March 6 Received six tumblers, six cups and saucers, 12 plates, 6 lbs. candles, 3 lbs. gunpowder, two candle sticks, six knives and forks, five balls cotton, 6 lbs. pepper, 1 lb. ——, two hammers, six tea spoons, six table spoons.

Appendix 5

A Voyage from Hobart Town to Launceston

June to August 1837

Saturday 3 June 1837 At 10.00 p.m. weighed and proceeded down the river. Light variable winds. Midnight calm and cloudy weather. At 4.00 a.m. squally from the S.W. with rain. At 10.30 a.m. tacked ship to S.E. Light breezes S.W. Stowed the anchors. Pumped ship every 24 hours.

Sunday 4 June At 12.30 p.m. Cape Raoul E. by N. 12 miles. Strong gales with rain. Stowed the jib, took two reefs in the fore-topsail, foresail and mainsail. A heavy cross-sea and the ship labouring, occasions her to be pumped every hour from this time. At 4.00 p.m. Cape Pillar N. 5 miles. At 5.20 the Hippolite Rock N.W. 8 miles. Strong gales and a heavy cross-sea, the vessel shipping much water. Stowed the mainsail. Midnight ditto weather. At 7.30 a.m. St. Patrick's Head N.W. 25 miles. More moderate. Set the mainsail single reef. Set the square sail, and one reef out of the topsail. At 12 out all reefs. Light winds clear weather. Pumped ship every hour.

Monday 5 June Forepart calm and clear weather. At 4.00 p.m. light airs. St. Patrick's Head S.W.½W. 12 miles and Eddystone Point N.W. by W. 18 miles. Midnight calm and clear weather. At 10.00 a.m. light airs. All sail set. At 12.00 took in the square sail. Light breezes. Pumped ship every hour.

Tuesday 6 June At 12.30 tacked ship to S.S.W. Fresh breezes and clear weather. At 4.00 tacked to the N.N.W. At 4.35 King George's Rocks N.W. 15 miles. Fresh breezes and clear weather. Midnight fresh breezes and hazy. Cone Point N. by E. 6 miles. Took one reef in the mainsail and topsail and stowed the topgallant sail and jib. Tacked ship every hour during the night. At 6.30 a.m. made sail. At 12.00 Black Reef S. by E. 5 miles. Swan Island bore W. by S. 2 miles. Pumped ship every hour.

Wednesday 7 June At 2.00 p.m. tacked ship to the S.W. At 3.30 tacked to the ——. At 4.32 Lookout Rock N.W.½W. 6 miles and Ringaroomah Point S.W.½W. 9 miles. Tacked ship every two hours during the night. Midnight stowed the jib and topgallant sail. Fore-topsail tie gave way. Cloudy with rain. At 9.00 a.m. stood close in under Waterhouse Island. Took two reefs in the foresail, mainsail and topsail. Down topgallant yard. Foggy with rain. Tacked to northward. Strong gales and a heavy sea from the westward. Pumped ship every hour.

Thursday 8 June Fore part strong gales and cloudy with rain. At 2.00 p.m. tacked to the S.W. At 5.15 north point of Waterhouse Island E. by N. 5 miles. Tacked to the northward. Tacked ship every two hours during the night. Midnight squally with rain. At 7.33 more moderate. Set the jib and one reef out of all sails. At 9.30 tacked ship to the northward. Ninth Island S.W. 1 mile. Pumped ship hourly.

Friday 9 June 1837 Forepart fresh breezes and hazy. At 5.30 p.m. Tenth Island E. by S. 4 miles. At 6.30 tacked ship. Fresh breezes, foggy with rain. Stowed the outer jib. Light S.S.E. 8 miles. At 8.00 p.m. strong gales, squally with rain and a heavy sea setting in upon the land. Close reefed the topsail, foresail and mainsail. Ship labouring and making an increase of water occasions one pump to be constantly worked. The light not visible. At 10.00 p.m. wore ship. At 11.30 wore ship. At 1.30 a.m. wore ship. Strong gales, very heavy squalls, rain and foggy. At 7.00 a.m. wore ship. At 8.00 a.m. in a heavy squall the standing jib blew from the boltrope, the topsail sheet parted and the sail parted from the footrope. Set the forestaysail and outer jib until topsail sheet was bent, set the topsail, the outer jib shattered in a squall. Stowed the remnant of the sail. At 12.00 wore ship. Ditto weather. Pumped ship constantly.

Saturday 10 June First two hours the same weather. At 2.00 p.m. the gale broke suddenly falling nearly calm. A heavy sea struck the vessel abaft, knocking away both the after quarter davits. At 2.30 p.m. strong gales, squally, with rain and hail alternately. Wore ship. At 4.45 p.m. Tenth Island bore southwest three miles. Wore ship. At 11.15 p.m. stowed the topsail, fore staysail and mainsail and hove-to under the reefed foresail. Strong gales with very heavy squalls, rain and foggy. Midnight wore ship. The same weather throughout the day and pumped ship hourly.

Sunday 11 June These 24 hours commence with the same weather. Vessel still hove to. At 6.00 wore ship to the N.W. Midnight wore ship to the southward. At 11.45 Waterhouse Island S.S.W. 5 miles. Set the mainsail, topsail and forestaysail and bore up for the Island of Preservation. Ditto weather. Pump ship hourly.

Monday 12 June Commence with strong gales, with rain and heavy squalls. At 3.15 anchored with the small bower in Hamilton Roads in 4 fathoms water, 60 fathoms chain. Midnight ditto weather. People employed repairing sails *etc*. The same weather throughout the day. Pumped ship hourly.

Wednesday 14 June Commenced with strong gales. People employed as necessary. Midnight more moderate. At 7.00 a.m. light airs from the N.E. Weighed and proceeded to sea. Ditto weather. Hazy. Up topgallant yard. Pumped ship every two hours.

Thursday 15 June Commences with light winds and hazy. Chapell Island N.E. by N. 6 leagues. Saw a brig standing to N.W. Midnight light winds and cloudy. At 3.00 a.m. thick foggy weather. Hauled off the land to N.W. At 5.00 a.m. tacked to the S.S.E. At 7.15 Stony Head S.S.E. 15 miles. Bore up for the Heads. At 10.00 Mr. Hunter came on board as pilot. The lighthouse E.S.E. a quarter mile. Light winds and cloudy. At 11.00 the harbour master from George Town came on board. At 12.00 anchored below Garden Island. Calm with rain.

Friday 16 June At 3.00 p.m. weighed and made sail up the river. Light winds N.W. At 9.15 anchored in Long Reach. Calm with rains. At 8.00 a.m. weighed and proceeded up the river. At 10.30 anchored in the Little Devil's Elbow below Whirlpool Reach. 15 fathoms water. 45 fathoms chain. Light winds easterly.

Saturday 17 June At 4.00 p.m. weighed and sailed. Fresh breezes N.W. At 7.30 anchored in 5 fathoms in Coulson's Reach. Foggy with rain. Midnight squally with rain. At 7.15 weighed and at 7.30 took the mud. Run lines across the river and hauled off. At 10.00 light airs N.W. At 12.00 the vessel ran on the mud in Monty's Reach. Fresh winds and rainy weather. Run the kedge out to haul off but found it useless.

Sunday 18 June At 2.00 p.m. the harbour master's boat came on board with five men to assist in getting the vessel up the river. Rain throughout the day. Midnight high water hove the vessel off with a kedge and anchored for the tide. At 7.00 a.m. weighed and proceeded up the river. At 12.00 anchored in Ti Tree Reach.

Monday 19 June 1837 Fore part light winds variable and foggy. Midnight ditto weather. At

10.00 a.m. weighed and proceeded over the bar with the assistance of the harbour master. Received on board 2 gallons of ——. Noted a protest.

Tuesday 20 June At 2.00 p.m. hauled alongside the wharf and moored ship. Strong southerly winds. Midnight calm and foggy. Employed discharging the cargo. Fresh southerly winds.

Thursday 22nd June Employed discharging the cargo. Carpenter employed caulking the counter. Unshipped the rudder, observing the main—— splintered.

Friday 23 June Employed discharging the cargo. Carpenter employed caulking the bows and fore scuttle.

Monday 26 June Employed cleaning the hold. Carpenter employed caulking, and repairing the rudder.

In the River Tamar. Tuesday 27 June 1837 Received on board 30 hogsheads ale and 117 bullock hides. Meat 12 lbs. Light westerly winds.

Friday 30 June Employed as yesterday. Ditto weather. John Blandford confined to his bed unwell. Employed two labourers.

Saturday 1 July Employed as yesterday. Discharged Thomas Phillips unwell. Two labourers employed. John Blandford unwell. Meat 39 lbs.

Monday 3 July Hauled off from the wharf. Shipped the rudder. Received on board one bag sugar, a quarter chest of tea. Shipped John Lawrence, cook.

Tuesday 4 July At 2.00 p.m. the pilot came on board and hauled the vessel over the bar. Strong winds N.W. Moored ship near ——. At 11.00 a.m. weighed and towed down to Pig Island.

Wednesday 5 July At 7.00 a.m. weighed and towed down to Fresh Water Point.

Thursday 6 July Heavy rain. At 2.30 p.m. weighed and proceeded down the river. At 6.00 p.m. anchored off Stony Creek. Fresh breezes N.E. Rain throughout the night. At 7.00 a.m. weighed and proceeded as far as Spring Bay. Squally with rain. Anchored in 6 fathoms. 35 fathoms chain.

Friday 7 July Commences with strong gales. N.E. heavy squalls with rain, hail, thunder and lightning. At 1.30 very heavy squalls with rain. Drove about 2 miles. Veered cable to 60 fathoms in 3 fathoms water. Midnight strong gales N.N.E. Heavy rain. At 7.00 a.m. more moderate. Weighed and worked down to Mary Anne's Creek in Whirlpool reach. At 11.30 moored ship.

Saturday 8 July Commenced with fresh breezes N.W. At 3.35 p.m. weighed and at 7.30 anchored below Middle Island in 6 fathoms. 35 fathoms chain. Midnight squally with rain. At 7.00 a.m. weighed. At 9.30 came to in Kelso Bay. Squally with snow and sleet. Rain. At 11.00 pilot went ashore. A heavy sea breaking across the harbour. John Blandford off duty.

Sunday 9 July Commences with strong gales, snow, sleet and rain. Wind W.S.W. At 5.00 p.m. calm. At 7.00 fresh breezes. At 7.30 p.m. pilot came on board. Weighed and proceeded to sea. Strong winds west and a heavy sea. At 9.30 am pilot left the ship. Lighthouse E.S.E.½ ——. At 10.50 Tenth Island S.E. 4 miles. Strong gales and heavy sea. All sail set.

Monday 10 July Commences with fresh gales and clear weather. At 1.00 p.m. Ninth Island S.E. 4 miles. At 3.10 Waterhouse Island S.E. by E. 3 miles. Saw a brig riding under the island. At 5.00 Swan Island S.E. by S. 8 miles. Midnight light wind clear weather. Cape St. Helens S.W. 8 miles. At 8.00 a.m. strong breezes. In topgallant sail. Tacked to the N.W. Cape Lodi W.S.W. 25 miles. John Blandford off duty.

Tuesday 11 July Light breezes and clear. Set topgallant sail. At 1.30 tacked to the southward. At 3.30 p.m. set square sail. At 5.00 Cape Tourville S.W.½W. 25 miles. Midnight fresh breezes and clear. Coxcomb head W.N.W. 9 miles. At 4.00 Cape Peron W.N.W. 7 miles. At 6.30

Hippolite Rock W. 4 miles. At 8.15 Cape Pillar W. 3 miles. At 10.30 Cape Raoul W.N.W. 5 miles. At 12.00 tacked to the northward.

Wednesday 12 July At 3.00 p.m. Cape Frederick Henry S.W. 2 miles. Light winds, Tacked ship occasionally. At 9.30 p.m. light winds with rain. At 11.35 Iron Pot Light N.E. 2 miles. At 2.35 a.m. anchored in Sullivan's Cove.

Thursday 13 July At 2.00 p.m. weighed and hauled alongside the wharf. At 4.00 Mr. Pitt, harbour master came on board. Midnight fresh breezes N.W. At 7.00 a.m. employed discharging cargo *etc*. The barque *Perthshire* carried away the main boom.

Friday 14 July Employed discharging cargo *etc*. Two men employed from Mr. Kelly's.

Saturday 15 July Employed discharging cargo *etc*. Two men employed from Mr. Kelly's yard. Meat 29 lbs.

Tuesday 18 July Employed discharging cargo, clearing the hold *etc*. At 6.00 p.m. Mr. William Fletcher, mate of the vessel, fell overboard from the starboard gangway and was drowned. At 8.00 p.m. picked up the body. 14 lbs. meat.

Wednesday 19 July Employed taking in casks, filling water *etc*. Discharged John Lawrence. Cook shipped, Thomas East. Received one bag potatoes, meat 13 lbs. John Blandford off duty.

Thursday 20 July Employed taking on board casks. Fully watered. Carpenters Jeffreys and Hebden employed fitting quarter davits *etc*. Received from Mr. Stokett[?] 4 lbs. 5-inch spikes, 2 lbs. 3-inch nails. 12 lbs. meat. Four bolts repaired. Ten rings, six forelocks from Morell. John Blandford off duty.

Friday 21 July Employed taking in casks. Received one skimmer, 14 lbs. meat. John Blandford ashore.

Saturday 22 July Employed taking in casks, stores *etc*. 12 lbs. meat, five casks pork, three and two-thirds casks beef, six bags sugar, three bundles cooper's flags. John Blandford off duty.

Monday 24 July John Blandford returned to duty. William Woodman commenced work. Shipped John Garland, seaman. Received on board ten half pipes, 20 bags potatoes, three ditto bread, eight ditto flour, 28 lbs. meat, five bundles hoops, one coil 1½-inch rope.

Tuesday 25 July At 5.00 p.m. unmoored and hauled off from the wharf. Midnight strong gales westerly. Veered out 70 fathoms small bower chain and let go best bower with 30 fathoms. At 9.00 a.m. more moderate. Weighed the best bower.

Wednesday 26 July Received 20 lbs. rivets, six bottles mustard, three bales cotton. At 3.00 p.m. squally. Weighed and sailed out in the stream. At 5.00 anchored in 14 fathoms. Squally with rain. At 9.00 a.m. weighed and sailed down the river. Fresh breezes, squally S.W. At 11.00 entered the passage.

Thursday 27 July Commences with squalls. Wind variable. Calm. At 6.35 p.m. anchored in 5 fathoms near the flats. At midnight squally. At 6.00 a.m. weighed. Fresh breezes S.W. At 8.00 passed the barque *William the Fourth*. At 9.00 squally.

Friday 28 July Commences with strong gales. At 2.00 p.m. split fore-topgallant sail. Martingale bolt broke. Lost the martingale. At 4.00 p.m. anchored under Partridge Island 12 fathoms water, in company with the *Royal William*. At midnight ditto weather. At 5.00 a.m. weighed and made sail. Light air, northerly.

Saturday 29 July Commenced light winds variable. At 4.00 p.m. anchored in Recherche Bay. Moored east and west in 5 fathoms of water. 60 fathoms of chain with bower anchors. Sent down topgallant yard and mast. At 9.00 a.m. commenced discharging casks. Squally wind W.S.W.

Wednesday 2 August Commenced with heavy squalls with rain and hail alternately. Employed as yesterday. Arrived the *Vansittart*. Strong gales S.W. Heavy thunder, lightning hail and rain. At 7.00 a.m. unmoored and moved nearer the fishery.

Monday 7 August Light breezes W.S.W. At 6.00 p.m. calm and fine weather. At 3.00 a.m. cloudy with rain. Employed landing casks, ballasting *etc*. Sailed the *Vansittart*.

Wednesday 9 August Commences with strong gales, W.S.W. Midnight, light airs. 7.00 a.m. boat left the vessel to fetch bark for repairing the huts.

Recherche Bay Thursday 10 August Fore part heavy rain. Light breezes west. Boat away after casks. At 6.00 p.m. arrived the brig *Amity*. Midnight calm. Ditto weather throughout the day.

Friday 11 August Commenced with fresh breezes S.W. Employed cleaning casks. Midnight calm. Hard frost. At 8.00 a.m. up topgallant yard. Bent jib. Picked up the best bower anchor. Fresh breezes N.E.

Saturday 12 August Commenced with fresh breezes N.E. Midnight, calm and frosty. At 8.00 a.m. sent on board the *Amity* three casks beef, four ditto pork, 19 bags potatoes, five bundles hoops, four ditto flags, 20 rivets. At 10.00 a.m. weighed and sailed. Light airs N.E.

Sunday 13 August Light airs N.E. Midnight, high wind N.W. At 1.00 a.m. passed South Port. Light airs throughout the day.

Monday 14 August Commenced with light airs N.W. 4.00 p.m. calm. Came to off Smoke Island in 7 fathoms. At 8.00 weighed and sailed. Squally W.N.W. At 9.00 calm. Midnight, calm and cloudy.

Tuesday 15 August Fresh breezes N.W. At 4.00 p.m. anchored in Sullivan's Cove. Midnight calm. At 8.00 a.m. heavy squalls with rain. Let go the best bower. Employed cleaning the hold. S. Garland off duty and unwell.

Wednesday 16 August Strong gales with rain. Received on board one whaleboat, three whale lines, 30 gallons wine, two bundles flags.

Thursday 17 August Commences with heavy squalls rain. Employed taking in casks. 10.00 a.m. received on board one bale slops. One bag shoes.

Friday 18 August Employed receiving on board casks, stores *etc*. At 7.00 a.m. weighed both anchors. At 10.00 sailed, squally.

Saturday 19 August Commences with heavy squalls. At 0.15 p.m. carried away the fore gaff and close reefed the topsail, mainsail and stowed the jib. At 3.30 anchored in the passage with 60 fathoms small bower. Midnight strong gales with rain. Let go the best bower with 50 fathoms and veered to 110 on the small bower. At 10.00 a.m. moderate. Weighed and sailed.

Sunday 20 August Light winds. At 6.00 p.m. anchored in 7 fathoms near the flats. Midnight light airs. At 6.00 a.m. weighed and sailed. Light airs.

Monday 21 August Light breezes, variable. At 8.00 p.m. anchored at Southport. The outer end. Off the S.E. 1½ miles. Midnight calm. At 5.00 a.m. light wind. Weighed and sailed. At 10.00 took a whale in tow.

Tuesday 22 August Light winds, variable. At 3.30 anchored the whale near Muttors[?] Reef. At 6.30 anchored in Recherche Bay. At 6.00 commenced discharging the casks.

Appendix 6

Whaling at Recherche Bay
August to November 1837

Wednesday 23 August 1837 Fresh breezes and clear weather. At 8.00 a.m. got under way and went up to Southport to cut in. At 2.00 p.m. came in to Southport. Brought up with 50 fathoms and the small bower. Got one whale alongside ready to cut in.

Thursday 24 August Fine pleasant weather. Employed in the schooner at Southport cutting in. Downing got fast but his line parted and loosed the whale. No whales seen at Southport.

Friday 25 August Pleasant breezes and clear weather. At 7.00 a.m. got under way and went down to Recherche Bay. Chase got one whale and towed his home. Rogers cutting in his half whale with the brig. Moored the schooner with 50 fathoms of both chains. Took one raft of blubber ashore then lighted the works.

Saturday 26 August Pleasant breezes and clear weather. Got in Chase's whale and moored her at the blubber moorings. Got blubber up ready for trying-out.

Sunday 27 August Commences with fine weather. At daylight the brig *Amity* got underway and went to town. Middle and latter parts strong gales and rainy weather. Trying-out all day.

Monday 28 August Commences with light breezes and light showers of rain. At daylight the boats went out. Middle and latter parts strong gales and showers of rain. Chase got fast but was obliged to pull. Loosed one iron. The works alight all day. Got one raft of blubber hacked up.

Tuesday 29 August Commences with strong gales and thick showers of rain and clear at intervals. At daylight the boats went out but saw no whales. The works alight all day. Got one raft of blubber up on the stage. Middle and latter parts ditto wind and weather.

Wednesday 30 August Commenced with strong gales and heavy squalls of wind and hailstones. At 7.00 a.m. the boats went out but saw nothing. The works alight all day. Samson knocked off and would not work. At 4.00 p.m. Archibald McMillen came down from the *Cheviot*. Left Cobb at Southport. Strong gales from the S.W.

Thursday 31 August Commenced with strong gales and heavy squalls of rain. All the boats out part of the day then they commenced building a new hut for the *Cheviot*'s crew. Middle and latter parts more moderate.

Saturday 2 September Fine pleasant breezes and clear weather. Four boats out all day. One whale seen and got by Bartens.

Sunday 3 September Fine pleasant weather throughout. One whale seen and got by Griffiths. All the boats out all day.

Tuesday 5 September Commenced with strong gales and thick showers of rain. No boats out all day. People employed getting bone out and getting bark for the try-works house. Middle and latter parts ditto winds and weather. No whales seen.

Thursday 7 September Light breezes and heavy weather throughout with a heavy sea setting in the bay from the S.E. All the boats out part of the day. Nothing seen. All hands getting bone out. Thomas Groves denied to do his duty and would not go in the boat.

Friday 8 September Commences with calms and clear weather. At daylight the schooner *Amity* came into the bay and the barque *William*. Griffiths got one whale. Middle and latter parts strong breezes and clear weather.

Saturday 9 September Commences with pleasant breezes and clear weather. At daylight the boats went out – chased one whale and Barton's party got her. Middle part strong breezes and hazy weather. Latter part light airs and calm.

Monday 11 September Strong breezes and clear weather throughout. At daylight the boats went out. Chase got a whale and towed her home.

Tuesday 12 September Commences with pleasant breezes and clear weather. At daylight the boats went out. Two whales got by the opposition parties. Middle and latter parts, strong breezes and squalls of wind and rain. Cut-in Chase's whale and got the blubber ashore and commenced trying-out.

Lying in Recherche Bay Black Whaling. Wednesday 13 September Commenced with pleasant breezes and clear weather. At daylight the boats went out. Mansfield got a whale, towed her home and cut her in and the works alight all day. Middle and latter parts, strong squalls and showers of rain.

Thursday 21 September Pleasant breezes and clear weather throughout. At daylight the boats went out. Chased one whale but did not get her. Henry Rodgers went to town in Petchy's cutter.

Saturday 23 September These 24 hours, pleasant breezes and clear pleasant weather. At daylight the boats went out. Three whales seen and two got by the opposition party. The schooner *Rob Roy* came in the bay.

Sunday 24 September These 24 hours, pleasant breezes and clear weather. At daylight the boats went out. Several whales seen. Downing got one. Sunk and anchored her. The barque *Lloyds of London* came in the bay for Griffiths' oil. The *Cheviot* went past the bay.

Monday 25 September These 24 hours, light breezes and rainy weather. At daylight the boats went out. Saw a good many whales. A. McMillan got one whale and Chase got a half ditto. Towed them home and anchored them. The spare hands employed getting oil off.

Tuesday 26 September Fine pleasant breezes and variable. At daylight the boats went out. The spare hands employed cutting-in. J. Mansfield got one whale and Cobb got another and Archibald McMillan got a half, getting stove, and Barrett got the other. Anchored all the whales. A great many whales seen and got.

Wednesday 27 September Strong gales and squalls of wind and rain. At daylight the boats went out. Several whales chased but none got by our party. At 2.00 p.m. the *Elisa*, government schooner, came in the bay. Middle and latter parts ditto wind and weather.

Friday 29 September Strong gales and heavy squalls. Towed Downing's whale and Mansfields's and Arch's and cut them in. Downing's whale turned out a dry skin. Middle and latter part more moderate.

Saturday 30 September Commences with strong gales and showers of rain. Towed Cable's whale out Southport. Cobb got fast to a cow and calf. Killed the calf but was obliged to cut, there being so much sea.

Sunday 1 October Lying in Recherche Bay black whaling. Strong breezes and hazy weather. At daylight the boats went out. At 7.00 a.m. unmoored the schooner and went up to South Port to cut in Cobbs's whale. At noon came to in South Port with 40 fathoms of the small bower in 10 fathoms of water. Then commenced cutting-in. At 8.00 p.m. let go the best bower and gave her 20 fathoms of ditto, it blowing hard.

Monday 2 October Commences with strong gales and showers of rain. At daylight hove up the best bower. At 9.00 a.m. got underway. At 1.00 p.m. came to in Recherche in 7 fathoms and moored ship. Then got out the blubber and took it ashore. Middle and latter parts light breezes and pleasant weather.

Tuesday 3 October Pleasant breezes and clear weather. At daylight the boats went out. Cobb got one whale and he sank and anchored her. The work alight all day. Middle and latter parts ditto winds and weather. —— Millar got a half ditto.

Wednesday 4 October Fine pleasant breezes and clear weather. At daylight the boats went out. Rodgers got one whale. Mansfield got but he got stove and loosed one whale. Middle and latter parts ditto wind and weather.

Thursday 5 October Pleasant breezes and showers of rain. The carpenter repairing Mansfield's boat. Latter parts ditto wind and weather. Employed ashore cutting-in.

Saturday 7 October Strong gales and heavy —— winds. At daylight the boats went out. Chase and McMillen got fast but their irons drew. John Mansfield got one whale and Cobb got another. Archibald McMillen got half and Downing got one whale. Was obliged to anchor them all it blowing so hard. Trying-out all day and getting blubber ashore.

Sunday 8 October Strong gales and heavy squalls throughout. At daylight the boats went out. Towed home Cobb's whale but could not tow the others there being so much sea. The work alight all day.

Monday 9 October Strong gales and squally with showers of rain. At daylight the boats went out. Archibald McMillen cutting-in the half whale. Chase got one whale and towed her home. The works alight all day. Cobb at home not well. The spare hands getting out the empty casks out of the brig *Amity*.

Tuesday 10 October Fine pleasant weather throughout. At daylight the boats went out but saw no whales. Cut-in Chase's whale with the spare hands. The works alight. Mansfield and Cobb not able to go out being not well.

Wednesday 11 October Fine pleasant weather throughout. At daylight four boats went out. Mansfield and Cobb not being able to go out. The works alight all day. Put on board the *Amity* six tun butts and six 180-gallon casks. No whales seen.

Friday 13 October Fine pleasant weather throughout. At daylight the boats went out. Mansfield got fast but his iron drew and Mackay[?] got the whale. Got off eight tun butts and 17 180-[gallon casks].

Sunday 15 October Fine pleasant weather throughout. Daylight the boats went out. Mansfield and Downing ashore getting the brig loaded and ready for sea. At 11.00 a.m. the *Amity* got underway for town. George Downing and —— went in the brig. Took Peter the —— on board to the doctor, being very bad. He gave him some medicine.

Saturday 21 October Strong breezes and rainy weather. Got the remainder of the oil on board the schooner, being about 30 tuns and ten casks empty.

Sunday 22 October Strong breezes and clear weather. At daylight unmoored the schooner and got underway for town with light airs from the S.E. When off the South Port the wind shifted round to the N.E. with strong breezes and hazy. At 4.00 p.m. pumped ship. At midnight was abreast of the buoys.

Monday 23 October Strong breezes and attended with showers of rain turning up the bay. At 2.00 p.m. a very heavy squall split the topgallant sail. At 5.00 p.m. came to anchor in Sullivan's Cove with 40 fathoms of the small bower.

Tuesday 24 October Strong breezes and clear weather. At noon the *Mariane* came in the harbour. Employed mooring ship. Middle and latter parts ditto wind and weather.

Wednesday 25 October Pleasant breezes and clear weather. Shifted the schooner alongside of the wharf ready for discharging.

Friday 27 October Fine pleasant weather throughout. Finished discharging and hauled off from the wharf. Received 16 lbs. fresh mutton.

Saturday 28 October Fine pleasant weather throughout. Loosed the sails and gave them the airs.

Monday 13 November Fine pleasant breezes and clear weather. Shipped Alfred Lang—— as chief mate and Andrew Thompson and Phillip Gillon. Received 14 lbs. of meat and 6 ——.

Wednesday 15 November Strong breezes and squally. Shipped William Wilson. Received 14 lbs. meat. Pickle employed as m——. Phillip absent.

Thursday 16 November Ditto wind and weather. Employed as yesterday. —— —— absent.

Friday 17 November Fresh breezes and variable. Employed tarring down the rigging. —— —— — absent.

Saturday 18 November Pleasant breezes and ditto weather. Employed as yesterday. John Williams came on board as cook.

Sunday 19 November Pleasant breezes and ditto weather.

Monday 20 November Strong breezes and clearing weather. People employed tarring and setting-up rigging.

Tuesday 14 November 1837 Shipped Andrew Thompson and Phillip Gillon. Shipped William Wilson on the 15th.

Appendix 7

Owners of the schooner Prince of Denmark

1822–1863

T. & D. Asquith	1822–1827
Thomas Raine	1827–1830
George Jack (or Black)	1830–1833
John Wallace Murdoch	1833–1834
Thomas Hewitt & John Wallace Murdoch	1834–1835
James Kelly	1835–1842
Thomas Brown & William Knight	1842–1843
Alfred Garret & George Watson	1843
George Watson & John Watson	1843–1845
George Watson	1845–1851
Richard Cleburne	1851–?
George Watson	?–1856
Hubert Beard Evans	1856–1858?
Charles McKellar	1858–1861
Isabella McKellar	1861–1862
J. C. Bennett & J. G. McDougall	1862–1863
John Charles Bennett	1863

Masters of the Schooner *Prince of Denmark*, 1822–1863

Peter Williams	1822–1823
William Stewart	1824–1827
Thomas Wright	1827–1828
Duncan Forbes	1828–1829
Philip Skelton	1829–1830
George Jack (or Black)	1830–1833
Henry Wishart	1833–1835
James Kelly	1835

James Young / John Young / Youngson	1835–1836
Thomas Gray / Gay	1836–1837
James Kelly	1838–1840
Captain Smith	1841
David Robert Comyn	1842–1843
Captain Smith	1843
Michael Connor II	1843–1844
Robert Heays	1845–1855
R. W. Johns	1855
Robert Heays	1856
Hubert Beard Evans	1856–1858
Charles McKellar	1858–1859
John Charles Bennett	1859–1863

Glossary

N.B. Some of the following definitions of terms used in the log of the *Prince of Denmark* reflect usage in the early 19th century rather than that which is current.

A.B. or A.B.S. Able-bodied seaman

aft of or **abaft** Behind, e.g. 'abaft the foremast' means 'behind the foremast', in the direction of the stern of a vessel.

ambergris A waxy substance found in the digestive system of the sperm whale.

backstay The piece of standing rigging which runs from the masthead of the mast which is furthest aft, to the stern of a vessel. It is secured to the stern by a metal plate or plates, bolted through the structure of the vessel.

baleen Whalebone

ballast Heavy material, such as stone, used to compensate for the loss of weight when a ship has no cargo.

barque A square-rigged vessel, with three, four or five masts, the after one of which is fore-and-aft rigged.

barquentine A three, four or five-masted vessel, only the foremast of which is square-rigged.

bending on Attaching sails to the various booms, gaffs, masts and yards, on which they are to be set.

bitts Immensely strong timber posts close to the windlass. The bowsprit normally passes between them and is held in place by them, but their main function is to provide a secure fastening for the anchor cable.

blocks A block consists of a wooden casing having one sheave inside (single block) or two sheaves (double block). Many different forms of blocks exist and are combined to form tackles when ropes are rove through their various parts.

bolt rope A rope sewn to, and reinforcing the edge of a sail.

bombasine Twilled, black worsted material for dressmaking.

boom A timber spar to which the lower part of a mainsail on a fore-and-aft rigged vessel is attached. The forward end of the boom is attached to, and pivots at, the mast, and the after end is secured and controlled by sheets.

bower The main anchor of a vessel.

brig A square-rigged vessel with two masts, the after one of which carries a lower fore-and-aft rigged sail with gaff and boom.

brigantine A true brigantine is similar to a brig, except that she carries a fore-and-aft rigged mainsail instead of a square-rigged one. When the square topsails on the mainmast are replaced with a gaff topsail, such a vessel is still sometimes called a brigantine, but is also known as a hermaphrodite brig.

bulls' eyes Pieces of timber, often *lignum vitae* wood, in the form of a sleeve secured by a strop. They are used to divert the angle of a rope with a minimum of friction.

bulwarks The sides of a vessel above deck level.

burgee A small flag or pennant, usually triangular, flown at the masthead, and often used to denote the ownership or identity of a vessel.

burthen or **burden** The carrying capacity of a vessel.

butt A large cask or barrel capable of holding 108 imperial gallons.

carvel built Planked with timber, fitted edge-to-edge, so that a flush finish is presented to both the outside and the inside of the planking.

caulking The sealing of a joint in planking such as that which forms the hull or the deck of a timber vessel. This is achieved by driving oakum into the joint with a caulking iron, then finishing off the joint with pitch.

chain plate A metal plate fastened to the outside of a ship's hull and bolted through its timbers. It provides the fixing point for the deadeyes to which the lower shrouds are attached and hence secures the mast.

clew The lower and after corner of a fore-and-aft rigged sail, and either lower corner of a square sail.

counter That part of the stern of a vessel which is aft of the rudderpost, and overhangs the water.

cutter A small one-masted fore-and-aft rigged vessel with two headsails.

cutting-in The process of stripping blubber from a whale carcase prior to trying-out.

davits The small cranes used to raise and lower boats to and from a ship. They are arranged in pairs, and each carries either the bow or the stern of the boat.

deadeyes Pieces of timber, usually *lignum vitae*, each pierced with three holes. They come in pairs, and the upper deadeye is attached to an eye in the lower end of a shroud. The lower deadeye is bolted to a chain plate in the side of the ship's hull. A lanyard rove through the various holes in the two deadeyes is then used to tension and set up the standing rigging.

dimity Stout cotton fabric with raised stripes or a pattern woven into it.

dolphin striker A strong bar of wood or iron, hung down from the lower side of the bowsprit, at its extremity, inside the cap, and by which the martingale supports the jib boom.

ensign A rectangular flag, which identifies the nationality of a vessel. It is flown at the stern, or sometimes from the peak of the gaff of the aftermost fore-and-aft sail.

fairleads Fittings, usually of metal, used to alter the direction of running rigging or mooring lines.

false keel The outer part of the keel of a vessel. Usually in the form of a separate piece of timber, it is designed to be capable of replacement to remedy damage through grounding *etc.*, without necessarily compromising the strength of the hull.

fid A square metal bar with a shoulder, which forms part of the housing assembly at the top of a mainmast, used to support a topmast.

firkin A cask capable of holding 9 imperial gallons, or a quarter of a barrel.

fish A strong purchase composed of four parts: a pendant, block, hook and tackle. It is portable, and is used for a variety of heavy lifting tasks at sea.

flying jib A jib which is set, not on a stay, but so that it is free to take its own shape according to the wind. It is secured at the foot to the jib boom and is set by connecting a halyard to its head, and hoisting it to the masthead. It is set above and clear of all other headsails.

foremast On a two-masted schooner, the forward and smaller mast.

foresail On a schooner, the fore-and-aft rigged sail set on the foremast.

fore scuttle The forward hatch opening in the deck of a ship.

forestaysail A triangular sail, which on a schooner is set on a forestay, running from, the stem head to the top of the mainmast.

fore-topmast staysail A triangular sail set on a stay, running from the end of the bowsprit to the top of the fore-topmast.

freeboard The height of the deck of a vessel above sea level.

furling Wrapping or rolling a sail close up to its yard, mast, boom or stay, and fastening it up with ties.

G.R.T. Gross Registered Tonnage.

gaff A timber spar to which the upper part of the mainsail of a fore-and-aft rigged vessel is attached. The forward end of the gaff terminates in a fork, called the 'gaff jaws', which bear against the mast. The after end is called the peak. Halyards are attached to both the throat and the peak.

gaff-rigged A vessel is described as gaff-rigged when its mainsail incorporates a gaff.

gaff topsail A triangular sail set above a gaff mainsail.

gallery A balcony built outside the body of a ship. At the stern (stern gallery), or at the quarters (quarter gallery).

galloons Narrow braid used as a trimming, often made of lace, or embroidered.

gangway (1) A demountable section of the bulwarks of a ship, which enabled easy access to the shore for the loading, and unloading of cargo and passengers. (2) A moveable bridge from a ship to a wharf.

gunny A jute sack

gybe To alter course while running before the wind, to such an extent that the wind direction relative to the vessel's stern is shifted from one quarter to the other, causing the sails to suddenly fill on the opposite side from previously. In strong winds, gibing has to be undertaken with care, to avoid damage to spars, sails and crew.

halyards Ropes used for hoisting and lowering yards, sails and flags.

heaving down The process of causing a ship to lean extremely heavily to one side or the other, to enable maintenance to be carried out to the underside, as far as the keel. This was achieved by leading cables from the mastheads to the shore, while the vessel was alongside a wharf, and applying great tension. Before doing this, it was of course necessary to remove all cargo or ballast, and any other loose items from the vessel.

half pipe A cask. The capacity of a pipe was usually equivalent to 105 imperial gallons, or half a tun.

half whale When a whale was caught, it had frequently been pursued by the crews of several different vessels. In the event of more than one harpooner having been successful, the first two were each credited with a half whale.

hermaphrodite brig See Brigantine.

hide A leather container.

hogshead A large cask capable of holding 52.5 gallons (imperial measure).

hooping Narrow metal strapping used by coopers in the making of barrels.

hounds The fittings at the masthead, which include timber cheeks, which secure the rigging. The whole assembly also supports the topmasts.

hove-to A vessel is said to be hove-to when its sails are adjusted so that it makes a minimum of headway, but lies comfortably with the bows at 45 degrees or so to the wind and weather. This is usually done in either severe conditions, or when it is necessary to slow down, for example, to lower a boat. It is often achieved by hauling the headsails to the weather side so that they counter the effects of any other sails set. The process is referred to as heaving-to.

hyson-skin tea A fragrant kind of green tea.

jib A triangular sail set forward of the forestaysail, on a stay running from the bowsprit to the head of the mainmast.

jib boom A spar extending from a standing bowsprit, to enable a jib or jibs to be set from its forward extremity.

kedge *n.* The secondary anchor of a vessel. *v.* To move a vessel by laying out a secondary anchor and hauling in on the cable.

larboard The port, or left hand side of a vessel when viewed from the stern, looking forwards.

lateen A triangular sail, the leading edge of which is secured to a long flexible spar. This form of sail and rig is characteristic of Mediterranean vessels.

latitude The angle by which any point on the surface of the globe is positioned north or south of the equator.

letter of marque The official document which authorises the captain of a vessel to act as a privateer.

longitude The angle by which any point on the surface of the globe is positioned east or west of the Greenwich Meridian.

main gaff topsail On a gaff-rigged schooner, the fore-and-aft rigged sail set above the mainsail, on the main topmast.

mainmast On a two-masted schooner, the after and larger mast.

mainsail On a schooner, the fore-and-aft rigged sail set on the mainmast.

main topmast staysail On a schooner, the triangular sail set on a stay running from the top of the main topmast to the top of the foremast.

martingale The name of the rope extending downwards from the jib boom end to the dolphin striker. Its purpose is to hold down the jib boom.

mat A textured material woven from spun yarn or strands of rope and used to prevent chafe on masts, spars and yards.

mizzle A combination of mist and drizzle.

O.S. Ordinary seaman

offing An area of the sea that is visible from the shore, but a long way off.

polacre An adjective generally used to describe a vessel, the mast of which consists of a single spar.

ports Large openings in the bulwarks of a ship to permit the quick egress of water in the event of a heavy sea having come on deck. Ports were sometimes fitted with hinged port-lids, which acted as non-return valves.

privateer A privately-owned armed vessel, having official authority to attack the merchant ships of a hostile nation.

puncheon A large cask capable of holding 120 gallons (imperial measure).

quadrant A navigational instrument used to measure angles, particularly the angle between the sun and the horizon.

quarter pipe A cask. The capacity of a pipe was usually equivalent to 105 Imperial gallons, or half a tun.

ratlines or **rattling** Small ropes which cross the shrouds horizontally, at equal distances, from the deck upwards. They are used to form ladders to provide access to and from the mastheads.

reef To reef a sail is to reduce its area by rolling up and tying securely a section of its lower part. A sail would usually be capable of reduction by two or three sections: (1st reef, 2nd reef and 3rd reef).

reeving (past tense, **rove**) The process of rigging running rigging by threading it through the various necessary blocks, bull's-eyes and fairleads.

running or **running before the wind** Sailing with the wind either directly over the stern, or on either of the stern quarters and in the general direction of travel.

running rigging All movable rigging, used to hoist sails or spars, and to control or otherwise adjust them.

schooner A fore-and-aft rigged vessel, generally with two masts, the after one of which was taller than the foremast. Larger schooners often had three or four masts, and many schooners carried one or more topsails.

setting-up Adjusting the tension of all standing rigging to align the masts and spars correctly and to best advantage.

sheave A pulley wheel.

sheers These are often formed by a pair of heavy spars, such as the topmasts of a vessel, and are used to lift out the mainmasts, for major maintenance. The foot of each sheer leg is secured on opposite sides of the deck, and they are lashed together at the top. A tackle from the top is then used to lift out the mast. The sheers must be sufficiently long that the weight of that part of the mast to be lifted that is below the tackle exceeds the weight of that part which is above it.

sheets Ropes which control the set of a sail.

ship A vessel, square-rigged on each of her three or four masts.

shrouds A range of large ropes extending from the masthead to the port and starboard sides of a vessel to support the masts.

slops A random collection of clothing and footwear, normally the property of the ship, but available for the crew to purchase where the need arises. Slops were kept in the 'slop-chest'.

spermaceti A waxy substance obtained from the head of a sperm whale.

square sail A sail of quadrilateral shape, bent on to a yard. On a schooner it would have been set on the lower portion of the foremast, and would have been highly effective when running.

stage A working platform in the form of a raft, which was brought alongside a vessel to permit maintenance of the outside of the hull.

standing bowsprit A spar projected from the bows of a vessel, to carry a headsail and to support rigging from the foremast, and permanently secured in that position.

standing rigging The fixed and permanent rigging, which supports the mast or masts of a vessel.

starboard The right-hand side of a vessel when viewed from the stern, looking forward.

stove (**stove-in**) When said of a boat, having the hull pierced or shattered by impact.

strop A loop of rope spliced around a block, a yard, or any large rope by which a tackle might be connected to it.

studding sail A narrow sail, often rectangular, set outside the edge of a square sail on extensions of the yards.

tack To tack is to alter the course of a sailing vessel so that the wind changes from being on one side of the bows to being on the other. This is achieved by swinging the ship's head directly into the wind and allowing its momentum to carry it to the desired new course.

taken aback A sailing ship is described as taken aback when the wind changes suddenly and fills the sails on the opposite side from that which they are set to respond to.

tierce A cask capable of holding 42 gallons of liquid (imperial measure).

topgallant A square sail set above the upper topsail, on its own topgallant mast.

topgallant mast A mast, which is separate from and lighter than a topmast, and extends its height by being housed in fittings at its masthead.

topmast A mast, which is separate from and lighter than the mainmast, and extends its height by being housed in fittings at its masthead.

topping lift A rope running from the outer end of a boom or gaff to a block mounted at the hounds or at the mast head, and thence to the deck, enabling the weight of the boom or gaff to be supported when the sail is not set, or to relieve the pressure exerted on the sail by the weight of the boom in a light wind.

topsail A square sail set above the mainsail. Some vessel had both lower and upper topsails.

topsides Those parts of a ship's hull that are above the waterline.

treenails or **trunnels** Timber pegs used to secure a ship's planking to the timbers of its hull. They have a slot at the outer end into which a wedge is driven to hold them securely in place.

trying-out The process of producing oil in the try-works.

try-works A group of large metal pots set on a brick base, which are used to boil up a whale's blubber and to produce oil.

tun A large cask or barrel capable of holding 252 imperial gallons.

wear ship To change from one tack to another by turning the ship's stern through the direction of the wind and gybing. (In tacking, the ship's bow is turned through the direction of the wind). The process of tacking is undertaken using the momentum or 'way' of the ship. The process of wearing ship does not rely on momentum, but is driven by the wind. Wearing ship takes more sea room and involves a lot more effort on the part of the crew. It might be deployed when heavy seas and reduced sail resulted in insufficient momentum to tack.

weigh In the case of an anchor, to hoist it up from the seabed.

windlass A large winch, normally situated at the inner end of the bowsprit, close to the bows of a vessel. It is used mainly for weighing and lowering the anchor, but can also be utilised for any heavy haulage work on board ship.

works *see* **try-works**.

yard A horizontal spar, suspended from a mast at its mid-point, on which a square sail can be bent.

Information sources

Books, journals, articles and logs

A brief Narrative of the remarkable History of Barnet Burns, an English Sailor. Barnet Burns (1835).

Association Fortunes de Mer Caledoniennes, Patrimoine Maritime Caledonien (December 1989).

Blue Gum Clippers and Whale Ships of Tasmania. Will Lawson (1949).

Busby, James (1802–1871). Claudia Orange, in the *Dictionary of New Zealand Biography Vol. I., 1769–1869* (1990).

Cape York's Wild White Man, The Story of Narcisse Pellatier. William MacFarlane in *Cummins and Campbell Journal* (1948).

Captain Henry Wishart of Port Fairy Bay. Jenny Fawcett (2005).

Captain James Kelly of Hobart Town. K. M. Bowden (1964).

Chronological List of Antarctic Expeditions and Related Historical Events. Robert K. Headland (1989).

Cleburne, Richard (1799–1864). John Reynolds, in the *Australian Dictionary of Biography, Vol. I.* (1966).

Cochrane, The Life and Exploits of a Fighting Captain. Robert Harvey (2000).

CRC World Dictionary of Plant Names. Umberto Quattrochi (1999).

Decisions of the Superior Courts of New South Wales, 1788–1899.

Fast Sailing Ships, Their Design and Construction, 1775–1875. David R. MacGregor (1973).

Historic Poverty Bay and the East Coast, North Island, New Zealand. Joseph Angus Mackay (1949).

Historical Records of Australia, Vol. VI. Frederick Watson (1923).

Historical Records of New Zealand, Vol. I. Edited by Robert McNab (1908).

History of Botany in South Australia (1800–1895). D. N. Kraehenbuehl (1986) in *Flora of South Australia* 4th Edition, J. P. Jessop & H. R. Toelkin (editors).

Hongi Hika, (1772–1828). Angela Ballara, in the *Dictionary of New Zealand Biography Vol. I., 1769–1869* (1990, updated 2007).

In Tasmania. Nicholas Shakespeare (2004).

In the Heart of the Sea. Nathaniel Philbrick (2000).

Kelly, James (1791–1859). E. R. Pretyman, in the *Australian Dictionary of Biography, Vol. II* (1967).

Kendall, Thomas (1778–1832). Judith Binney, in the *Dictionary of New Zealand Biography Vol. I., 1769–1869* (1990, updated 2007).

King's Cutters and Smugglers. E. Keble Chatterton (1912).

Kirkcudbright, an Alphabetical Guide to its History. David R. Collin (2003).

Kirkcudbright Old Parish Registers. Transcribed by Howard Sproat (1992). Copies in the Stewartry Museum, Kirkcudbright.

Les Mers du Sud, m'ont raconte... Jean Guillou (2009).

Life in Old Van Diemen's Land. Joan Goodrick (1978).

Log of Logs Vol. I., A Catalogue of Logs, Journals, Shipboard Diaries, letters, and all forms of Voyage Narratives, 1788–1988 for Australia and New Zealand and Surrounding Oceans. Ian Nicholson (1989).

Log of the schooner Prince of Denmark, *1835–1836* (original in the Archives Office of Tasmania).

Log of the Schooner Prince of Denmark, *1842–1852* (original in the Archives Office of Tasmania).

Marsden, Samuel (1764–1838). A. T. Yarwood, in the *Australian Dictionary of Biography, Vol. II.* (1967).

Marsden, Samuel (1765–1838). G. S. Parsonson, in the *Dictionary of New Zealand Biography Vol. I., 1769–1869* (1990, updated 2007).

Merchant Sailing Ships, 1815–1850. David R. MacGregor (1984).

Merchant Sailing Ships, 1850–1875. David R. MacGregor (1984).

Moby Dick. Herman Melville (1851).

Morgan, John (c.1807–1865) from *An Encyclopaedia of New Zealand*, edited by A. H. McLintock (1966).

Murihiku: A History of the South Island of New Zealand and the Islands Adjacent and Lying to the South, from 1642–1835. Robert McNab (1909).

New Zealand. Reginald Horsley, Romance of Empire series, edited by John Lang (1908).

On the Tide 2: More Stories of the Tamar. Edited by Peter Richardson (2003).

Pelletier The Forgotten Castaway of Cape York. Stephanie Anderson (2009).

Petchy, John ([?]–1850). W. E. Goodhand, Vol. II., in the *Australian Dictionary of Biography* (1967).

Pitcairn: The Island, the People and the Pastor; with a Short Account of the Mutiny of the Bounty. Rev. Thomas Boyles Murray M.A. (1853).

Records of W.A. botanists. J. H. Maiden, in the *Journal of the Western Australian Natural History Society*, Number 6 (1909).

Remarkable Incidents in the Life of the Rev. Samuel Leigh, Missionary to the Settlers and Savages of Australia and New Zealand. Rev. Alexander Strachan (1855).

Sailing Ships. Bjorn Landstrom (1969).

Sails through the Centuries. Sam Svensson (1962).

Shipping Arrivals and Departures – South Australia, 1627–1850. R. T. Sexton (1990).

Shipping Arrivals and Departures – Sydney, 1826–1840. Ian H. Nicholson (1977).

Shipping Arrivals and Departures – Tasmania, 1803–1833. Ian H. Nicholson (1983).

Shipping Arrivals and Departures – Tasmania, 1834–1842. Ian H. Nicholson (1985).

Shipping Arrivals and Departures – Tasmania, Vol. III., 1843–1850. Graeme Broxom (1998).

Ships Employed in the South Seas Trade, 1775–1861. A. G. E. Jones / Ian H. Nicholson (1991).

Solway Sailing Vessels. James Copland, in *Sea Breezes* (1930).

Stewart, Captain William W. (c.1776–1851) from *An Encyclopaedia of New Zealand*, edited by A. H. McLintock (1966).

Tasmanian Heritage Council, Heritage Bulletin (November 2007).

The Art of Rigging. George Biddlecombe (1848).

The Comprehensive Atlas and Geography of the World. W. G. Blackie (1882).

The Convict King – Being the Life and Adventures of Jorgen Jorgenson. Jorgen Jorgenson and James Francis Hogan (1891).

The Early Journals of Henry Williams, 1826–1840. L. M. Rogers (1961).

The English Dane. Sarah Bakewell (2006).

The Fatal Shore. Robert Hughes (1987).

The Old Whaling Days: A History of Southern New Zealand from 1830–1840. Robert McNab (1913).

The People of Kirkcudbright in 1786 and 1788. Edited by Innes F. Macleod (2002).

The Rosanna Settlers, a manuscript by Hilda McDonnell (2002), held in the Mitchell Library, State Library of N.S.W., Sydney.

The Scottish Smuggler. Gavin D. Smith (2003).

The Ship Thieves. Sian Rees (2006).

The Three Cutters. Captain Frederick Marryat (1836).

Thierry, Charles Philippe Hippolyte de, (1793–1864). J. D. Raeside, in the *Dictionary of New Zealand Biography Vol. I., 1769–1869* (1990, updated 2007).

Thomas Burr's Journal, published in *The Journal of the Royal Geographical Society of London, Volume 15* (1845).

Trois Naufrages Aux Iles Chesterfield au Siecle Dernier, by Jean Guillou, *Article publie dans le* bulletin no 55 (*2 trimestre* 1983) *de la Societe d'Etudes Historique de la Nouvelle Caledonie*.

Whalers and Free Men: Life on Tasmania's Colonial Whaling Stations. Susan Lawrence (2006).

Who Discovered Lake Alexandrina? by Thomas Gill, in the *Proceedings of the Royal Geographical Society of Australasia, South Australian Branch 8* (Sessions 1904/05–1905/06).

William Stewart, Sealing Captain, Trader and Speculator. John O. C. Ross (1987).

Williams, Henry (1782–1867), from *An Encyclopaedia of New Zealand*. Edited by A. H. McLintock (1966).

Willis, Joseph Scaife (1808–1897). G. P. Welsh, in the *Australian Dictionary of Biography, Vol. VI.* (1976).

Newspapers and periodicals

Australian
Brisbane Courier
Cleveland Bay Express
Colonial Times
Colonial Times and Tasmanian Advertiser
Cornwall Chronicle
Daily Southern Cross, Vol.XIX., Issue 1872, (17 July 1863)
Evening Post, Wellington
Gladstone Observer
Hobart Courier
Hobart Town Advertiser
Hobarton Courier
Hobart Town Daily Mercury
Hobart Town Gazette
Hobarton Mercury
Launceston Examiner
Maitland Mercury and Hunter River General Advertiser
Nelson Examiner and New Zealand Chronicle, Vol. I., issue 45, (14 January 1843)
New Zealander
New Zealand Spectator and Cook's Strait Guardian, Vol. IV., Issue 308, (12 July 1848)
North Otago Times
Otago Witness
Perth Gazette and Western Australian Journal
Portland Guardian
Queensland Guardian
Shipping Gazette and Sydney General Trade List
Surabaya Haudelsblad
Sydney Empire
Sydney Gazette and New South Wales Advertiser
Sydney Herald
Sydney Monitor
Sydney Morning Herald
South Australian Advertiser
Southern Australian

Internet

Australian Newspapers – http://trove.nla.gov.au/newspaper
Australian Shipping Arrivals and Departures, 1788–1968 –www.blaxland.com/ozships/index.htm
Mariners and ships in Australian Waters – http://mariners.records.nsw.gov.au/
National Oceanic Atmospheric Administration, Department of Commerce, U.S.A. – www.photolib.noaa.gov/
New Zealand Newspapers – http://paperspast.natlib.govt.nz
Old Bailey Proceedings Online – www.oldbaileyonline.org, 2 January 2008; 23 October 1828, Trial of Stilman White, ref. t18281023-156.

Museums, art galleries and libraries

Alexander Turnbull Library, New Zealand
Allport Library and Museum of Fine Arts, State Library of Tasmania, Australia.
Auckland City Library, New Zealand
Australian National Maritime Museum
Broughton House Museum and Library, Kirkcudbright, Scotland
Ewart Library, Dumfries, Scotland
Fiji Museum, Suva, Fiji
Fortune de mer, Noumea, New Caledonia
Kirkcudbright Library, Kirkcudbright, Scotland
Library and Archives, Canada
Maritime Museum of Tasmania, Australia
Memorial University of Newfoundland, Canada.
Merseyside Maritime Museum, England, U.K.
Mitchell Library, State Library of New South Wales, Australia
National Library of Australia
National Library of New Zealand
National Maritime Museum, Greenwich, England, U.K.
New Zealand Electronic Text Centre
Queen Victoria Museum and Art Gallery, Launceston, Tasmania, Australia
Royal Historical Society of Queensland, Australia
Scottish Maritime Museum, Irvine, Scotland, U.K.
State Archives of Tasmania, Australia
State Library of New South Wales, Australia
State Library of Queensland, Australia
State Library of Tasmania, Launceston, Australia
State Library of Victoria, Australia
Stewartry Museum, Kirkcudbright, Scotland, U.K.
University of Massachusetts, U.S.A.
W. L. Crowther Library, State Library of Tasmania, Australia

Credits

NOAA (National Oceanic and Atmospheric Administration) United States Department of Commerce. NOAA Photo Library
1. A ship on the northwest coast of America cutting in her last right whale. Drawing by H. W. Elliott from a French lithograph designed by B. Russell. Image ID: figb0208, NOAA's Historic Fisheries Collection Credit: NOAA National Marine Fisheries Service
2. Stripping sea elephant blubber and rolling it in barrels to try-works, southwest beach, Herd's Island. Drawing by H. W. Elliott after Capt. H. C. Chester. Image ID: figb0230, NOAA's Historic Fisheries Collection Credit: NOAA National Marine Fisheries Service
3. In: '*Voyage au pole sud et dans l'Oceanie...*' by the French ships *Astrolabe* and *Zelee* under the command of Dumont D'Urville. Plate 81. Grand Place d'Apia, Ile Opoulou. Library Call Number Q115 .D9 1842, pt.1, Atlas, t.1. Image ID: libr0292, Treasures of the NOAA Library Collection Photographer: Archival Photograph by Mr. Steve Nicklas, NOS, NGS.

State Archives of Tasmania, Australia
1. Richard Cleburne – Allport Library and Museum of Fine Arts, Tasmanian Archive and Heritage Office
2. Thomas Gay Sketch – Archives Office of Tasmania
3. Pages of log – Archives Office of Tasmania

Mitchell Library, State Library of New South Wales, Australia
1. Panel 3 of *Panorama of Hobart* – *c*.1825, watercolour by Augustus Earle. Original item no. DGD 14/3. Digital order no. a1541003
2. Major Lockyer – 1886(?) William Macleod. Call no P2/152. Digital order no. a1528097
3. The *Success* hove down to the *Couizer* – *c*.1829–1830. Original item no. PX★D 41/8. Digital order no. a1120008
4. George French Angas – naturalist and painter, London, 1868, pre-1955 photograph. Call no P1/42. Digital order no. a4157042

State Library of Victoria, Australia
1. Seal hunting at the Auckland Islands – Grosse, Frederick, 1828–1894, engraver Ebenezer and David Syme, Melbourne, 3 March 1868. State Library of Victoria
2. Cape Pillar near the entrance of the River Derwent – by Joseph Lycett *c*.1775–1828 (published 1824). State Library of Victoria.
3. Cutting up a stranded whale – wood engraving from *The Australasian Sketcher* (published 1879). State Library of Victoria.

Alexander Turnbull Library, New Zealand
1. The Rev. Thomas Kendall, and the Maori chiefs Hongi Hika and Waikato, 1820 – oil painting by James Barry, 1818–1846. Alexander Turnbull Library, Wellington, N.Z.
2. HMS *Herald* in Sylvan Cove, Stewarts (*sic*) island, 1840 (n.d.) – pencil drawing by Edward Marsh Williams, 1818–1909. Alexander Turnbull Library, Wellington, N.Z.
3. Rev. Archdeacon Henry Williams (1782–1867). He came to New Zealand in 1823 – photograph by unknown photographer. Alexander Turnbull Library, Wellington, N.Z.
4. Rev. Samuel Marsden. First missionary to New Zealand. Born 1764. Died 1838. (Between 1832 and 1838) – oil painting by Joseph Backler, 1815–1897. Alexander Turnbull Library, Wellington, N.Z.
5. James Busby, 1832 – photograph of miniature oil painting by Richard Read, 1765(?)–*c*.1843. Alexander Turnbull Library, Wellington, N.Z.

6. Barnet Burns – wood engraving, artist unknown (London, R. & D. Read, 1844). Alexander Turnbull Library, Wellington, N.Z.

State Library of Queensland, Australia
1. George Harris MLC, Queensland *c.*1870 – John Oxley Library, State Library of Queensland, Neg:19218

Royal Historical Society of Queensland, Australia
1. Narcisse Pelletier – Collection of the Royal Historical Society of Queensland, P51287

Auckland City Library, New Zealand
1. Baron De Thierry (young) – Ref 7-A10827 Special Collections, Auckland City Libraries (NZ)
2. Baron De Thierry (old) – Ref 7-A11526 Special Collections, Auckland City Libraries (NZ)

Auckland Libraries, New Zealand
1. Sir George Edward Grey – Sir George Grey, Special Collections, Auckland libraries, 4-1341

Australasian Pioneers' Club, Sydney, Australia
1. Captain Thomas Raine – photograph by John Langer of an original portrait in the collection of the Australasian Pioneers' Club, Sydney, Australia

University of Massachusetts, U.S.A.
1. *Hamlet's Ghost* – from the Walter B. Woodbury Photographic Collection (PH3) *Hamlet's Ghost*, Surabaya, Java (boat with passengers and crew), *c.*1865, from the Special Collections Department, W. E. B. Du Bois Library, University of Massachusetts, Amherst. U.S.A.

Library and Archives Canada
1. Sir John Franklin – engraving: Sir John Franklin, Arctic explorer, *c.*1845, by Negelen. **Source:** Library and Archives Canada/C-001352

Queen Victoria Museum and Art Gallery, Tasmania, Australia
1. Captain James Kelly – miniature portrait of Captain James Kelly, QVM.1962.61.2 Collection: Queen Victoria Museum and Art Gallery, Launceston, Tasmania

Edinburgh Napier University, Scotland
1. HMS *Beagle* – permission granted by the trustees of the Edward Clark Collection at Edinburgh Napier University

Royal Geographical Society, London
1. A Chinese funeral in Cooktown, Australia – Royal Geographical Society and the Institute of British Geographers

National Maritime Museum, London
1. Barque *Rory O'More*

***Fortune de Mer*, New Caledonia**
1. Whalebone at *Prince of Denmark* wreck site, Chesterfield Islands – photograph by Pierre Larue of *Fortune de Mer*, New Caledonia
2. Examining try-pots at *Prince of Denmark* wreck site, Chesterfield Islands – photograph by Pierre Larue of *Fortune de Mer*, New Caledonia

Wikipedia / Wikimedia Commons
1. Kelly Street Hobart – Wikimedia Commons, photograph by Frances 76, creative commons attribution – share alike 3.0 license

Stewartry Museum, Kirkcudbright, Scotland
1. Kirkcudbright, 1792 – the Moat Brae, Kirkcudbright, drawing by A. Reid, engraved by W. and J. Walker and published in London on 1 October 1792. Image courtesy of Stewartry Museum, Kirkcudbright
2. Kirkcudbright *c.*1840 – published by J. Nicholson. Image courtesy of Stewartry Museum, Kirkcudbright

Collin Family collection
1. Ladies with prams and parasols at Burntisland – photograph (*c.*1905)
2. Lady with crinoline and child at Adelaide – photograph (*c.*1860)
3. "Pango Pango Harbour, Tutuila" by Edward Whymper, an illustration in *The Cruise of the Mary Rose* by W.H.G. Kingston (circa 1910)

Index